Lecture Notes in Computer Science 10374

Commenced Publication in 1973
Founding and Former Series Editors:
Gerhard Goos, Juris Hartmanis, and Jan van Leeuwen

More information about this series at http://www.springer.com/series/7408

Esther Guerra · Mark van den Brand (Eds.)

Theory and Practice of Model Transformation

10th International Conference, ICMT 2017
Held as Part of STAF 2017
Marburg, Germany, July 17–18, 2017
Proceedings

 Springer

Editors
Esther Guerra (iD)
Department of Computer Science
Universidad Autónoma de Madrid
Madrid
Spain

Mark van den Brand
Eindhoven University of Technology
Eindhoven
The Netherlands

ISSN 0302-9743   ISSN 1611-3349 (electronic)
Lecture Notes in Computer Science
ISBN 978-3-319-61472-4   ISBN 978-3-319-61473-1 (eBook)
DOI 10.1007/978-3-319-61473-1

Library of Congress Control Number: 2017945378

LNCS Sublibrary: SL2 – Programming and Software Engineering

Printed on acid-free paper

This Springer imprint is published by Springer Nature
The registered company is Springer International Publishing AG
The registered company address is: Gewerbestrasse 11, 6330 Cham, Switzerland

Foreword

Software Technologies: Applications and Foundations (STAF) is a federation of leading conferences on software technologies. It provides a loose umbrella organization with a Steering Committee that ensures continuity. The STAF federated event takes place annually. The participating conferences may vary from year to year, but they all focus on foundational and practical advances in software technology. The conferences address all aspects of software technology, from object-oriented design, testing, mathematical approaches to modeling and verification, transformation, model-driven engineering, aspect-oriented techniques, and tools.

STAF 2017 took place in Marburg, Germany, during July 17–21, 2017, and hosted the four conferences ECMFA 2017, ICGT 2017, ICMT 2017, and TAP 2017, the transformation tool contest TTC 2017, six workshops, a doctoral symposium, and a projects showcase event. STAF 2017 featured four internationally renowned keynote speakers, and welcomed participants from around the world.

The STAF 2017 Organizing Committee would like to thank (a) all participants for submitting to and attending the event, (b) the Program Committees and Steering Committees of all the individual conferences and satellite events for their hard work, (c) the keynote speakers for their thoughtful, insightful, and inspiring talks, and (d) the Philipps-Universität, the city of Marburg, and all sponsors for their support. A special thanks goes to Christoph Bockisch (local chair), Barbara Dinklage, and the rest of the members of the Department of Mathematics and Computer Science of the Philipps-Universität, coping with all the foreseen and unforeseen work to prepare a memorable event.

July 2017   Gabriele Taentzer

Preface

This volume contains the papers presented at ICMT 2017: the 10th International Conference on Model Transformation held during July 17–18, 2017, in Marburg, Germany, as part of the STAF 2017 (Software Technologies: Applications and Foundations) conference series. ICMT is the premier forum for researchers and practitioners from all areas of model transformation.

Modeling is key in reducing the complexity of software systems during their development and maintenance. Model transformations elevate models from passive documentation to first-class artifacts of the development process, and play a key role in analyzing models to reveal flaws and in integrating heterogeneous data and tools.

Model transformation includes approaches such as: model-to-text transformation, e.g., to generate code or other textual artifacts from models; text-to-model transformations, e.g., to derive models from structured text such as legacy code; and model-to-model transformations, e.g., to normalize, weave, analyze, optimize, simulate, and refactor models, as well as to translate between modeling languages.

Model transformation encompasses a variety of technical spaces including modelware, grammarware, dataware, and ontoware; a variety of model representations, e.g., based on different types of graphs; and a variety of transformation paradigms including rule-based transformations, term rewriting, and model manipulation using general-purpose programming languages.

The study of model transformation includes foundations, structuring mechanisms and properties (e.g., modularity, composability, reusability, and parameterization of transformations), transformation languages, techniques, and tools. An important goal of the field is the development of high-level model transformation languages, providing transformations that are amenable to higher-order model transformations and analysis mechanisms, or tailored to specific transformation problems. The efficient execution of model queries and transformations by scalable transformation engines on top of large graph data structures is also a key challenge in different application scenarios. Novel algorithms as well as innovative (e.g., distributed) execution strategies and domain-specific optimizations are sought in this respect. Model transformations have become artifacts that need to be managed in a structured way, resulting in developing methodology and tools to deal with versioning, (co-)evolution, etc. Correctness of model transformations has to be guaranteed as well.

This year ICMT 2017 received 31 submissions. Each submission was reviewed by three Program Committee members. After an online discussion period, the Program Committee accepted ten full papers and two short papers as part of the conference program. These papers included regular research, application, and tool demonstration papers presented in the context of four sessions on model transformation languages, model transformation tools, developing model transformations, applications of model transformations, and the future of the field.

A lot of people contributed to the success of ICMT 2017. We are grateful to the Program Committee members and reviewers for the timely delivery of thorough reviews and constructive discussions under a very tight review schedule. We also thank our keynote speaker, Ramon Schiffelers, for his excellent talk on the use of model transformations in an industrial context. Last but not least, we would like to thank the authors, who constitute the heart of the model transformation community, for their enthusiasm and hard work.

The organization of STAF made for a successful conference. We thank the local organizers, and in particular the general chair, Gabriele Taentzer, and the local chair, Christoph Bockish, for their hard work; and we thank Philipps-Universität Marburg for hosting us.

July 2017   Esther Guerra
                                                  Mark van den Brand

Organization

Program Committee

Jordi Cabot	ICREA - UOC (Internet Interdisciplinary Institute), Spain
Rubby Casallas	University of los Andes, Colombia
Antonio Cicchetti	Mälardalen University, Sweden
Tony Clark	Sheffield Hallam University, UK
Benoit Combemale	IRISA, Université de Rennes 1, France
Juan De Lara	Universidad Autonoma de Madrid, Spain
Davide Di Ruscio	Università degli Studi dell'Aquila, Italy
Gregor Engels	University of Paderborn, Germany
Jesus Garcia-Molina	Universidad de Murcia, Spain
Holger Giese	Hasso Plattner Institute at the University of Potsdam, Germany
Martin Gogolla	Database Systems Group, University of Bremen, Germany
Jeff Gray	University of Alabama, USA
Reiko Heckel	University of Leicester, UK
Soichiro Hidaka	Hosei University, Japan
Ludovico Iovino	Gran Sasso Science Institute, Italy
Frédéric Jouault	TRAME Team, ESEO, France
Timo Kehrer	Humboldt-Universität zu Berlin, Germany
Marouane Kessentini	University of Michigan, USA
Dimitris Kolovos	University of York, UK
Jochen Küster	IBM Research Zurich, Switzerland
Yngve Lamo	Bergen University College, Norway
Philip Langer	EclipseSource Services GmbH, Austria
Tanja Mayerhofer	Vienna University of Technology, Austria
James McKinna	University of Edinburgh, UK
Richard Paige	University of York, UK
Alfonso Pierantonio	University of L'Aquila, Italy
Istvan Rath	Budapest University of Technology and Economics, Hungary
Arend Rensink	University of Twente, The Netherlands
Bernhard Rumpe	RWTH Aachen University, Germany
Houari Sahraoui	DIRO, Université De Montréal, Canada
Andy Schürr	TU Darmstadt, Germany
Eugene Syriani	Université de Montréal, Canada
Jesús Sánchez Cuadrado	Universidad de Murcia, Spain
Massimo Tisi	AtlanMod team (Inria, Mines Nantes, LINA), France
Tijs Van Der Storm	Rijks Universiteit Groningen, The Netherlands
Pieter Van Gorp	Eindhoven University of Technology, The Netherlands

Dániel Varró   Budapest University of Technology and Economics,
                              Hungary
Gergely Varró   TU Dramstadt, Germany
Janis Voigtländer   University of Nijmegen, The Netherlands
Edward Willink   Willink Transformations Ltd., UK
Manuel Wimmer   Vienna University of Technology, Austria
Steffen Zschaler   King's College London, UK
Albert Zündorf   Kassel University, Germany

Additional Reviewers

Anjorin, Anthony   Leblebici, Erhan
Batot, Edouard   Nagy, András Szabolcs
Desai, Nisha   Polack, Fiona
Ergin, Huseyin   Raco, Deni
Fritsche, Lars   Semeráth, Oszkár
Hegedüs, Ábel   Szárnyas, Gábor
Hilken, Frank   Sánchez-Barbudo Herrera, Adolfo
Kluge, Roland

Empowering High Tech Systems Engineering Using MDSE Ecosystems (Invited Talk)

Ramon Schiffelers

ASML, Eindhoven University of Technology

Abstract. ASML is the world's leading provider of complex lithography systems for the semiconductor industry. To keep up with the increasing performance, evolvability and predictability requirements, ASML increasingly adopts model driven engineering methods and techniques within its development processes.

Models are developed and used for different purposes in several phases of the development process. There is not a single modeling language and analysis tool to address all these use cases. Instead, so-called Multi-Disciplinary Systems Engineering (MDSE) ecosystems are developed that seamlessly integrate dedicated (modeling) languages and tools for a given domain of interest. More specific, a MDSE ecosystem is an intuitive integrated development environment that consists of domain specific languages (DSLs) formalizing the domain in which engineers can model their system at hand. It contains transformations to transform these models automatically to one or more aspect models that form the inputs for (COTS) tools for rigorous analysis of (non)-functional properties, and synthesis tools to generate (code) artifacts to be used at run-time. Here, model transformations formalize and automate the relations between the various domain and aspect models.

Several of such MDSE ecosystems have been developed and introduced in the development processes and products of ASML, each for a specific domain. This presentation discusses both the technical and organizational challenges that have been overcome to develop these MDSE ecosystems, and have them adopted in a demanding industrial environment. Furthermore, it discusses challenges that need to be addressed to enable efficient development, analysis and synthesis of next generation industrial scale MDSE ecosystems.

Contents

Transformation Paradigms, Languages, Algorithms and Strategies

Experimentation with a Big-Step Semantics for ATL Model Transformations

Artur Boronat[✉]

Department of Informatics, University of Leicester, Leicester, UK
aboronat@le.ac.uk

Abstract. Formal semantics is a convenient tool to equip a model transformation language with precise meaning for its model transformations. Hence, clarifying their usage in complex scenarios and helping in the development of robust model transformation engines. In this paper, we focus on the formal specification of a model transformation engine for the declarative part of ATL.

We present an implementation-agnostic, big-step, structural operational semantics for ATL transformation rules and a rule scheduler, which form the specification of an interpreter for ATL. Hence, avoiding a complex compilation phase. The resulting semantics for rules enjoys a compositional nature and we illustrate its advantages by reusing an interpreter for OCL. The semantics discussed has been validated with the implementation of an interpreter in Maude, enabling the execution of model transformations and their formal analysis using Maude's toolkit. We also present an evaluation of the interpreter's performance and scalability.

Keywords: ATL · Big-step semantics · Model transformation · Maude

1 Introduction

Model(-to-model) transformation is a core asset in model-driven engineering (MDE) to manage complexity in scenarios such as DSL development, code generation, system interoperability and reverse engineering [5]. Demonstrating the reliability of such model transformations and of the generated software is a crucial step for MDE to succeed. Recent surveys [1,2] provide an outline of verification techniques applied to model transformations, ranging from lightweight approaches based on testing to automated and interactive theorem proving.

Our goal in this paper is to provide a formalization of ATL [9] using a big-step structural operational semantics that equips model transformation rules with a precise semantics that is independent of any implementation language. This semantics is nonetheless geared for functional programming languages with referential transparency and immutability. We focus our study on out-place ATL model transformations with one target domain and declarative rules, including OCL, `resolveTemp` expressions, matched and lazy rules. The formalization also includes a rule scheduler with small-step operational semantics. The whole approach has been validated by implementing an interpreter prototype in Maude [7]

© Springer International Publishing AG 2017
E. Guerra and M. van den Brand (Eds.): ICMT 2017, LNCS 10374, pp. 3–18, 2017.
DOI: 10.1007/978-3-319-61473-1_1

that follows the semantics specification faithfully. The interpreter allows for the analysis of ATL model transformations using Maude's verification toolkit, such as bounded model checking of invariants. The interpreter has been validated with a representative case study of out-place model transformations [10], which is also helpful to compare its performance and scalability against other approaches.

Maude has already been used as a rewriting engine for executing declarative model transformation rules [4,14] where models are encoded as configurations of objects using an associative, commutative binary top symbol with an identity, and model transformation rules are encoded as conditional rewrite rules. That is, models become graphs when the term representing the configuration of objects is interpreted modulo associativity and commutativity, and rewrite rules operate on the whole models. As already observed in [14], this approach does not scale very well for large models ($\sim$7K$-$10K objects) in out-place model transformations.

Our semantics of ATL relies on Focussed Model Actions (FMA) [3], a DSL modelling the typical side effects found in a model transformation (object creation and destruction, and setting and unsetting structural features $-$ which can be attribute values, and possibly bidirectional cross-references and containments) in functional contexts where models can be either represented as sets of objects or as sets of nested objects. Our semantics (FMA-ATL) allows for an alternative lower level encoding of ATL model transformations in Maude that decouples the query mechanism from the model transformation part in a model transformation rule. We analyse its performance and show that it scales better than previous Maude-based approaches in certain scenarios, allowing for the verification of a larger class of out-place ATL model transformations.

In what follows, we present: the case study that has been used to validate the interpreter; the FMA-ATL semantics, including support for OCL, matched and lazy rules, and resolveTemp expressions; performance and scalability experiments based on the FMA-ATL interpreter for the case study; a detailed comparison with a previous Maude-based formalization of ATL; and final remarks including lessons learnt from building an interpreter for ATL.

2   Case Study

We have borrowed the case study [10] that transforms class diagrams into relational schemas as it is representative of out-place model-to-model transformations and it facilitates a comparison of results with other approaches that implement a semantics for ATL in Maude. The metamodels have been extended by adding the meta-classes *Package*, which contains classifiers, in the metamodel *Class*, and by adding the meta-class *Database*, which contains tables, in the metamodel *Relational*, as shown in Fig. 1. An additional rule has been included to transform packages into databases, where the tables generated for the classes in the package are contained by the generated database.[1]

---

[1] The other ATL rules used in the case study are available at [10] or by accessing the experiment resources at https://github.com/arturboronat/fma-atl-experiments.

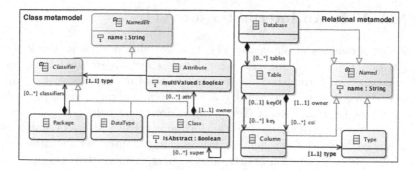

Fig. 1. Metamodels.

```
rule Package2Database { from p : Class!Package
  to out : Relational!Database ( name <- p.name,
    tables <- p.classifiers->select(c | c.oclIsKindOf(Class!Class)) -> union(
    p.classifiers ->select(c | c.oclIsKindOf(Class!Class))
    ->collect( c | c.attr )->flatten()
    ->collect(c | thisModule.resolveTemp(c,'out'))))}
```

We have developed an additional version of the Class2Relational transformation to discuss various aspects of our approach. In this version, all the matched rules are declared as lazy but for the rules that transform data types and packages. The rule that transforms packages calls the lazy rules that transform classes and multivalued attributes into tables as follows:

```
rule Package2Database { from p : Class!Package
  to out : Relational!Database ( name <- p.name,
    tables <- p.classifiers->select(c | c.oclIsKindOf(Class!Class))
    -> collect( c | thisModule.Class2Table( c ) )
    -> union( p.classifiers -> select(c | c.oclIsKindOf(Class!Class))
    -> collect( c | c.attr ) -> flatten()
    -> select( a | a.type.oclIsKindOf(Class!DataType) and a.multiValued )
    -> collect( a | thisModule.MultiValuedDataTypeAttribute2Column(a) )
    ) -> union (
    p.classifiers -> select(c | c.oclIsKindOf(Class!Class))
    -> collect( c | c.attr ) -> flatten()
    -> select( a | a.type.oclIsKindOf(Class!Class) and a.multiValued )
    -> collect( a | thisModule.MultiValuedClassAttribute2Column(a) )))}
```

The rule that transforms classes into tables calls the rules that transform single valued attributes into columns as follows:

```
lazy rule Class2Table { from c : Class!Class
  to out : Relational!Table ( name <- c.name,
    col <- Sequence {key} -> union(
        c.attr -> select( a |
          a.type.oclIsKindOf(Class!DataType) and not a.multiValued
        ) -> collect( a | thisModule.DataTypeAttribute2Column(a) )
      ) -> union (
        c.attr -> select( a |
          a.type.oclIsKindOf(Class!Class) and not a.multiValued
        ) -> collect( a | thisModule.ClassAttribute2Column(a) )),
    key <- Set {key}),
  key : Relational!Column (
    name <- 'objectId', type <- thisModule.objectIdType )}
```

3   FMA-ATL: An Interpreter for ATL

The big-step semantics of out-place ATL transformation rules is developed by using FMA, a DSL modelling the typical side effects performed by a model transformation. Our formalization covers a subset of declarative ATL, namely: matched and (non-unique) lazy rules, one *in-pattern* element, several *out-pattern* elements, filters, OCL and resolveTemp expressions, and helpers.

Given an out-place ATL model transformation, the FMA-ATL interpreter parses matched/lazy rules and helpers, initializing the interpreter configuration. This includes the computation of attribute helpers, caching their result. It then computes all enabling matches for matched rules, by considering their *in-target* element and their filter condition. This is achieved by retrieving all the instances of the class involved in the in-pattern element and by evaluating the filter condition for each instance using an OCL select expression.[2] Then the scheduler starts the model transformation by selecting one enabling match and the corresponding ATL matched rule. The execution of a matched rule involves the interpretation of both a FMA statement representing the side effects in the target model and of a trace statement that instructs what trace links need to be created in the trace store. After these side effects are applied, the scheduler updates the pool of pending matches by disabling those matches in which the transformed object was participating and continues the execution with the next enabling match.

Our formalization covers most of the out-place ATL model transformations expressible in the original ATL but it also introduces a number of constraints trading a small subclass of ATL model transformations for better scalability: when executing a matched rule for a given object, the source model where OCL expressions, appearing in binding statements of the *out-pattern* elements, are evaluated is reduced to the root container of the matched object;[3] a lazy rule can only be called under a containment reference and the result must be a collection of objects whose type must be compatible with that of the containment reference;[4] and `resolveTemp` expressions in a lazy rule can only be resolved with objects produced by matched rules other than the one calling that lazy rule.

By using big-step structural operational semantics for ATL rules, each matched rule application corresponds to one big transition containing all the computations associated with the fine-grained side effects that are applied both to the target model and to the trace store. When verifying the correctness of model transformations, this is helpful for keeping the state space isomorphic to the one that is generated when using normal declarative rules, in a graph

---

[2] The extension to several *in-pattern* elements does not necessarily affect the order of magnitude of the performance obtained in the experiments in Sect. 4. In practice, matching different in-pattern elements in the model consists of independent queries together with the evaluation of the filter condition, whose cost may become the dominating factor.

[3] This constraint does not apply to OCL expressions in the filter condition.

[4] Lazy rule recursion is conditioned by the containment structure specified in the metamodel, including infinite recursive structures, as in the composite design pattern.

transformation sense. Next, we explain the phases used by the FMA-ATL interpreter to execute an ATL transformation after an introduction to FMA.

3.1 Focussed Model Actions (FMA)

FMA constitutes a formalization of the typical model actions that can be found in the EMF API for manipulating models at the object level in order to implement model transformations in functional programming languages. Specifically, it constitutes an abstraction layer to implement the side effects of model transformations in declarative languages like Maude where the actions of a rewriting rule are represented in a term with variables in the right-hand side of the rule together with equationally-defined functions. Thus, one does not have to manually deal with different combinations of term patterns for each type of model action in order to make sure that the model is left in a consistent state (e.g. without dangling edges, containment integrity, etc.) after the transformation.

FMA is not Turing complete and it only includes two types of statements: model actions **ActStmt** including `create`, `set`, `setCmt`, `unset`, `let`-binding, the `snapshot2` operator, sequence with the separator symbol ';' and the no-op symbol $*$; and FMA statements **Stmt**, including `create`, `delete`, sequence with the separator symbol ';', the no-op symbol (), `let`-binding and the operation `snapshot` x {$s2$} for an object variable x and a model action $s2$. In FMA, the `snapshot` operator is used to focus the interpreter on an object for manipulating it locally by applying the sequence $s2$ of model actions to the set of properties of the object referenced by x, reducing the amount of model traversals required to apply each model action. The `snapshot2` operator enables updates in contained objects of the object under focus without having to invoke `snapshot` again. FMA also provides support for declaring procedures and for evaluating expressions, which include values (String, Int, Bool, references to objects of a particular type), variables and `let`-binding and procedure calls. While FMA expressions evaluate to a value, FMA statements apply model actions to a model and they evaluate to the corresponding no-op symbol.

The following example is a FMA statement representing the side effects of the rule `DataType2Type`, in which an object of type `Type` is created and its attribute `name` is set to the result of evaluating the OCL expression DT . name where DT is the object variable matched in the left-hand side of the rule.

```
let T = create(Relational ! Type) in () ;
snapshot (T){
  set(name, (DSL#String) DT . name)
}
```

The semantics of the FMA interpreter consists of two main components: the interpreter configurations (the interpreter state together with the statement being evaluated) for the two types of statements and for expressions; and big-step semantic rules describing its behaviour. Figure 2 describes the configuration classes of the FMA interpreter for FMA statements **Stmt**, for model actions **ActStmt**, and for FMA expressions. Each configuration class has a

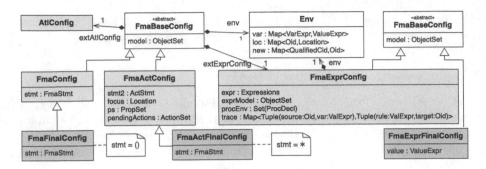

Fig. 2. FMA configurations.

subclass describing what the final configurations are for each type of statement and expression.

Model action configurations FmaActConfig contain the statement stmt2 to be interpreted, the focus location of the object being manipulated, the set of properties ps (attributes, references and containments) of the object under focus and a set pendingActions of pending model actions for setting non-containment opposite references. Pending actions are used for updating opposite references automatically when the other end is set. Final configurations of the interpreter for model actions are given by those states whose statement is the no-op symbol *. Expression states contain the model exprModel to be queried, an environment procEnv of procedure declarations, the expression expr to be evaluated, a trace map exprTrace to be used for the ATL expression resolveTemp, and an environment with a substitution for the free variables in the expression expr and with the location store attaching a location in the model exprModel to each object identifier. Final configurations for FMA expressions only contain a value.

Big-step rules specify an evaluation relation for a particular type of configurations and are defined in terms of transitions from a configuration of a particular type of statements or expressions to a final configuration of the corresponding type. Transition rules are represented using the following form:

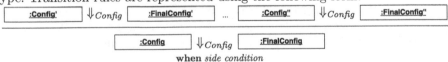

when *side condition*

The transition appearing in the conclusion (below the bar) is valid if the transitions appearing in the premise of the rule (above the bar) also hold and if the side conditions when, placed below the rule for the sake of readability, are satisfied. A side condition is a conjunction of boolean predicates, assignments $T = F(T_1, .., T_n)$ involving n-ary functions F, and transitions from other evaluation relations as we will see in the next sections. Side conditions are evaluated from left to right, a boolean predicate is satisfied when there is a valid substitution for its variables, an assignment is satisfied when the function returns a value with the shape indicated in the term T (usually assigning values to variables appearing in T)[5] and a transition is satisfied when the right-hand side of the transition can be reached (possibly initializing variables) by using transition rules for the corresponding configuration type. In the case of transitions, these will always be *one-step* transitions in practice owing to the design of the big-step rules. A rule without any premise is an axiom and simply asserts a fact, i.e. that a transition from a configuration to a final configuration holds if the side conditions are satisfied as explained above.

As an example, we define the semantic rule that defines the integration of the mOdCL [11] interpreter into the FMA interpreter for evaluating OCL expressions. OCL expressions can be defined in FMA using the FMA expression (T:Scalar) OCL:OclExp, which indicates the type of the OCL expression being used and the OCL expression OCLE:OclExp using mOdCL syntax. The semantic rule E-OclExp in Fig. 3 evaluates such an expression by calling the mOdCL interpreter with: the OCL expression, the model MODEL to be queried, the variable store and the location store from the environment. For the integration to work correctly we have also had to extend some of mOdCL operations with a few equations specifying the behaviour of the allInstances() expression and of navigation expressions using attributes.

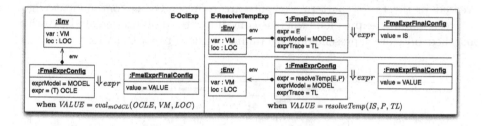

Fig. 3. FMA-ATL semantics of OCL and resolveTemp expressions.

In the following subsections, we describe the following extensions to FMA in order to provide support for ATL. Procedure declarations are extended with ATL helpers; FMA expressions are extended with helper calls and with resolveTemp expressions; and FMA statements are extended with lazy rule calls.

3.2 Initialization

To execute a model transformation, the FMA-ATL interpreter first initializes the interpreter state from the transformation declaration, loading each rule into a rule store and helpers into a helper store. Once rules are available in the store it computes all matches for non-lazy rules, as ATL does, but without creating

---

[5] This notation is a convenient representation both for executing a function and for decomposing its results with projections. Hence, unification is not required.

any objects. This allows FMA-ATL to work with declarative rules that have causal dependencies among them when the expression `resolveTemp` is used in the variable bindings of an ATL rule.

Rule initialization. When an ATL rule is initialized, FMA-ATL obtains an FMA statement that represents the model transformation to be applied in the target model from the variable bindings in the target pattern elements. Additionally, it also obtains a trace statement that indicates what trace links should be added to the trace store. This initialization is performed by extracting a graph from the set of target pattern elements where nodes are FMA expressions and where there are two types of named edges: reference edges and containment edges. When defining an edge, a source node is always a variable expression referring to a variable appearing in the target pattern elements of the rule.

This initialization process is illustrated in Fig. 4. For each target pattern element, FMA traverses its binding statements introducing: (a) a node with a variable expression referring to the object being created and (b) either a reference edge, when the binding corresponds to an attribute or to a non-containment reference, or a containment edge, when the binding corresponds to a containment reference. When defining containment edges, variables corresponding to a target element are extracted from OCL expressions so that containments to objects created in the target pattern elements are represented as containment edges between variable expressions whereas containments to objects created by other matched rules are represented as containment edges to an FMA expression.

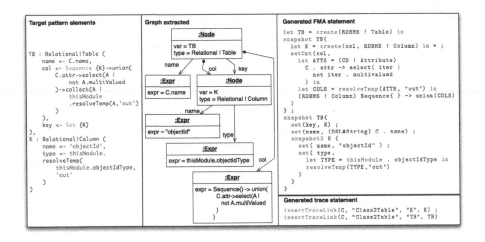

Fig. 4. Translation of Class2Table ATL target pattern elements.

Once the graph is generated, FMA-ATL walks it from its root objects following containment edges twice: first, it obtains an FMA statement that creates a tree of objects that initializes their containment references; second, for each object created in the first traversal, it initializes their attributes and non-containment references as mandated by the rule. Finally, FMA-ATL traverses the nodes that are variables and obtains a trace statement as a sequence of insertions of trace links into the trace store. The free variables used in the trace statement are those that are initialized in the execution of the FMA statement.

Helpers. The helper store is initialized with the helpers defined in the transformation. Helpers with context are simply copied into the helper store but attribute helpers are computed and FMA-ATL caches their value at declaration time by introducing their value together with the attribute helper.

3.3   Scheduling

In this section, we describe the behaviour of the FMA-ATL interpreter and the semantics of ATL matched rules. We start by introducing the main configuration types and we then continue by describing the main rules that specify the behaviour of the FMA-ATL interpreter and the big-step semantics of matched rules. Both the configuration model of the FMA-ATL interpreter and the rules mentioned above are depicted in Fig. 5, where small-step and big-step transition rules are denoted by ⇒ and ⇓, respectively. In the representation of semantic rules, the notation has been simplified by collapsing references to collections of objects in an attribute whose value is a set of objects.

Configurations of the FMA-ATL interpreter have: a `ruleStore` and a `helperStore` with the set of ATL rules and the set of helpers, respectively, that are defined in the transformation; a `queryDomain` pointing to the domain that contains the source model and a set of `domains` that correspond to the different target models that are created by the transformation; a set of `resolveTempClasses` that corresponds to the type names of those classes whose objects may be involved in `resolveTemp` expressions; a `globalTrace` map including all the trace links that are generated by the model and a `localTrace` map that contains the trace links of those objects that may participate in `resolveTemp` expressions − that is, those objects that are instance of a class involved in a `resolveTemp` expression. Each domain contains a `model`, a location store `loc` giving the locations for each object in that model and a factory `new` of fresh identifiers, which is used to create new objects. In addition, there are three specialized types of configurations: `AtlMatchingConfiguration`, used in the rule `E-Schedule` and which has a pointer to a pool of enabled matches; and the corresponding type of final configurations defined as those whose pool of enabled matches is empty; `AtlConfiguration`, used in the rule `E-RuleSideEffects` and which has a pointer to a specific match; and the corresponding type of final configurations defined as those with no match; `AtlDomainConfiguration`, used in the rule `E-DomainActions` and which has an environment of variables containing the match, and a set of domain actions corresponding to those defined in the rule that is being applied; and the corresponding type of final configurations defined as those with an empty set of domain actions.

Once the pool of matches has been computed and linked to an object `AtlMatchingConfig`, FMA-ATL starts applying ATL rules by choosing a match from this pool in the rule `E-Schedule`. This rule selects the root container of the matched object (and the corresponding locations) from the query domain model and uses it as the source domain model for executing the rule. It then applies the matched rule with the selected match via the rule `E-RuleSideEffects`. The resulting target domain and trace maps are updated with the results from executing the matched rule and the pool of enabled matches is updated by disabling all matches involving the matched object (according to the ATL semantics it cannot be transformed any longer as it appears in a trace link).

The semantics of ATL matched rules is given by two big-step semantic rules: `E-RuleSideEffects`, which executes the model actions defined for a domain in that ATL rule[6] via the rule `E-DomainActions`, creating an `AtlFinalConfig` object with updated target domain and trace maps, and deleting the match; and `E-DomainActions`, which applies the model actions for a particular domain by executing the FMA statement in the target domain and the trace statement for creating trace links in the global and local trace maps, creating an `AtlDomainFinalConfig` without any pending domain actions.

3.4   ResolveTemp Expressions and Lazy Rules Call Statements

ResolveTemp expressions. To consider `resolveTempExpr` expressions we have extended the set of FMA expressions with `resolveTemp(E,P)`, where E is an expression that evaluates to a collection of object references and P is the name of the target variable to be used when exploring trace links. The semantics of such an expression, defined by the big-step semantic rule `E-ResolveTemp` in Fig. 3, evaluates the expression E to a set IS of object identifiers and then, for each object identifier SO in IS, it obtains the set of target identifiers TO by getting the value for the key (SO,P) in the local trace map TL in the function `resolveTemp`.

Lazy rule call statements. We have modelled calls to lazy rules as statements instead of modelling them as expressions as in FMA an expression cannot perform changes in a model. Thus we have extended FMA model actions with the statement `setCmtLazyRule(P,RN,O)` where P is the containment reference to contain the newly created objects, RN is the name of the lazy rule, and O is the matched object to be used. In the translation from ATL rules to FMA statements illustrated in Subsect. 3.2, a lazy rule call expression is translated into an FMA model action. In FMA-ATL, a lazy rule is used to expand containments under an object under focus (that is, in a snapshot statement) and its semantics is that of a matched rule as described by the rules `E-RuleSideEffects` and `E-DomainActions`. The only difference is the way in which they are invoked as the match is fixed by the call statement and not by the scheduler.

---

[6] At the moment, we only consider one target domain. To consider more than one target domain, we only need to add an additional rule to iterate over the different domain actions appropriately.

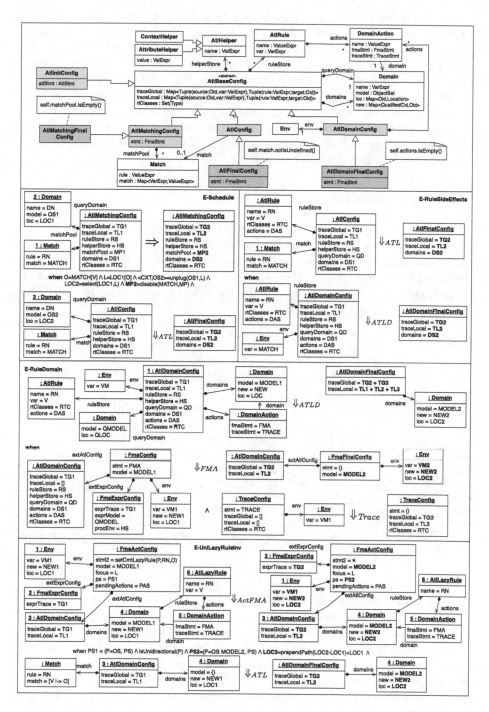

Fig. 5. FMA-ATL semantics: configurations and scheduling rules.

The way in which we have allowed the interaction between FMA and FMA-ATL while preserving the semantics of the former, is by means of the extension point `extFmaConfig` of class `AtlConfigs` in Fig. 2 which allows the FMA model action `setCmtLazyRule` to invoke a FMA-ATL rule with an appropriate configuration as shown in rule `E-UniLazyRuleInv` in Fig. 5 for uni-directional containment references. This rule prepares the configuration for executing the lazy rule as a matched one with an empty target model and stores the results in the extended configuration `extAtlConfig`. Bi-directional containment references are handled similarly but a new model action is added to the set of pending actions in order to update the opposite reference.

4 Experimentation

In this section, we compare the efficiency of our interpreter against ATL 3.6 using two experiments: one for the transformation without lazy rules and one for the transformation with lazy rules. For the experiments we have developed a model with one package containing 5 classes, each of which containing 4 attributes of each particular type in order to exercise all the rules in the transformation.[7] The results are summarized as follows:

| | | Flat models with Maude rules | | | Structured models with FMA-ATL | | | |
| | | Without lazy rules [14] | | | Without lazy rules | | With lazy rules | |
Classes	Attributes	ATL 3.0	Maude	Optimized	ATL 3.6	FMA-ATL	ATL 3.6	FMA-ATL
125	500	0.3″	15″	4″	0″	35.6″	0″	3.3″
250	1000	0.5″	1′ 37″	15″	0.1″	2′ 38.2″	0.1″	7.1″
375	1500	0.8″	5′ 53″	40″	0.1″	6′ 12″	0.1″	10.9″
500	2000	1.1″	16′ 9″	1′ 37″	0.2″	11′ 44.1″	0.2″	14.9″
750	3000	2″	58′ 28″	4′ 2″	0.3″	28′ 5.3″	0.3″	22.6″
1000	4000				0.5″	54′ 3.8″	0.4″	31.6″
1250	5000	3″	3h 16′ 49″	16′ 37″	0.6″	1h 32′ 51.8″	0.5″	41.4″
2000	8000	5″	17h 57′ 15″	1h 4′ 19″	1″	4h 46′ 17.6″	0.8″	1′ 20″
2500	10000				1.3″		1.1″	1′ 43.9″
5000	20000				2.7″		2.2″	5′ 14″
10000	40000				6.6″		4.8″	17′ 16.7″
15000	60000				11″		7.5″	36′ 43.2″

In both experiments, ATL shows better performance and scalability. However, simulating transformations in Maude has an additional advantage as it provides analysis techniques that can be used for reasoning about ATL model transformations, such as bounded model checking of invariants.

The scalability of ATL model transformations in FMA-ATL using structured models and plain configurations of objects with graph-based rewriting rules has been compared by using the experiment results presented in [14]. Their formalization has two variants: an original one [13] and an optimized one [14]. The

---

[7] The case study and the resources for the experiments performed can be found at https://github.com/arturboronat/fma-atl-experiments.

comparison of the scalability of the FMA-ATL interpreter for the ATL transformations in the case study with the implementations of the transformation in
Maude presented in [14] has to be considered with the following validity threats
in mind: the authors used ATL 3.0, an older machine, and the input models
that were used are different − e.g. ours include one additional package per five
classes. Given that both Maude implementations are less efficient than ATL,
the comparison is based on the unitary additional cost of executing an ATL
transformation in each approach with respect to the time obtained in the corresponding experiment. In this way, we mitigate the two first threats to validity.
In the graphs below we show the model size (without counting packages) on the
X axis and the additional unitary cost on the Y axis for ATL transformations
with matched rules only (left) and with lazy rules (right).

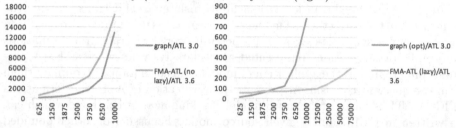

On the one hand, the FMA-ATL interpreter shows a worse performance when
dealing with model transformations without lazy rules. However, its performance
is actually comparable to that of the transformation (without optimization) on
flat models. The main reason for FMA-ATL to perform worse in the first transformation is that every containment that is set to an object created by a separate
matched rule requires searching the object in the model and its performance
worsens as the size of the output model grows.

On the other hand, the execution of the transformation with lazy rules in
FMA-ATL scales better than the optimized ATL transformation with unstruc-
tured models.[8] When using lazy transformations in FMA-ATL, the whole composite object (database) is created in one rule (Package2Database) and all containments are created under the corresponding container object without having
to perform any search in the output model − drastically improving the scalability of the approach. This performance could be improved by a constant factor
by making the compilation Maude-specific. That is, by using model patterns to
implement side effects and it is done in the right-hand side of a rewrite rule in
order to avoid the computation performed by FMA operations. However, this
would lose the advantages of the layer of abstraction that FMA provides.

---

[8] Note that the authors also showed how to implement lazy rules in [14] as functions
although there are no experimental results. However, such semantics for lazy rules
differs from that of FMA-ATL where the semantics of a lazy rule is exactly the same
as that of a matched rule, including the production of trace links.

5   Related Work

In [8], the AMMA platform was extended with abstract state machines using XASM for specifying the semantics of DSLs, including the semantics of ATL. As far as we are aware, there was no empirical evaluation of the performance of the code generated from XASM specifications for ATL. We have focussed on the use of FMA for specifying a structural operational semantics of the ATL transformation language by following a more declarative approach. That is, in our specification there is no explicit code to control the firing of semantic rules (e.g. choose and for all statements). In addition, transition rules in FMA-ATL faithfully reflect their representation in rewrite theories in Maude, enabling the automated analysis of ATL (out-place) model transformations.

In [12], ATL model transformations are translated to DSLTrans enabling the verification of the correctness of model transformations using pre-/post-condition contracts via a symbolic-execution property prover. DSLTrans transformations are graph transformations represented as declarative rules whereas FMA programs only represent the application of model transformations, decoupling them from the query mechanism. At present, the verification of ATL transformations in FMA-ATL is based on bounded model checking against contracts, which can be written in OCL, from a given source model. Focussing on other bounded model checking approaches, [6] the semantics of ATL transformations is captured in ATL transformation models using OCL constraints and reduces the verification of their partial correctness to a satisfiability problem in Alloy.

A rewriting logic semantics of ATL using Maude has been proposed in [13,14], as discussed from a quantitative point of view in Sect. 4. From a qualitative point of view, their representation of models is based on sets of plain objects. ATL model transformation rules are represented using conditional rewrite rules using Maude as a high-level declarative rule-based language. Their formalization requires a compiler from ATL to their encoding of ATL transformation rules, which may require non-trivial program transformations for the optimized version, as acknowledged by the authors. Our approach is based on an interpreter for ATL that reuses FMA to encode the model transformation actions of each rule, encapsulating all the cases that would need to be implemented in the compiler in the other approach. This design decision allows us to represent the semantics of ATL in a small set of rules, implementing an interpreter, while retaining the analysis facilities that Maude's toolkit provides. Therefore, these two approaches differ in the way they deal with abstraction when capturing ATL semantics in rewriting logic. Both approaches use mOdCL [11] as their OCL interpreter.

6   Conclusions

In this paper, we have presented a big-step structural operational semantics for out-place ATL model transformation rules and the specification of a simple ATL interpreter. The conditional rewrite rules implementing the FMA-ATL interpreter in Maude facilitate the verification of ATL model transformations.

The formalization and design of the interpreter has helped us detect that calls to lazy rules in ATL expressions cannot be modelled as FMA expressions since they do not simply evaluate to a value. They also update other components of the interpreter configuration and have to be considered as FMA statements.

FMA-ATL enables the execution − and, thus, verification − of a larger class of out-place ATL model transformations than previous approaches (increasing the size of models from 10 K objects to 78 K objects) when working with models that consist of objects with containments and lazy rules aggregating the side effects of several dependent matched rules. The formalization in [14], based on compilation from ATL to Maude, is more appropriate for models without containments or when dealing with many interdependent matched rules. In future work, we are going to apply the lessons learnt from transformations with lazy rules for making ATL transformations with matched rules more scalable. On the other hand, we plan to address in-place model transformations and unique lazy rules in order to cover a larger gamut of ATL model transformations.

References

1. Ab. Rahim, A., Whittle, J.: A survey of approaches for verifying model transformations. Softw. Syst. Model. **14**(2), 1003–1028 (2015)
2. Amrani, M., Combemale, B., Lucio, L., Selim, G.M.K., Dingel, J., Traon, Y.L., Vangheluwe, H., Cordy, J.R.: Formal verification techniques for model transformations: a tridimensional classification. JOT **14**(3), 1:1–43 (2015)
3. Boronat, A.: Well-Behaved Model Transformations with Model Subtyping. CoRR abs/1703.08113 (2017)
4. Boronat, A., Heckel, R., Meseguer, J.: Rewriting logic semantics and verification of model transformations. In: Chechik, M., Wirsing, M. (eds.) FASE 2009. LNCS, vol. 5503, pp. 18–33. Springer, Heidelberg (2009). doi:10.1007/978-3-642-00593-0 2
5. Brambilla, M., Cabot, J., Wimmer, M.: Model-Driven Software Engineering in Practice. Morgan & Claypool Publishers (2012)
6. Büttner, F., Egea, M., Cabot, J., Gogolla, M.: Verification of ATL transformations using transformation models and model finders. In: Aoki, T., Taguchi, K. (eds.) ICFEM 2012. LNCS, vol. 7635, pp. 198–213. Springer, Heidelberg (2012). doi:10.1007/978-3-642-34281-3_16
7. Clavel, M., Durán, F., Eker, S., Lincoln, P., Martí-Oliet, N., Meseguer, J., Talcott, C.: All About Maude - A High-Performance Logical Framework. LNCS, vol. 4350. Springer, Heidelberg (2007)
8. Di Ruscio, D., Jouault, F., Kurtev, I., Bézivin, J., Pierantonio, A.: Extending AMMA for Supporting Dynamic Semantics Specifications of DSLs. Laboratoire d'Informatique de Nantes-Atlantique, LINA (2006)
9. Jouault, F., Allilaire, F., Bézivin, J., Kurtev, I.: ATL: a model transformation tool. Sci. Comput. Program. **72**(1–2), 31–39 (2008)
10. Lawlew, M., Duddy, K., Gerber, A., Raymond, K.: Language Features for Re-Use and Maintainability of MDA Transformations. In: OOPSLA & GPCE Workshop (2004). adapted in. https://www.eclipse.org/atl/atlTransformations/# Class2Relational
11. Roldán, M., Durán, F.: The mOdCL evaluator: Maude + OCL (2013). http://maude.lcc.uma.es/mOdCL/. Accessed 3 Mar 2016

12. Oakes, B.J., Troya, J., Lucio, L., Wimmer, M.: Fully verifying transformation contracts for declarative ATL. In: ACM/IEEE MoDELS 2015, pp. 256–265 (2015)
13. Troya, J., Vallecillo, A.: Towards a rewriting logic semantics for ATL. In: Tratt, L., Gogolla, M. (eds.) ICMT 2010. LNCS, vol. 6142, pp. 230–244. Springer, Heidelberg (2010). doi:10.1007/978-3-642-13688-7_16
14. Troya, J., Vallecillo, A.: A rewriting logic semantics for ATL. J. Object Technol. **10**(5), 1–29 (2011)

Reducing the Verbosity of Imperative Model Refinements by Using General-Purpose Language Facilities

Christopher Gerking[1]([✉]), David Schubert[2], and Ingo Budde[2]

[1] Heinz Nixdorf Institute, Paderborn University, Paderborn, Germany
christopher.gerking@upb.de
[2] Fraunhofer IEM, Paderborn, Germany

Abstract. Refinements are model transformations that leave large parts of the source models unchanged. Therefore, if refinements are executed outplace, model elements need to be copied to the target model. Refinements written in imperative languages are increasingly verbose, unless suitable language facilities exist for creating these copies implicitly. Thus, for languages restricted to general-purpose facilities, the verbosity of refinements is still an open problem. Existing approaches towards reducing this verbosity suffer from the complexity of developing a higher-order transformation to synthesize the copying code. In this paper, we propose a generic transformation library for creating implicit copies, reducing the verbosity without a higher-order transformation. We identify the underlying general-purpose language facilities, and compare state-of-the-art languages against these requirements. We give a proof of concept using the imperative QVTo language, and showcase the ability of our library to reduce the verbosity of an industrial-scale transformation chain.

Keywords: Model refinement · Implicit copy · Imperative languages

1 Introduction

In model-driven engineering (MDE), imperative transformation languages are widely used as vehicles for creating operational model transformations [4]. By including facilities known from general-purpose languages, imperative languages enable [26] the specification and execution of fit-for-purpose model transformations.

One major purpose of model transformation is *refinement* [25], with use cases such as desugaring [15], aspect weaving [17], or synthesis [7]. According to the terminology used in [20], a model refinement "preserves large parts of the source model and adds additional information". Therefore, a refinement is *endogenous* because source and target models are based on the same metamodel. Furthermore, refinements in MDE often need to preserve the source models as primary, immutable artifacts. Thus, one possible approach is to create a temporary one-to-one copy of the source model (e.g., a file copy) in order to refine the copy using

© Springer International Publishing AG 2017
E. Guerra and M. van den Brand (Eds.): ICMT 2017, LNCS 10374, pp. 19–34, 2017.
DOI: 10.1007/978-3-319-61473-1_2

an *inplace* transformation. However, this approach lacks end-to-end traceability and leads to redundant copies of the changing elements. Therefore, refinement transformations are often required to execute *outplace* [26] and need to copy the unchanged elements during the refinement.

This paper addresses the problem that imperative languages are increasingly verbose when used for outplace model refinements. The reason is that users need to copy the unchanged elements explicitly by iterating over all links of each element, resulting in a huge amount of *boilerplate* code that users must write and maintain. Nowadays, maintainability of model transformations is already considered as a critical factor [1]. A well-known approach for reducing this verbosity is the *implicit copy* design pattern [24], proposing a mechanism for creating copies implicitly. However, such a mechanism must be supported by the transformation language in use. Therefore, Lano and Kolahdouz-Rahimi request "suitable language facilities to be present" [24]. On the one hand, languages such as ATL [18] or Epsilon Flock [29] provide special-purpose facilities for implicit copies. On the other hand, languages restricted to general-purpose facilities still suffer from an increased verbosity because users need to create all copies explicitly.

In literature, other approaches exist towards reducing this verbosity [12,13,22]. These related works regard the copying as *schematic-repetitive code* [30], and use a *higher-order transformation* (HOT, [32]) to synthesize the boilerplate code. However, such approaches suffer from the intrinsic complexity of developing a HOT [31], and from the maintenance burden of re-executing the HOT to update the boilerplate code in case of metamodel evolution [28].

In this paper, we demonstrate that general-purpose facilities are sufficient to realize the implicit copy pattern in imperative languages. Thereby, the language facilities requested by Lano and Kolahdouz-Rahimi [24] are made explicit. We regard the copying as *generic code* [30] and propose a transformation library that provides implicit copies to reduce the verbosity of model refinements. We identify an amount of four underlying language facilities that enable our approach, and check state-of-the-art imperative languages against these facilities. Thereby, we assess their ability to realize our library. In contrast to related work, we propose a generic library that is reusable as-is for different metamodels, saving users from the effort of developing a HOT and maintaining the synthesized boilerplate code.

As a proof of concept, we realize our library using the QVT Operational Mappings language (QVTo, [27]), and showcase the ability of our library to improve the maintainability of an industrial-scale transformation chain.

In summary, this paper makes the following contributions:

- We provide a concept for an implicit copy library that reduces the verbosity of model refinements written in imperative transformation languages.
- We illustrate the required language facilities, and compare state-of-the-art imperative languages against these requirements.
- We give a proof of concept using the imperative QVTo language.

Paper Organization: Sect. 2 introduces a motivating example, before we discuss related work in Sect. 3. In Sect. 4, we present our implicit copy library and compare existing languages against the required facilities. We use QVTo to provide a proof of concept in Sect. 5, before concluding in Sect. 6.

2   Motivating Example

As an illustrative example of a model refinement, we consider a statemachine dialect that requires *desugaring*, i.e., semantics-preserving normalization to a more basic syntactic form. In our dialect, every state of a statemachine may refer to a *do* activity which is a behavior executed periodically. The activity is released for execution in a fixed time interval (the period) and executes once per period. In Fig. 1a, we show an excerpt from a statemachine including a state A with a do activity named a() and a fixed period of 50 milliseconds.

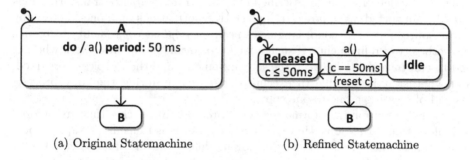

(a) Original Statemachine   (b) Refined Statemachine

Fig. 1. Example refinement of statemachine models

When transforming such models to an execution platform, the declarative specification of a do activity needs to be refined to an equivalent operational form. For example, in Fig. 1b, we replaced the declaration of the do event by a submachine with two substates and one clock c, measuring the time that has already passed during the current period. Initially, the submachine is in state Released, denoting a situation in which the behavior a() was released for execution, but has not yet been executed in the current period. At latest after 50 ms, the invariant $c \leq 50ms$ forces the submachine to execute the behavior a() by switching to state Idle. In this state, the submachine waits until the clock constraint $c == 50ms$ is fulfilled, i.e., the end of the current period. At this time, the activity is released for execution again. Therefore, the submachine switches back to Released and resets the clock c to zero.

Our example refinement affects only states with do activities, whereas all other model elements (e.g., transitions) remain unchanged. Copying the unchanged model elements explicitly requires boilerplate code to iterate over all elements and copy all their links to other elements. In language families like UML with a multitude of different types included, the number of unchanged elements might increase drastically, and lead to an advanced verbosity of the boilerplate code for refinements. Thus, according to the *implicit copy* pattern, the transformation language in use should provide a mechanism to specify explicitly only the refinement of states. All other unchanged model elements should be copied implicitly.

3   Related Work

In the following, we first review existing transformation approaches with respect to built-in refinement support (cf. Sect. 3.1). Then, we discuss approaches using a HOT for refinements in languages without built-in support (cf. Sect. 3.2).

3.1   Refinement as Built-in Language Facility

In Table 1, we check existing transformation approaches against the core requirements for model refinements described in Sect. 1. First, *outplace* transformations must be supported, as opposed to inplace transformations on a one-to-one copy of the source model. Second, languages need an *implicit copy* facility to reduce the verbosity of refinements. If such a facility is available, we also check whether end-to-end *traceability* between the source elements and their copies is provided, and whether it is possible to execute a *refinement* during the copy process, instead of creating a one-to-one copy.

The field of graph transformation (GT) provides approaches that are tailored to inplace transformations. However, languages such as Henshin [3] support outplace transformations as well, connecting models by means of a dedicated trace model that provides traceability between source and target elements. Whereas no implicit copy facility is given in general, Krause et al. [23] propose dynamically typed graph transformations that enable the specification of concise and generic rules for implicit copies[1].

In contrast, approaches based on triple graph grammars (TGG) address outplace transformations, connecting source and target models by means of a correspondence graph. The correspondence graph ensures traceability between source and target elements. Anjorin et al. [2] address refinement support for TGG by enabling specialization of basic transformation rules. However, in general, no mechanism for creating implicit copies is available.

The Epsilon Wizard Language (EWL, [21]) is a task-specific language for manipulating user-defined selections of model elements. EWL is restricted to inplace transformations. Therefore, no outplace transformations and no implicit copies are supported.

The task of refining a model can also be viewed as a special case of model migration to compensate metamodel evolution. In this field of model/metamodel co-evolution, a large body of knowledge is already existing and surveyed in [14, 16, 28]. In fact, the majority of approaches uses outplace transformations [16]. For example, Epsilon Flock [29] creates implicit copies using a conservative copy strategy. The approach provides traceability and allows to execute refinements as user-defined migrations during the copy process.

---

[1] http://www.ckrause.org/2013/04/copying-emf-models-with-henshin.html

Similar to Flock, ATL provides a *refining* execution mode that implicitly copies all the unchanged model elements from the source model to the target model. The refining mode provides traceability and also allows to execute refinements during the copy process because user-defined transformation rules override the default copy behavior.

The QVT standard provides languages with support for outplace transformations. Whereas QVTr supports no implicit copies, QVTo provides a copy mechanism in terms of its *deepclone* operation [27]. However, this operation does not provide traceability between the source elements and their copies, and does not allow to execute refinements during the copy process.

Table 1. Comparative overview on refinement support

	GT	TGG	EWL	Flock	ATL	QVTr	QVTo
Outplace	(✓)[a]	✓	✗	✓	✓	✓	✓
Implicit Copy	(✓)[b]	✗	✗	✓	✓	✗	✓
-Traceability	(✓)[c]	-	-	✓	✓	-	✗
-Refinement	✗	-	-	✓	✓	-	✗

[a]Outplace is supported by graph transformation languages such as Henshin.
[b]Languages such as Henshin provide a trace model.
[c]Implicit copies are supported by dynamically typed graph transformations [23]

3.2   Refinement Using Higher-Order Transformations

The work by van Gorp et al. [13] extends graph transformations with declarative copy annotations for elements to be copied. A HOT is used to transform these implicit annotations into executable graph transformations with an explicit copy behavior. The use of annotations reduces the verbosity of the transformations, and also allows to specify refinements to be executed during the copy process.

Unlike the above approach that uses graph transformations as inputs for the HOT, Goldschmidt et al. [12, 19, 20] generate a full set of copy rules from a specific metamodel, one rule for each type. The copy rules generated by the HOT are based on the declarative QVTr language. In order to execute refinements during the copy process, it is possible to override specific copy rules with custom refinement rules. Furthermore, the authors also discuss the possibility of using another HOT to weave the refinement rules into the copy rules, receiving a single comprehensive refinement transformation.

Whereas the above approaches focus on declarative languages, the work by Kraas [22] addresses an imperative transformation language in terms of QVTo, similar to the scope of this paper. The author uses a HOT to generate an imperative copy transformation for a specific metamodel. Similar to the declarative case, one copy operation for each type inside the metamodel is generated. These default copy operations can be overridden by user-defined refinement operations.

A common drawback of the above approaches is that developing a HOT is generally considered a tedious task [31]. Furthermore, if the HOT can not be re-exccuted automatically, frequent metamodel evolution can easily evolve into serious maintenance efforts to update the generated code manually. Nevertheless, in this paper, we consider the HOT-based approach described by Kraas [22] as our baseline due to its focus on imperative transformations.

4   A Generic Library for Implicit Copies

In this section, we present our approach towards reducing the verbosity of imperative model refinements. In Sect. 4.1, we describe our conceptual approach based on a generic transformation library that provides implicit copies. In Sect. 4.2, we extrapolate the required language facilities, and compare state-of-the-art imperative languages against these requirements.

4.1   Conceptual Approach

Our approach enables model refinements based on general-purpose facilities of imperative transformation languages. Instead of using a HOT, we provide a generic library implementation that encapsulates the repetitive copying behavior, and is reusable by arbitrary user-defined refinement transformations.

As an example, Fig. 2a shows a metamodel excerpt for statemachines. We assume a type Element to be the implicit supertype of all model elements, similar to the Object class in Java. The only type affected by the normalization introduced in Sect. 2 is State because additional substates and transitions are added to replace the declarative do Activity. The elements of type Transition and any other types omitted in Fig. 2a should be copied without changes.

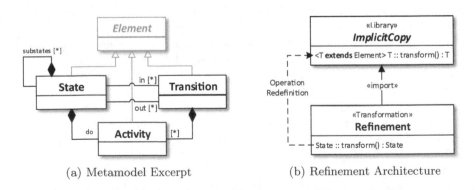

(a) Metamodel Excerpt   (b) Refinement Architecture

Fig. 2. Application scenario for model refinement

Figure 2b illustrates our approach at the architectural level. We introduce a transformation library named ImplicitCopy that can be imported by arbitrary Refinement transformations. Our library consists of a single operation named transform that receives an arbitrary model element. In its basic form, the operation returns a one-to-one copy of the element, including copies of all cross-linked elements. To make our operation applicable to arbitrary elements, the context type T (representing the received element) is a generic subtype of Element. Since transform returns a copy, T also acts as the return type. In Fig. 2b, we use a double colon to separate the operation's context type from the operation name, whereas a single colon separates the operation name from its return type.

In our example, the Refinement transformation includes a redefinition of the generic transform operation for elements of type State. By returning a subtype of Element, the operation makes use of covariant return types. On the right-hand side of Fig. 3, we depict the pseudocode implementation. To avoid duplicate copies, our library holds a cache of copied elements. The cache is a map between the originals and their copies, providing the default get and put operations to obtain or add a copy. Using the cache, the transform operation first checks for an existing copy and, if present, returns it. Otherwise, it creates a new instance of the same type as the received element, which is denoted by self. The new instance is assigned to the result variable, and added to the cache immediately.

Subsequently, the operation reflectively traverses all features of the self element, representing links to other elements. For each feature, the operation obtains the current values (representing the linked elements), and invokes transform recursively on each of them. At this point, we apply the *recursive descent* design pattern for model transformations [24]. In order to avoid duplicate copies in a recursive invocation, it is of crucial importance that every result is added to the cache immediately after its creation. Thereby, we also ensure termination

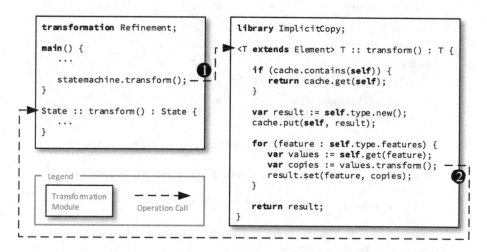

Fig. 3. Interaction of refinement transformation and implicit copy library

because the recursion takes place only during the first execution of the operation for a particular element. Finally, the resulting copies are assigned to the respective feature of the result, which is returned at the end of the operation.

On the left-hand side of Fig. 3, we depict a transformation using our library to refine statemachine models. From its main operation, the refinement invokes transform on a statemachine, as depicted by ❶. Accordingly, the library implementation of the operation executes. However, when invoking the operation recursively on a State contained in the statemachine, a virtual operation call depicted by ❷ ensures that the redefining implementation executes instead. Thereby, we ensure that refinements can be executed during the copy process.

4.2   Language Facilities

The concept described in Sect. 4.1 requires four core facilities of imperative languages in order to apply our approach successfully. In the following, we extrapolate these facilities (F1-F4) from our conceptual approach.

(F1) Module Superimposition [33] is the ability to layer separate transformation modules by means of importing. Thereby, it is possible for arbitrary transformations to import and reuse our implicit copy library.

(F2) Dynamic Dispatch of virtual operations is required to distinguish at runtime between the generic copying behavior implemented by our library, and the user-defined refinement behavior. The default copying operation needs to be polymorphic in order to support redefinitions for specific model

Table 2. Comparative overview on language facilities

	Xtend	K3	ATL	ETL	QVTo
Built-In Facility	✗	✗	✓	✗[a]	✗[b]
Module Superimposition (F1)	✓	✓	✓	✓	✓
Dynamic Dispatch (F2)	✓	✗[c]	✓	✓	✓
Reflection (F3)	✓	✓	✗[d]	✓	✓
Generic Return Types (F4)	(✓)[e]	✗[f]	✗	✗	✗
Successful Implementation	✓	✗	✗	✓	✓

[a] The Epsilon family provides refinement facilities in terms of Epsilon Flock.
[b] QVTo provides a *deepclone* operation that is restricted to one-to-one copies.
[c] Kermeta 3 does not support dynamic dispatching for methods of aspect classes.
[d] ATL provides no access to the reflective API of the EMF modeling framework.
[e] Xtend supports generic return types, but not in combination with dynamic dispatch.
[f] Kermeta 3 does not support generic return types for methods of aspect classes.

element types. At runtime, the executing implementation depends on the actual type of the element that the operation has been invoked on.

(F3) Reflection of the underlying modeling framework. Given an element of a concrete type, the copy operation needs to create a new instance of the same type, which is only known at runtime. Furthermore, reflective access to all features of an element's type is required.

(F4) Generic Return Types (optional) to infer the type of a copied element statically. When invoking the copy operation on an element of a certain type, it is beneficial to obtain the identical return type at compile time. Otherwise, type casting is required to establish type compatibility.

In order to point out the generality of our approach, we attempted to implement our library in five state-of-the-art imperative transformation languages, namely Xtend, Kermeta 3 (K3), ATL, ETL, and QVTo, covering two of the most widely used de-facto standards [4]. In Table 2, we check these languages against the facilities F1-F4. We also indicate if an built-in facility is already provided, and if our concept could be implemented successfully.

5   Proof of Concept

We realized our concept of a generic implicit copy library using QVTo [27] as one of the languages that lacks a built-in facility, and provides the mandatory facilities F1-F3 identified in Sect. 4.2. QVTo enables the specification and execution of imperative model-to-model transformations, consisting of modules that can define operations and import other modules. In QVTo, `mapping` operations are used to transform a source element into a target element.

5.1   Library Implementation Using QVTo

We provide a reference implementation of our concept as a transformation library for Eclipse QVTo, which is based on the Eclipse Modeling Framework (EMF). Our library is ready to use and publicly available at an Eclipse update site[2]. In QVTo, we use a `mapping` to implement the default `transform` operation. Since QVTo does not support generic return types (F4), we use the implicit supertype `Element` as both context and return type of our mapping. Below, we show the mapping declaration and its implementation in QVTo.

---

[2] http://muml.org/implicitcopy/updates

```
mapping Element :: transform() : Element {
    init {
            var type := self.oclAsType(EObject).eClass();
            var factory := type.ePackage.eFactoryInstance;
            result := factory.create(type);
    }

    type.eAllReferences->select(modifiable())->forEach(r) {
            var values := self.oclAsType(EObject).eGet(r);
            var copies := values.oclAsType(Element).map transform
                ();
            result.oclAsType(EObject).eSet(r, copies);
    }
}
```

For the received element denoted by self, our mapping creates a new instance of the same type inside the init section, which allows to assign the instance to the predefined result variable. By using EMF's reflective API, we obtain the concrete type of the self element, and use the corresponding factory to create a new instance. QVTo does not require the manual implementation of the caching mechanism introduced in Sect. 4.1. Instead, a built-in traceability mechanism [27] records a trace link between the self and the result elements at the end of the init section. If the mapping is invoked on an element for which a trace record exists already, the copy will be obtained from the trace automatically without executing the mapping again.

Subsequently, we link the result to the copies of all cross-linked elements. For each modifiable reference r of the type, we obtain the collection of cross-linked values using EMF's eGet operation. We create the copies by casting each of the values to the required type Element and invoking transform recursively. Finally, we use a EMF's eSet operation to create the links between the result and the copies of the cross-linked elements.

5.2   Refinement Implementation Using QVTo

Transformations may use the identifier org.muml.ImplicitCopy to import our library. As an example, we illustrate how we implemented the normalization of do activities for statemachine models introduced in Sect. 2. Below, we show a QVTo transformation named DoActivity operating on statemachine models of type SM. In the main operation, the transformation starts the refinement by invoking the imported transform mapping on all root elements of type StateMachine.

For elements of type State, an additional mapping declared in the refinement transformation is automatically executed instead of the default copying operation. Inside this mapping, the state name as well as all incoming/outgoing transitions and embedded regions of the state are preserved by recursively invoking transform. Since the return type is Element, we use the oclAsType operation to cast the copies to the required type. The do activity of a state is not preserved, as it is replaced by an additional region that is created by the mapping `DoActivity2Region` (omitted below). This new region contains the additional states and transitions described in Sect. 2.

```
import org.muml.ImplicitCopy;

transformation DoActivity(in source : SM, out target : SM);

main() {
    source.objects()[StateMachine]->map transform();
}

mapping State :: transform() : State {

    name := self.name;

    incoming := self.incoming->
        map transform().oclAsType(Transition);
    outgoing := self.outgoing->
        map transform().oclAsType(Transition);

    regions := self.regions->map transform().oclAsType(Region)
        ;
    regions += self.map DoActivity2Region();
}
```

5.3 Validation

The objective of our validation is to demonstrate the progress of our implicit copy library in terms of maintainability, compared to the baseline approach of using a HOT (cf. Sect. 3.2). To this end, we consider a refinement scenario in the context of MECHATRONICUML [5,11], a model-driven software design method for cyber-physical systems. Since MECHATRONICUML combines numerous domain-specific languages, the resulting domain models are based on a large, industrial-scale metamodel. A key feature of MECHATRONICUML is domain-specific model checking of the system behavior [9], which is modeled using a real-time variant of UML statemachines. To this end, MECHATRONICUML uses model refinements to align its statemachines to the syntax of the model checker in use. This refinement is based on a QVTo transformation chain consisting of eight refinement steps for statemachine models [9]. Each step refines only a particular syntactic feature, namely (1) scaling of time units, (2) disambiguation of identifiers, (3) normalizing transition deadlines, (4) normalizing transitions of composite states, (5) normalizing of do activities, (6) flattening of hierarchical states, (7) normalization of entry/exit activities, and finally (8) normalizing of urgency properties of transitions.

Setting the Hypothesis. We argue that our approach outperforms the baseline by reducing the size of transformation code that requires maintenance in case of metamodel evolution. According to the quality model for QVTo proposed in [10], we use lines of code for the quantification of transformation size. In particular, we chose source lines of code (SLOC) as our base metric, which represents the overall number of lines of code, excluding whitespace and comments. On the basis of SLOC, we compute three different response variables:

1. *Overall code size* which is the total number of SLOC.
2. *Handwritten code size* as the number of SLOC that was written manually.
3. *Evolving code size* which is the number of SLOC that is metamodel-specific, including both handwritten and generated code.

Our evaluation hypothesis is that our approach improves the maintainability of the transformation chain by significantly reducing the *evolving code size* compared to the baseline approach of using a HOT.

Planning. To conduct our validation, we implement each of the eight refinement steps in four different stages, differing in what type of library is used to enable implicit copies. The stage *none* denotes a naive implementation stage without a copy library. All transformation steps implement the copying on their own, resulting in huge code duplication between the different steps. For the stage *boilerplate*, we avoid code duplication. Here, the copying is outsourced to a central library containing the handwritten boilerplate code. In contrast, the *HOT-generated* stage uses a HOT to generate this boilerplate code automatically. Finally, the *generic* stage denotes the approach of using an implicit copy library as proposed in this paper.

Validating the Hypothesis. We validate our hypothesis by traversing the four aforementioned stages of implementation. The stages *none* and *boilerplate* comprise manually implemented code only. For the stage *HOT-generated*, we manually implement a HOT in QVTo that traverses an arbitrary Ecore metamodel and generates the abstract syntax tree of a QVTo copy library. We refer the reader to [22] for structural details on the synthesized code. In the *generic* stage, we implement the implicit copy library as proposed in this paper.

After every stage, we count the SLOC of all transformation modules involved. The respective modules include (1) the eight refinement steps, (2) a copy library as used in all stages except *none*, and (3) a HOT as used only in the *HOT-generated* stage. Finally, on the basis of SLOC values for all modules and all different implementation stages, we calculate the response values for our variables by distinguishing between manually implemented and generated modules, and between metamodel-specific and metamodel-independent modules.

Analyzing the Results. In Table 3, we list the results of our validation procedure. For each implementation stage and each transformation module involved, we show the resulting number of SLOC. In the rightmost columns, we present the resulting values of our response variables. In particular, we also show percentage values indicating the increase/decrease compared to the preceding implementation stage. According to our results, the *boilerplate* approach reduces all three variables by 71.3% compared to the type *none*. Whereas the *HOT-generated* library leads to a minor increase of the overall transformation size by 4.0% compared to the boilerplate approach, it further decreases the handwritten code size significantly by another 31.4%. With respect to the evolving code size, no difference compared to the *boilerplate* approach is detected because the additional HOT implementation is metamodel-independent. Finally, the *generic* approach reduces the overall code size by another 37.7%, and the handwritten code size slightly by 5.5%. Furthermore, we also detect a reduction of the evolving code size by 36.2%. According to this significant reduction, we regard our evaluation hypothesis as fulfilled.

Table 3. Resulting SLOC Values and Response Variables

Library Type	Time Units	Identi fiers	Dead lines	Transi tions	Do Acti vities	Hier archy	Entry/ Exit	Ur gency	Lib rary	HOT	Over all	Hand written	Evol ving
None	1062	1033	1198	1235	1281	1755	1082	1261	N/A	N/A	9907	9907	9907
Boilerplate	53	24	189	226	272	746	73	252	1009	N/A	2844 -71.3%	2844 -71.3%	2844 -71.3%
HOT-generated	53	24	189	226	272	746	73	252	1009	115	2959 +4.0%	1950 -31.4%	2844 ±0%
Generic	53	24	196	226	272	746	73	224	29	N/A	1843 -37.7%	1843 -5.5%	1814 -36.2%

Threats to Validity. A threat to the validity of our findings is that SLOC represents only the overall size of the transformation modules. Thus, it reflects the potential vulnerability to metamodel evolution, but does not capture the actual maintenance efforts over time in a real evolution scenario. Therefore, in case of infrequent metamodel evolution or limited change impact, the benefits of our approach might be less obvious. Furthermore, if it is possible to re-execute the HOT automatically (e.g., by means of continuous integration), the evolving code size might not be the crucial variable to measure maintenance effort. In this case, the handwritten code size is a more meaningful metric.

Another threat is that the HOT we developed is a model-to-model transformation and, therefore, generates an abstract syntax tree. Instead, using a model-to-text transformation to generate the concrete syntax is expected to be less cumbersome. However, since we restrict our validation to QVTo as a model-to-model approach, involving an additional model-to-text engine would lead to incomparability of the transformation size.

6   Conclusion and Future Work

In this paper, we present a transformation library that provides implicit copies for imperative transformation languages without special-purpose refinement facilities. Thereby, we significantly reduce the verbosity of refinement transformations written in such languages restricted to general-purpose facilities. We also discuss the generality of the approach by elaborating the core facilities that imperative languages must provide in order to realize our approach. We give an overview on state-of-the-art imperative languages with respect to the core facilities. Thereby, we assess the applicability of our approach to these languages. Our proof of concept demonstrates how a reduced verbosity contributes to an improved maintainability of refinement transformations.

Our approach is beneficial for imperative transformation developers with recurring model refinement tasks, provided that their favored transformation language supports the identified facilities. If so, developing an implicit copy library will eventually save development efforts, compared to the approach of writing the boilerplate code manually for each refinement transformation. Furthermore, compared to the approach of using a HOT to synthesize the boilerplate code, our approach also saves maintenance efforts in scenarios with frequent metamodel evolution. Finally, language engineers might use our approach to provide transformation languages with a built-in standard library for implicit copies. For now, we make a ready-to-use library available to QVTo developers.

Future work on our approach includes a more fine-grained specification of refinements. Currently, refinement operations are specified per type and need to address all of the type's features, i.e., links to other types. In contrast, specifying refinements per feature is a promising extension to our approach. At the technological level, our library implementation in QVTo could benefit from generic return types for copy operations, as one of the language facilities identified in this paper. In order to avoid type casting in case of such generic, type-preserving operations, QVTo might adopt the `OclSelf` pseudo type proposed by Willink [34] as an extension to OCL. Finally, we plan to extend the scope of our work towards refining declarative transformation models [6], addressing also exogenous transformations. In particular, we intend to combine our approach with generic execution algorithms [8], assisting in situations where complex mapping models can not be executed by an algorithm, and therefore need to be refined manually using an imperative language.

Acknowledgments. The authors thank Marie Christin Platenius and Anthony Anjorin for helpful comments on earlier versions of the paper, and Mario Treiber for assisting in our validation.

References

1. Amstel, M.F., Brand, M.G.J.: Model transformation analysis: staying ahead of the maintenance nightmare. In: Cabot, J., Visser, E. (eds.) ICMT 2011. LNCS, vol. 6707, pp. 108–122. Springer, Heidelberg (2011). doi:10.1007/978-3-642-21732-6_8
2. Anjorin, A., Saller, K., Lochau, M., Schürr, A.: Modularizing triple graph grammars using rule refinement. In: Gnesi, S., Rensink, A. (eds.) FASE 2014. LNCS, vol. 8411, pp. 340–354. Springer, Heidelberg (2014). doi:10.1007/978-3-642-54804-8_24

3. Arendt, T., Biermann, E., Jurack, S., Krause, C., Taentzer, G.: Henshin: advanced concepts and tools for in-place EMF model transformations. In: Petriu, D.C., Rouquette, N., Haugen, Ø. (eds.) MODELS 2010. LNCS, vol. 6394, pp. 121–135. Springer, Heidelberg (2010). doi:10.1007/978-3-642-16145-2_9

4. Batot, E., Sahraoui, H.A., Syriani, E., Molins, P., Sboui, W.: Systematic mapping study of model transformations for concrete problems. In: MODELSWARD 2016, pp. 176–183. SciTePress (2016)

5. Becker, S., Dziwok, S., Gerking, C., Heinzemann, C., Schäfer, W., Meyer, M., Pohlmann, U.: The MechatronicUML method. In: ICSE Companion 2014, pp. 614–615. ACM (2014)

6. Bézivin, J., Büttner, F., Gogolla, M., Jouault, F., Kurtev, I., Lindow, A.: Model transformations? transformation models!. In: Nierstrasz, O., Whittle, J., Harel, D., Reggio, G. (eds.) MODELS 2006. LNCS, vol. 4199, pp. 440–453. Springer, Heidelberg (2006). doi:10.1007/11880240_31

7. Denil, J., Cicchetti, A., Biehl, M., Meulenaere, P.D., Eramo, R., Demeyer, S., Vangheluwe, H.: Automatic deployment space exploration using refinement transformations. Electronic Communications of the EASST 50 (2011)

8. Freund, M., Braune, A.: A generic transformation algorithm to simplify the development of mapping models. In: MoDELS 2016, pp. 284–294. ACM (2016)

9. Gerking, C., Dziwok, S., Heinzemann, C., Schäfer, W.: Domain-specific model checking for cyber-physical systems. In: MoDeVVa 2015, pp. 18–27 (2015)

10. Gerpheide, C.M., Schiffelers, R.R.H., Serebrenik, A.: Assessing and improving quality of QVTo model transformations. Software Qual. J. **24**(3), 797–834 (2016)

11. Giese, H., Tichy, M., Burmester, S., Schäfer, W., Flake, S.: Towards the compositional verification of real-time UML designs. In: ESEC/FSE 2003, pp. 38–47. ACM (2003)

12. Goldschmidt, T., Wachsmuth, G.: Refinement transformation support for QVT relational transformations. In: MDSE 2008 (2008)

13. Gorp, P., Keller, A., Janssens, D.: Transformation language integration based on profiles and higher order transformations. In: Gašević, D., Lämmel, R., Wyk, E. (eds.) SLE 2008. LNCS, vol. 5452, pp. 208–226. Springer, Heidelberg (2009). doi:10.1007/978-3-642-00434-6_14

14. Hebig, R., Khelladi, D., Bendraou, R.: Approaches to co-evolution of metamodels and models: a survey. IEEE Trans. Softw. Eng. **43**(5), 396–414 (2016)

15. Hemel, Z., Kats, L.C.L., Groenewegen, D.M., Visser, E.: Code generation by model transformation: a case study in transformation modularity. Softw. Syst. Model. **9**(3), 375–402 (2010)

16. Herrmannsdörfer, M., Wachsmuth, G.: Coupled evolution of software metamodels and models. In: Mens, T., Serebrenik, A., Cleve, A. (eds.) Evolving Software Systems, pp. 33–63. Springer, Heidelberg (2014)

17. Jézéquel, J.M.: Model driven design and aspect weaving. Softw. Syst. Model. **7**(2), 209–218 (2008)

18. Jouault, F., Allilaire, F., Bézivin, J., Kurtev, I.: ATL: a model transformation tool. Sci. Comput. Program. **72**(1–2), 31–39 (2008)

19. Kapová, L., Goldschmidt, T.: Automated feature model-based generation of refinement transformations. In: SEAA 2009, pp. 141–148 (2009)

20. Kapová, L., Goldschmidt, T., Happe, J., Reussner, R.H.: Domain-specific templates for refinement transformations. In: MDI 2010, pp. 69–78. ACM (2010)

21. Kolovos, D.S., Paige, R.F., Polack, F., Rose, L.M.: Update transformations in the small with the Epsilon Wizard Language. J. Object Technol. **6**(9), 53–69 (2007)

22. Kraas, A.: Realizing model simplifications with QVT operational mappings. In: OCL 2014, pp. 53–62 (2014)
23. Krause, C., Dyck, J., Giese, H.: Metamodel-specific coupled evolution based on dynamically typed graph transformations. In: Duddy, K., Kappel, G. (eds.) ICMT 2013. LNCS, vol. 7909, pp. 76–91. Springer, Heidelberg (2013). doi:10.1007/978-3-642-38883-5_10
24. Lano, K., Kolahdouz Rahimi, S.: Model-transformation design patterns. IEEE Trans. Softw. Eng. **40**(12), 1224–1259 (2014)
25. Lúcio, L., Amrani, M., Dingel, J., Lambers, L., Salay, R., Selim, G.M.K., Syriani, E., Wimmer, M.: Model transformation intents and their properties. Softw. Syst. Model. **15**(3), 647–684 (2016)
26. Mens, T., van Gorp, P.: A taxonomy of model transformation. Electron. Notes Theor. Comput. Sci. **152**, 125–142 (2006)
27. Object Management Group: Meta Object Facility (MOF) 2.0 Query/View/Transformation Specification. No. formal/15-02-01 (2015)
28. Paige, R.F., Matragkas, N.D., Rose, L.M.: Evolving models in model-driven engineering: State-of-the-art and future challenges. J. Syst. Softw. **111**, 272–280 (2016)
29. Rose, L.M., Kolovos, D.S., Paige, R.F., Polack, F.A.C., Poulding, S.M.: Epsilon Flock: a model migration language. Softw. Syst. Model. **13**(2), 735–755 (2014)
30. Stahl, T., Völter, M.: Model-driven software development: technology, engineering, management. Wiley (2013)
31. Tisi, M., Cabot, J., Jouault, F.: Improving higher-order transformations support in ATL. In: Tratt, L., Gogolla, M. (eds.) ICMT 2010. LNCS, vol. 6142, pp. 215–229. Springer, Heidelberg (2010). doi:10.1007/978-3-642-13688-7_15
32. Tisi, M., Jouault, F., Fraternali, P., Ceri, S., Bézivin, J.: On the use of higher-order model transformations. In: Paige, R.F., Hartman, A., Rensink, A. (eds.) ECMDA-FA 2009. LNCS, vol. 5562, pp. 18–33. Springer, Heidelberg (2009). doi:10.1007/978-3-642-02674-4_3
33. Wagelaar, D., van der Straeten, R., Deridder, D.: Module superimposition: a composition technique for rule-based model transformation languages. Softw. Syst. Model. **9**(3), 285–309 (2009)
34. Willink, E.D.: Modeling the OCL standard library. Electronic Communications of the EASST 44 (2011)

Decision Points for Non-determinism in Concurrent Model Synchronization with Triple Graph Grammars

Frank Trollmann[✉] and Sahin Albayrak

Faculty of Electrical Engineering and Computer Science,
DAI-Labor, TU-Berlin, Berlin, Germany
{Frank.Trollmann,Sahin.Albayrak}@dai-labor.de

Abstract. Model synchronization is one of the core activities in model driven engineering. One of the challenges is non-determinism when multiple valid solutions exist. This is exasperated in triple graph based approaches, where additional non-determinism may arise from the alignment of the synchronized changes and the grammar. Non-determinism is often the result of multiple decision points during the synchronization process. Handling these decisions where they occur can reduce the overall complexity of dealing with non-determinism. In this paper we analyse a triple graph based synchronization approach to identify these decisions, extend the approach to clearly separate them and discuss the relation to formal properties of model synchronization.

Keywords: Model synchronization · Triple graphs · Model driven engineering

1 Introduction

In modelling environments consistency between models is often a concern. Model synchronization is a model transformation that synchronizes changes between models to re-establish consistency [15]. However, in many cases the correct synchronization result is not unique, which causes non-determinism.

Model synchronization with triple graph grammars (TGGs) also suffers from this problem. Here, non-determinism can be handled in different ways, e.g., by producing only one result or imposing conditions to reduce non-determinism [10, 11]. These approaches may produce the wrong result or may have overly restrictive conditions. A different approach is to produce all results [12] or a representation of all results [14]. While these approaches contain the correct result, the selection is not trivial since the results are caused by multiple decisions during the synchronization process whose rationale is not available after the synchronization.

In this paper we analyse the approach of Gottmann et al. [12] to identify these decisions. The goal is to identify decision points that lead to non-determinism and relevant information to make these decisions. To enable a clear separation of these decisions we extend the synchronization algorithm.

To familiarize the reader with model synchronization in TGGs, Sect. 2 gives a summary of formal definitions and related work. Sections 3 and 4 analyse decision

© Springer International Publishing AG 2017
E. Guerra and M. van den Brand (Eds.): ICMT 2017, LNCS 10374, pp. 35–50, 2017.
DOI: 10.1007/978-3-319-61473-1_3

points for non-determinism and extend the synchronization algorithm. Section 3 considers a simplified problem, in which synchronized changes align with the TGG and leave no residual elements. Section 4 considers additional non-determinism introduced by residual elements. The decision points are discussed and related to formal properties of model synchronization in Sect. 5. Section 6 concludes the paper and discusses future research directions.

2   Model Synchronization with Triple Graph Grammars

This section describes model synchronization with TGGs. Formal definitions of triple graphs can be found in [7]. As running example we assume two related models: a class diagram and a database model, representing a table structure to store the classes. We discuss the example from the perspective of human software developers who merge changes in these two models. This enables us to focus on decision points and required information by abstracting from how the decision is made by the developer. Nevertheless, we will discuss formal policies for each decision point in Sect. 5.

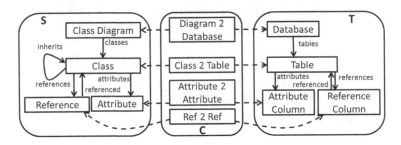

Fig. 1. Type graph of the running example

A **triple graph** $S \xleftarrow{s} C \xrightarrow{t} T$ represents two related models [16]. These models are represented by two graphs, called source S and target T. The relation is represented by a third graph, called correspondence C, and two monomorphisms s and t. These morphisms relate each element in C to one element in S and T.

The running example uses typed triple graphs. The type graph (Fig. 1) is a triple graph which specifies node and edge types. A class diagram (S) contains classes, which contain attributes and references and can inherit other classes. A database (T) consists of tables, with columns, that can contain elementary attributes or references to other tables. C expresses relations between class diagram and database, classes and tables, attributes and attribute columns and references and reference columns.

A **triple rule** is a triple graph monomorphism $L \rightarrow R$ between triple graphs L and R that describe substitution of subgraph L by R. A triple rule can only create and not delete any elements.

A **triple graph grammar** ($St, Rules$) consists of a start object St and a set of triple rules $Rules$. It defines a language of two related models consisting of all triples that can be reached from *St* via repeated application of rules from *Rules*. This defines a consistency relation *Rel* which contains all triples in the language.

For the running example *St* will consist of one related class diagram and database and no other elements. The rules are depicted in Fig. 2, where *L* is depicted on the top and *R* is depicted on the bottom. They are typed over the type graph in Fig. 1. Rule (a) creates a class together with a related table. Rule (b) assumes two classes and inserts a reference between them, together with a related reference column. Rules (c) and (d) add a new class that inherits from an existing class. They are identical in their class diagram component but differ in how they represent the inheritance in the database. Rule (c) creates a new table and references a base object from the superclass via a reference column. Rule (d) adds the new subclass to the table of the superclass and adds a new attribute to distinguish the objects of the subtype on the data level.

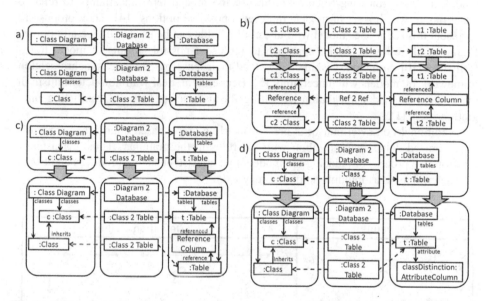

Fig. 2. Rules of the running example. Names are given where necessary to disambiguate morphisms.

The purpose of model synchronization is to derive a consistent triple that encompasses given changes, e.g., to re-establish a state where the database model can be used to store objects defined by the class diagram after both models have been altered. Diskin et al. distinguish between symmetric and asymmetric synchronization [3]. In the asymmetric case one model is an abstraction of the other one. An example is the approach by Vogel et al. that synchronizes a source model, containing all information, with target models that contain partial information for a specific concern [18]. In the symmetric case both models contain information not reflected in the other model. This is the case in the running example. Symmetric synchronization is the harder case [4]. Diskin et al. advocate representing changes as deltas [3]. Formally a delta $\Delta = M_0 \xleftarrow{d} M_0' \xrightarrow{a} M_1$ is a span of morphisms, where d represents deletion and a represents creation of elements. In the figures we distinguish deltas from normal morphisms by arrows with a point in their source.

Furthermore, one can distinguish non-concurrent and concurrent synchronization. In the concurrent case updates in both models are synchronized at the same time [13]. Conflicts between these updates may occur and cause additional non-determinism.

Non-determinism is a general problem in model synchronization and related areas, not limited to triple graph grammars. Eramo et al. analyse non-determinism in model synchronization at design time, via translation into a reasoning language, to detect and avoid non-determinism [9]. Cicchetti et al. reduce non-determinism by using logical constraints to reduce the options for model transformation [2]. In the scope of general model driven engineering Michalis et al. use the related term uncertainty to refer to situations in which a set of models represents possible options [14]. They propose to represent this set in one "model with uncertainty" that can be used to derive all options. Eramo et al. follow a similar approach to represent possible results of model transformation [10]. Similarly, Diskin et al. extend their lense-based model synchronization framework by models with uncertainty [5]. Becker et al. deal with non-determinism in the context of model integration by letting the user select between conflicting integration rules [1].

Additional non-determinism is present in triple-graph based approaches since the synchronized deltas may not align with the rules in the grammar. Thus, consistency creation, the process of reducing the models to a consistent state, introduces additional non-determinism, as multiple solutions may exist.

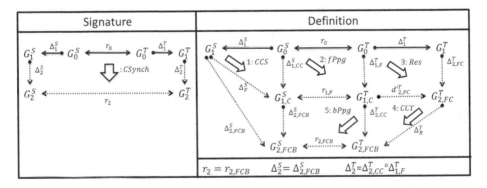

Fig. 3. Signature and definition of the concurrent synchronization operation

For our analysis of non-determinism we selected the approach of Hermann et al. [13], since it is delta-based, able to deal with symmetric and concurrent cases and has already been analysed for non-determinism [12]. Hermann et al. define the concurrent synchronization operation as illustrated in Fig. 3 [13]. Its signature is $CSynch :$ $(Rel \otimes \Delta_S \otimes \Delta_T) \rightsquigarrow (Rel \times \Delta_S \times \Delta_T)$ (Fig. 3, left). Given a consistent triple and a delta on source and target side it produces the synchronized triple and deltas leading to it. The operation is non-deterministic, indicated by $\rightsquigarrow$.

The Definition of *CSynch* follows the steps proposed by Xiong et al. [19]. It propagates the source delta to the target model (i), merges it with the target delta while resolving conflicts (ii) and propagates the merged result back to the source model (iii). The operations used to implement these steps are shown in the right part of Fig. 3. In step (i) the source delta is reduced to a consistent model via operation *CCS* (consistency creation in source). The result is propagated to the target model using operation *fPpg* (forward propagate). Step (ii) merges the deltas and resolves conflicts via operation *Res* (resolve). The result of the conflict resolution is an updated target delta (iii). Analogous to (i), the target delta is reduced to a consistent model via operation *CCT* (consistency creation in target) and propagated to the source model via operation *bPpg* (backward propagate).

Since the original triple rules modify both models at the same time these operations are based on derived rules. These rules can be used to create one of the models at a time (source/target rule) [7], to propagate the changes from one model to the other model (forward/backward rule) [ibid.] or to establish the correspondence when both models already exist (integration rule) [8]. Hermann et al. also extended these rules to operate on translation attributes to remember parsed elements [13].

Gottmann et al. discuss non-determinism in this algorithm [12]. They allow non-determinism in the operations *fPpg* and *bPpg* (which is excluded via an assumption in the original algorithm), such that all operations can produce multiple results. The correct result is then assumed to be selected via some selection mechanism.

In our running example the developer is available as external selection mechanism. However, the decision between all results is complicated by the fact that the options are determined by decisions at several points during the algorithm. For the developer it would be easier to provide answers to those decisions at the relevant points in the algorithm since the information concerning the decisions is available there. The next two sections identify and discuss these decision points.

3 Non-determinism Without Residual Elements

The mismatch between deltas to be synchronized and the language produced by the TGG adds complexity and non-determinism due to the need for consistency creation. In this section we abstract from this process to focus on the remaining decisions. We assume the synchronized deltas $\Delta = M_0 \overset{d}{\leftarrow} M_0' \overset{a}{\rightarrow} M_1$ to be parseable, i.e., the morphisms d and a can be parsed by sequences of source/target rules and M_0' and M_1 are consistent. We also assume that the conflict resolution produces a parseable delta. This simplified situation could appear in cases where consistency is ensured before merging models, e.g., by means of a parser/compiler. This assumption implies that the consistency creating operations (*CCS* and *CCT*) produce an identity since the model is already consistent.

The other sources of non-determinism remain: $fPpg$ and $bPpg$ may have multiple options to propagate the input delta and *Res* may have multiple options to unify two deltas. From the point of view of the developers four decisions can be identified.

During forward propagation the first decision (D_{fPpg}) is to select which of the possible results is the correct one. During backward propagation the dual decision (D_{bPpg}) has to be made. Multiple results exist if the mapping between both models is not bijective. The running example is not deterministic. Figure 4 illustrates this in a specific situation. The figure shows a triple graph, and two deltas. To save space the deltas are represented by annotations in the graph, where dotted green edges represent added elements and crossed out red elements denote removed elements. The delta on class diagram side contains the creation of class $c2$, inheriting from class $c1$. While propagating this structure, the developer has the choice (D_{fPpg}) to propagate this structure via rule c or rule d. Similarly, the delta for the database model contains the creation of a reference column between table $t2$ and $t3$. The developer has the choice (D_{bPpg}) to propagate this as new subclass (rule c) or as reference (rule b).

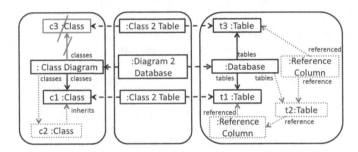

Fig. 4. Deltas for the Running example. Green dotted edges denote added elements, red crossed out elements denote deleted elements. (Color figure online)

For the conflict resolution we can identify two decisions. The first one is derived from the fact that developers coordinate their editing process and thus changes in both models may be related. This requires to decide (D_{Int}) which changes in both deltas to identify. In the running example in Fig. 4, the creation of table $t2$ and class $c2$ could be interpreted as the same object and thus be integrated via rule c. The second decision during conflict resolution (D_{Res}) is how to resolve conflicts. The running example in Fig. 4 contains a potential conflict, since the removal of class $c3$ implies the removal of the related table $t3$, while $t3$ is referenced by the added reference column from table $t2$. The operation *Res* by Hermann et al. prefers creation over deletion and thus would have preferred to revoke the removal of class $c3$ over the non-insertion of the reference column. The operation does not deal with decision D_{Int} and thus would not have integrated class $c2$ with table $t2$. However, this is only one possible implementation of a resolution strategy.

Decisions D_{Int} and D_{Res} are independent, although they are made in the same operation. Furthermore, decision D_{fPpg} influences decision D_{Int} since an integration on target side (D_{Int}) is dependent of how the source model has been propagated (D_{fPpg}).

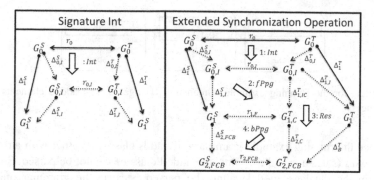

Fig. 5. The signature of the integration operation *Int* (left) and integration into the synchronization operation (right).

For these reasons we chose to decouple decision D_{Int} from the conflict resolution operation and add it before D_{fPpg}.

Figure 5 (left) shows the signature of the new operation *Int*, which integrates a triple graph and two deltas. The integration result is a triple graph $r_{0,I}$, deltas $\Delta_{0,I}^S$ and $\Delta_{0,I}^T$ that represent the integrated changes, and deltas $\Delta_{1,I}^S$ and $\Delta_{1,I}^T$ that represent the changes that have not been integrated.

The remaining synchronization process is based on the integrated triple $r_{0,I}$, and deltas $\Delta_{1,I}^S$ and $\Delta_{1,I}^T$. Figure 5 (right) shows the extended synchronization operation. *CCS* and *CCT* have been omitted since they have no effect. All other steps are implemented as in the previous algorithm. The conflict resolution can now assume that the resolved deltas contain no redundancy.

4   Non-determinism with Residual Elements

In this section we relax the assumption of parseability of synchronized deltas $\Delta = M_0 \xleftarrow{d} M_0' \xrightarrow{a} M_1$. This implies that d and a may not be parseable by the grammar and that M_0' and M_1 may not be consistent. Consistency creation is the purpose of the operations *CCS* and *CCT*. This relaxation introduces additional non-determinism since the operations *CCS* and *CCT* may not be deterministic. This leads to decisions D_{CCS} and D_{CCT}, which define which consistent model is the right one.

Inconsistency of M_1 implies residual elements that are left over when trying to parse M_1 via the respective source/target rules of the grammar. For a software developer a reasonable restriction would be to produce consistent models. In this case residual elements imply an error. They could either represent wrongly added elements or forgotten elements that should have been added together with other elements. Reasonable resolution options are to remove wrongly added or add missing elements.

Figure 6 illustrates handling residual elements on the running example. The figure shows a triple graph and two deltas, where added elements are indicated by green dotted edges. Neither delta is parseable. The delta on the class diagram side cannot be

Fig. 6. Deltas for the Running example. Green dotted edges denote added elements. (Color figure online)

parsed since the running example grammar only adds classes together with a reference of type *classes* (rules a, c and d). Thus, the added class *c1* cannot be parsed. Similarly, the delta in the database model cannot be parsed because the grammar only adds references of type *tables* together with exactly one table (rules a, c and d). For this reason there cannot be two such references to the one table *t1*.

The operations *CCS* and *CCT* proposed by Hermann et al. remove residual elements. They calculate a maximal consistent submodel and remove all elements that are not present in this submodel. The characterization of the maximal consistent submodel is depicted on the left hand side in Fig. 7. It is maximal in the sense that no rules can be applied to the submodel to parse any of the residual elements without also creating new elements. In the running example in Fig. 6 this leads to the removal of class c1 by *CCS*, since it cannot be parsed, and the removal of one of the references *tables* by *CCT*, since only one can be parsed. This algorithm treats all residual elements as wrongly created elements. It is not able to add forgotten elements.

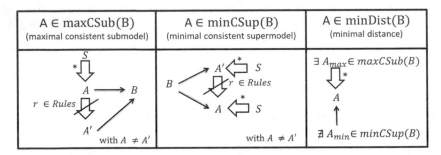

Fig. 7. Characterization of consistency creation options. Small arrows denote monomorphisms, big arrows denote application of one or a set of (*) rules.

Creating forgotten elements can be achieved by using the dual notion to the maximal consistent submodel, the minimal consistent supermodel (see Fig. 7, centre). This model is a supermodel of the original model but contains only those additional elements that are created alongside elements in the original model. It only creates forgotten elements and is not able to remove wrongly created elements. In the running example in Fig. 6 the class *c1* could be completed to a minimum consistent supermodel by adding the missing reference of type *classes*. The running example also shows that the minimum consistent supermodel may not always exist. Since there is no way of adding two references of type *tables* via our grammar this structure cannot be contained in any consistent model that is supermodel of this model.

For the developer the resolution of errors may require creation and removal of elements. Thus, the result is something "in between". For example, if the two changes in the running example both occurred in the class diagram (meaning that in addition to one class without a *classes* reference there is another class with two *classes* references) the natural solution would be to delete one of the redundant references but add a new references to keep the unreferenced class. We characterize this as minimal distance (Fig. 7, right hand side). A model is of minimal distance if it contains a maximal consistent submodel but not more than a minimal consistent supermodel. We use the maximal consistent submodel and minimal consistent supermodel as bounds since they exclude unnecessary removal and creation of elements.

In the algorithm by Hermann et al. handling of residual elements is done at the beginning of the algorithm on source side (*CCS*) and after merging the propagated changes on target side (*CCT*). Extending these operations along the lines discussed above is straightforward. Finding models of minimal distance can be based on maximal consistent submodels and applying source/target rules that parse at least one of the remaining elements until minimum consistent supermodels are reached. The adapted operations are identical in signature, but produce a larger set of options to choose from. We call the adapted operations *CCS'* and *CCT'*.

If *CCS'* and *CCT'* are applied in the original places of *CCS* and *CCT* the operation *Int* has to integrate non-parseable deltas with residual elements. *CCS'* and *CCT'* could also be applied before *Int*, with the caveat that *CCT'* may have to be applied again to make the result of *Res* consistent. We chose to apply *CCS'* and *CCT'* after *Int* because the integration process may make use of the residual elements during the integration. For example, *Int* may choose to integrate the class c1 and database model in the running example in Fig. 6. During this process it may integrate class *c1* and table *t1*. This integration could be done via rule a, which would also add the reference of type *classes* to contain *c1*.

To enable handling residual elements the signature of *Int* has to be adapted, since it can remove and create new elements as side-effects to integrating the models. The signature and definition of the integration operation can be found in Fig. 8. The signature uses the original triple graph and two deltas as input and creates a new triple graph and deltas $\Delta^S_{1,I}$ and $\Delta^T_{1,I}$. The operation handles the removing and adding part of the deltas separately. In the removing part the morphisms d^S_1 and d^T_1 are parsed via rules from the grammar, which are then reversed from the original triple graph, leading to the sequence of triple graphs r_1 to r_n. To account for residual elements that should have been deleted the parsing rules may contain additional deletions. The result of this parsing process with additional deletion is r_n. One side-constraint is that r_n is consistent. A similar parsing process is executed for the adding morphism. To retrieve adding morphisms from r_n we create pushouts (PO1) and pushout complements for (PO2), to arrive at the morphisms $a^S_{r,n}$ and $a^T_{r,n}$. These morphisms can now be parsed to integrate the adding part of the deltas and create r_{n+1} to r_m. Again, we allow for additional creation of objects. Triple graph r_m is the result $r_{0,I}$ of the integration.

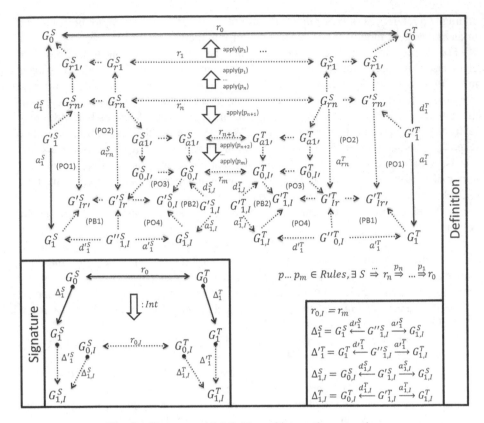

Fig. 8. Signature and definition of integration operation.

The remaining deltas $d_{1,I}^{S/T} = G_{0,I}^{S/T} \xleftarrow{r_{1,I}^{S/T}} G'^{S/T}_{1,I} \xrightarrow{a_{1,I}^{S/T}} G_{1,I}^{S/T}$ can be calculated via pullbacks (PB1), pushouts (PB3) and (PB4) and then pullback (PB2).

The above construction is possible if the underlying models form a weak adhesive HLR category [6]. The formal properties are required for the construction of the pushouts and pullbacks along monomorphisms. The complements of PO2 and PO4 may not exist. Their non-existence indicates conflicts between the additional creations and deletions and the original delta.

Since the integration is able to operate on non-consistent deltas the operations CCS' and CCT' can be placed in their usual position in the algorithm by Hermann et al. after the integration. The resulting algorithm is depicted in Fig. 9. This algorithm works as the original algorithm if Int does not integrate and CCS' and CCT' choose maximal consistent submodels. Thus, it still encompasses all results produced by the algorithm by Herman et al. However, the algorithm now produces more results, due to integration and extended handling of residual elements. We will discuss this in the next section in the scope of the consistency requirements for synchronization.

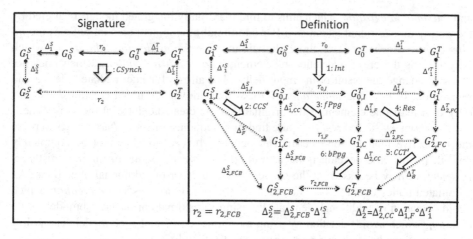

Fig. 9. Final algorithm with integration of *Int* and extension of *CCS'* and *CCT'*

5 Discussion

Sections 3 and 4 identified decision points that cause non-determinism. We added the operation *Int*, to explicitly align these decisions with the underlying synchronization operations. Summarizing, the developer has the following decisions:

- D_{Int}: Which parts of the source and target delta correspond to each other?
- $D_{CCS'}$: How to establish consistency in the source delta?
- D_{fPpg}: How to propagate the source delta?
- D_{Res}: How to solve conflicts between propagated and original target delta?
- $D_{CCT'}$: How to establish consistency in the target delta?
- D_{bPpg}: How to propagate the target delta?

In the following we discuss these decisions from the point of view of the developer and indicate policies that could be used for automated decision making.

Decision D_{int} requires finding correspondences between the synchronized deltas. This decision is made based on the deltas, the rules that can be used to integrate them and the additional elements created/removed by these rules. A pure integration (without any additional creation/removal) can be implemented using derived integration rules. Taking into account additional creation or deletion either requires applying the full rule and deriving these elements via comparison or partially matching the rule. The developer can make decisions based on a comparison of the deltas and the rules to select ones that implement the intended integration. An automated mechanism could tackle this decision via policies that specify which changes to match or which rules to select. Preferably, these decisions can be based on the context of the synchronization (e.g., knowing which elements should correspond to each other). Context independent policies could refer to the amount of integrated elements or the amount of additional alterations. For the integrated elements straightforward candidates are *no integration*, which does not integrate anything and behaves like the algorithm by Hermann et al.

and *maximal integration*, which aims to find maximally integrated models restricted by the policy on additional alterations. For additional alterations potential policies are *no alterations*, which does not allow alterations, *no creating/deleting alterations* which only forbids the creation/deletion of elements, *no result alterations,* which does not allow to change the result of the input deltas, but allows for intermediate deletion and reinsertion, or *no stand-alone alterations*, which allows additional creations/deletions only if at least one element of the original delta is created/deleted at the same time.

Decisions $D_{CCS'}$ and $D_{CCT'}$ require finding a sequence of source/target rules to parse the respective model. Non-determinism occurs when a model cannot be completely parsed. In this case developers have to choose between options of minimal distance. A selection may be based on the sequences of rules or on additional alterations. An automated policy could be based on these alterations. Examples are *no creation,* which avoids creation of additional elements by using a maximal consistent submodel, or *no deletion*, which avoids deletion by using a minimal consistent supermodel. The policy *no creation* results in the original operations *CCS* and *CCT*.

Decisions D_{fPpg} and D_{bPpg} requires choosing between different propagations of a source/target model. For the developer the propagated models are likely of more interest than the parsing sequences. The decision is which target model best reflects the intended changes on source model side. An automated policy may also base this decision on structural considerations, e.g., *prioritizing* certain rules over others or *maximizing similarity* between the propagated and the target delta.

Decision D_{Res} requires conflict resolution. Since this step can be implemented in different variations, it is hard to consider specific policies. In general, the selection is between multiple results of conflict resolution. The operation implemented by Hermann et al. represents a policy that *prefers creation* over deletion.

In addition, developers have to decide on a direction of synchronization. While the operation *Int* is symmetrical and leads to the same result for both directions, the remaining algorithm is not. Thus, it has to be decided whether to start with the source or target model. This decision could be based on which model the developer is more familiar with, on structural conditions, e.g., which model contains more changes, or used as backtracking point in case one direction does not deliver a good result.

In the scope of model synchronization the definition of "right" synchronization result has been subject to discussion and has been expressed as formal properties of the synchronization mechanism. These properties could be used to further reduce non-determinism by eliminating options that violate them. In the remainder of this section we discuss the relation of these properties to our algorithm (assuming the resolution operation *Res* as specified by Hermann et al. [13]). We will discuss whether our algorithm guarantees these properties in all results ($\forall$) or can be expected to produce at least one result that fulfils them ($\exists$). In addition, we discuss the relation between the policies mentioned above and the properties, i.e., which policies are required/excluded by which properties. As basis we will use the properties defined by Orejas et al. [15]. In the scope of propagation based synchronization these properties are:

- **Consistency:** The synchronization result is consistent.
- **Identity:** If the model is already consistent and source and target updates are identities the synchronization does not change anything.

- **Hippocraticness:** If source and target are consistent with respect to the grammar and with respect to each other they are not altered.
- **Soundness:** The synchronization results contain only changes from the synchronized deltas or changes that result from propagation of the synchronized deltas.
- **Strong soundness:** There is a submodification of the synchronized deltas such that the synchronization result only contains changes from this submodification or changes that are propagated from this submodification.
- **Maximal preservation:** The synchronization result contains any consistent sub-delta of the synchronized delta as well as all elements that are caused from propagation of this sub-delta.

The algorithm by Hermann et al. satisfies consistency and identity [13]. In the following we discuss which properties can be fulfilled by our algorithm. Figure 10 summarizes the discussion.

Consistency holds for all results ($\forall$) since the operation $bPpg$ always produces a consistent result when provided with the consistent target model produce by CCT'.

Identity is only preserved if the integration operation provides an identity ($\exists$). Although the algorithm by Hermann et al. fulfils this property, it is influenced by the integration operation, specifically the ability to create/remove elements. The property can be preserved by the policy *no alterations* since it forbids alterations. It is also preserved by the policy *no stand-alone alterations* since an identical update contains no changes to add/remove additional elements along with. Operations CCS' and CCT' do not influence the property since a consistent model is the only model of minimal distance to itself. Accordingly, CCT' and CCS' provide identities as would CCT and CCS. As in the original algorithm, the other operations preserve identity.

		Consistency	Identity	Hippocraticness	(Strong) Soundness	Maximal Preservation
Algorithm		$\forall$	$\exists$	$\exists$	~	~
Operations	**Int**		*no stand-alone alterations*	*maximal integration* $\wedge$ *no result alterations*	*no creating alteration*	~
	CCS'				*no creation*	~
	fPpg				~	~
	Res					~
	CCT'				*no creation*	~
	bPpg				~	~

Fig. 10. Relation between properties of model synchronization, the extended algorithm and its operations. ~ means there may be no option that fulfils the property.

Hippocraticness requires an already consistent update to not change source or target model. This is not fulfilled in general, but can be fulfilled ($\exists$). A consistent update implies that both deltas can be integrated to a consistent triple graph. This can be produced in the operation *Int*. However, since the deltas may not be aligned with the grammar this may include additional deletion and creation of elements. In the worst case the operation has to completely reduce the current model to the start object of the grammar and reconstruct the changed model. All elements can be integrated via policy *maximal integration*. Combined with policy *no result alterations*, which forbids additional alterations, this implies that the integration completely integrates source and target and produces identical deltas. As discussed in the scope of identity, these identical deltas are not changed by the other operations.

Soundness requires that all modifications produced by the synchronization are included in the synchronized delta or propagated from parts of that delta. This does not hold in general since *Int*, *CCS'*, *CCT'*, *fPpg* and *bPpg* can create additional elements. Via policies *no creating alterations* for operation *Int* and the policies *no creation* for *CCS'* and *CCT'* we can restrict the first three operations to not create additional elements. However, since the propagated delta may not be aligned with the TGG, operations *fPpg* and *bPpg* parse the whole integrated model. During this process a different selection of rules in the parsing process may result in the creation of new elements that are not directly contained or caused by the changes in the delta. These elements could be detected and avoided in a policy, but the application of this policy may yield no results when there is no parsing sequence that does not add additional elements. The same argumentation applies for strong soundness, where the modifications have to be derived from a specific submodification and its propagation.

Maximum preservation is also not fulfilled in general and not necessarily fulfilled for any result. The property requires that any sub-delta and its propagation is contained in the synchronization result. At every decision point a set of alternatives are discarded. These alternatives may have led to the propagation of additional elements not contained in any propagation for the selected alternative. However, this is not directly caused by the decision points themselves, since the property requires these elements to be contained in the same result, which require that the TGG enables such a result in the first place. If this cannot be guaranteed the property cannot be guaranteed solely by making the right decisions during synchronization.

Summarizing, the extended algorithm fulfils the property of consistency. Identity and Hippocraticness can be fulfilled by choosing policies on the integration operation. (Strong) soundness and maximal preservation are not necessarily fulfilled. In comparison with the original algorithm, the property identity is not always guaranteed to be fulfilled, but can be fulfilled via policies. The property Hippocraticness, which does not hold for the original algorithm, can be fulfilled by the integration operation.

6 Conclusion and Future Work

In this paper we discuss non-determinism in model synchronization with triple graphs and derive decision points within the synchronization algorithm with the aim to resolve the decisions. We extended the algorithm by Hermann et al. [13] to be aligned with the decisions by adding an additional integration operation.

Although the original intention was to find these decision points to reduce non-determinism, the adaptations proposed in Sect. 4 have increased the amount of options to choose from per decision. The additional options derive from the ability to integrate parts of the model (which is not done in the conflict resolution operation by Hermann et al. [13], but could be done by a different conflict resolution operation) and the ability to resolve non-consistency in deltas by adding additional elements. However, the operations can still produce all results producible by the original operation and can be forced to behave like the original algorithm by choosing suitable policies for the integration and consistency creation operation.

One major problem in synchronization with triple graphs is the discrepancy between deltas and rules in the triple graph grammar. This discrepancy is what causes problems with fulfilling properties like maximum preservation and soundness. Similar problems also exit in any other synchronization approaches where additional constraints restrict the state space of consistent deltas when compared to the state space of all possible deltas. We believe that in future work it is worth looking into approaches to formalize such properties making use of the restricted state space in the operations, e.g., by aligning the consecutive operations based on the parsing sequence instead of only the deltas and results.

In addition, we believe that the synchronization should be extended to more than two models. We extended the original algorithm by Hermann et al. to more than two models in [17]. The extended algorithm could be generalized analogously.

References

1. Becker, S.M., Lohmann, S., Westfechtel, B.: Rule execution in graph-based incremental interactive integration tools. In: Ehrig, H., Engels, G., Parisi-Presicce, F., Rozenberg, G. (eds.) ICGT 2004. LNCS, vol. 3256, pp. 22–38. Springer, Heidelberg (2004). doi:10.1007/978-3-540-30203-2_4
2. Cicchetti, A., Di Ruscio, D., Romina, E., Alfonso, P.: Logical constraints for managing non-determinism in bidirectional model transformations. In: International Workshop on Model-Driven Engineering, Logic and Optimization: Friends or Foes? (MELO 2011) (2011)
3. Diskin, Z., Xiong, Y., Czarnecki, K.: From state - to delta-based bidirectional model transformations: the asymmetric case. J. Obj. Technol. 10(6), 1–25 (2011)
4. Diskin, Z., Maibaum, T., Czarnecki, K.: Intermodeling, queries, and kleisli categories. In: Lara, J., Zisman, A. (eds.) FASE 2012. LNCS, vol. 7212, pp. 163–177. Springer, Heidelberg (2012). doi:10.1007/978-3-642-28872-2_12
5. Diskin, Z., Eramo, R., Pierantonio, A., Czarnecki, K.: Incorporating uncertainty into bidirectional model transformations and their delta-lens formalization. In: Bx@ ETAPS, pp. 15–31 (2016)
6. Ehrig, H., Ehrig, K., Prange, U., Taentzer, G.: Fundamentals of Algebraic Graph Transformation. Monographs in Theoretical Computer Science. An EATCS Series. Springer, Heidelberg (2006)
7. Ehrig, H., Ehrig, K., Ermel, C., Hermann, F., Taentzer, G.: Information preserving bidirectional model transformations. In: Dwyer, M.B., Lopes, A. (eds.) FASE 2007. LNCS, vol. 4422, pp. 72–86. Springer, Heidelberg (2007). doi:10.1007/978-3-540-71289-3_7
8. Ehrig, H., Ehrig, K., Hermann, F.: From model transformation to model integration based on the algebraic approach to triple graph grammars. Electron. Commun. EASST 10 (2008). https://journal.ub.tu-berlin.de/eceasst/issue/view/19, http://orbilu.uni.lu/handle/10993/5594
9. Eramo R., Marinelli R., Pierantonio A., Rosa G.: Towards analysing non-determinism in bidirectional transformations. In: Proceedings of the Analysis of Model Transformations Workshop (AMT2014) CEUR, pp. 76–85 (2014)

10. Eramo, R., Pierantonio, A., Rosa. G.: Managing uncertainty in bidirectional model transformations. In: Proceedings of the 2015 International Conference on Software Language Engineering. ACM (2015)
11. Giese, H., Wagner, R.: From model transformation to incremental bidirectional model synchronization. Softw. Syst. Model. **8**, 1:21–1:43 (2008). Springer
12. Gottmann, S., Hermann, F., Nachtigall, N., Braatz, B., Ermel, C., Ehrig, H., Engel, T.: Correctness and completeness of generalised concurrent model synchronisation based on triple graph grammars. In: Proceedings of the International Workshop on Analysis of Model Transformations 2013 (AMT 2013), CEUR Workshop Proceedings, vol. 1112, pp. 67–76 (2013)
13. Hermann, F., Ehrig, H., Ermel, C., Orejas, F.: Concurrent model synchronization with conflict resolution based on triple graph grammars. In: Lara, J., Zisman, A. (eds.) FASE 2012. LNCS, vol. 7212, pp. 178–193. Springer, Heidelberg (2012). doi:10.1007/978-3-642-28872-2_13
14. Michalis, F., Salay, R., Chechik, M.: Partial models: towards modeling and reasoning with uncertainty. In: Proceedings of the 34th International Conference on Software Engineering (ICSE2012), pp. 573–583. IEEE (2012)
15. Orejas, F., Boronat, A., Ehrig, H., Hermann, F., Schölzel, H.: On propagation-based concurrent model synchronization. Electron. Commun. EASST **57**, 19 (2013)
16. Schürr, A.: Specification of graph translators with triple graph grammars. In: Mayr, E.W., Schmidt, G., Tinhofer, G. (eds.) WG 1994. LNCS, vol. 903, pp. 151–163. Springer, Heidelberg (1995). doi:10.1007/3-540-59071-4_45
17. Trollmann, F., Albayrak, S.: Extending model synchronization results from triple graph grammars to multiple models. In: Van Gorp, P., Engels, G. (eds.) ICMT 2016. LNCS, vol. 9765, pp. 91–106. Springer, Cham (2016). doi:10.1007/978-3-319-42064-6_7
18. Vogel, T., Neumann, S., Hildebrandt, S., Giese, H., Becker, B.: Incremental model synchronization for efficient run-time monitoring. In: Ghosh, S. (ed.) MODELS 2009. LNCS, vol. 6002, pp. 124–139. Springer, Heidelberg (2010). doi:10.1007/978-3-642-12261-3_13
19. Xiong, Y., Song, H., Hu, Z., Takeichi, M.: Synchronizing concurrent model updates based on bidirectional transformation. Int. J. Softw. Syst. Model. (SoSyM) **12**(1), 89–104 (2013)

The Micromapping Model of Computation; The Foundation for Optimized Execution of Eclipse QVTc/QVTr/UMLX

Edward D. Willink[✉]

Willink Transformations Ltd., Reading, UK
ed_at_willink.me.uk

Abstract. It is 14 years since the first UMLX paper and 10 years since the QVT 1.0 specification was published. No useable UMLX implementation has appeared. QVTr implementations have been disappointing. The Eclipse QVTd project can now offer editing, optimization, execution and Java code generation for QVTc, QVTr and UMLX. This paper outlines the Micromapping Model of Computation used by the optimizations.

Keywords: Declarative model transformation · QVTc · QVTr · UMLX · Optimization

1 Introduction

The QVT specification introduced one imperative language, QVTo, and two declarative languages, QVTc and QVTr, as the solution to the early enthusiasm for model to model transformation. Only QVTo has a flourishing implementation. QVTc was never implemented despite the 'c' suggesting it is a core that 'o' and 'r' extend. The two QVTr implementations have not prospered.

The Eclipse QVTd project [9] has provided QVTc and QVTr editors for many years, but it is only recently[1] that any execution functionality has been available.

UMLX [5] was proposed a little before QVT [3]. UMLX extends UML-like object diagrams to specify the object patterns to be transformed. However three successive implementation attempts for UMLX foundered on the lack of an execution capability. UMLX and QVTr have now evolved to share some fairly obvious declarative principles enabling the Eclipse QVTd project to offer graphical UMLX as an interchangeable syntax for textual QVTr.

This paper describes the analyses and transformations that solve the problem; convert UMLX, QVTr and QVTc declarative forms to an optimized imperative representation suitable for interpreted or code generated execution. In Sect. 2, we contrast an imperative Procedure with a declarative Mapping[2]

---

[1] As part of the Eclipse Neon release in June 2016.
[2] A Mapping is also known as a Relation or a Rule.

© Springer International Publishing AG 2017
E. Guerra and M. van den Brand (Eds.): ICMT 2017, LNCS 10374, pp. 51–65, 2017.
DOI: 10.1007/978-3-319-61473-1_4

before introducing a Micromapping and its inter-Connection as the basis for the compile-time analysis described in Sect. 3. Section 4 presents some results, Sect. 5 related work and Sect. 6 the current status. Section 7 concludes.

2   Background

The familiar way in which a procedure interacts with its caller and objects is shown at the left of Fig. 1. The example procedure receives a *param1* parameter value from its caller, and executes, using the parameter to identify *object1*, whose *slot1* references an *object2* whose *slot3* contributes to some computation of a value to be assigned to *slot4* of *object3*. This is identified by *slot2* of *object1*. On completion, the procedure returns the *result1* value. The life cycle of the procedure is shown at the right of Fig. 1; the procedure is called, it executes and returns. If something goes wrong an exception may be thrown.

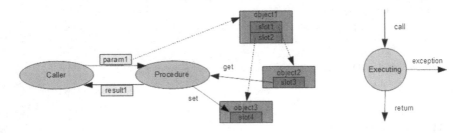

Fig. 1. Example procedure interactions and life cycle

In contrast, the invocation of a declarative transformation mapping need not be explicit. Rather, when objects are available, the mapping is invoked exactly once for each distinct permutation of suitable input objects. The interaction with objects shown at the right of Fig. 2 is similar to those of a procedure, however the life cycle is more complex. The *invoke, exception* and *success* transitions correspond to the *call, exception* and *return* transitions of a procedure. The *failure* transition occurs when the mapping's predicates or guards are not satisfied; no execution is required. The *not-ready* transition occurs for a premature access to an object or slot; the execution cannot proceed. A *re-invoke* may be attempted once the accessed object or slot is available.

Sequencing explicit procedure calls and slot accesses can be a challenging manual programming responsibility. Mappings are invoked automatically when the appropriate object slots are ready eliminating this opportunity for error.

These differences require the run-time for a declarative transformation to be aware of what has executed and which objects and slots are ready. Naively this could make the declarative transformation slower, however the restricted side effects offer significant opportunities for analysis, optimization and so enhanced performance.

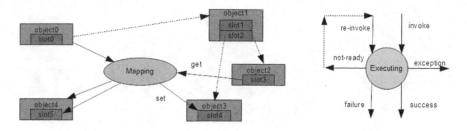

Fig. 2. Example declarative mapping interactions and life cycle

2.1 Micromappings

The simplest run-time for declarative mappings may just invoke all possible mappings for all possible object permutations, repeating the invocations for *not-ready* slot accesses. This is hideously inefficient. It may not even work since it assumes that there is at least one sequence of mapping executions that yields the required result. However a mapping may group multiple computations, generally to assist human readability. There is no prohibition on one mapping's slot access depending on another mapping's slot assignment and vice-versa, just the common sense prohibition on a pair of mappings such as $X1$ that computes $a = b + 1$ and $X2$ that performs a contradictory computation $b = a + 1$.

A mapping such as $X3$ that computes both $b = c + 1$ and $d = a + 1$ does not contradict $X1$ but it conflicts. $X1$ must wait for $X3$ to provide b, and $X3$ must wait for $X1$ to provide a. Partitioning $X3$ into $X3a$ and $X3b$, one for each computation, removes the conflict; $X1$ can be computed after $X3a$ and before $X3b$. We call these conflict-free partitioned mappings micromappings.

More formally, a micromapping is a guarded atomic computation. It comprises two active life cycle phases, shown in Fig. 3, a *fragile head* and a *robust tail*. The atomic *robust tail* may create or modify objects. The *fragile head* may bypass execution if a predicate is not satisfied or defer execution if a memory access is premature. The *fragile head* may be executed as many times as necessary to obtain the values needed by the *robust tail*. Since the *fragile head* makes no changes, there is never any need to roll-back inadvertent changes. The *Waiting* pre-state and the *Failure/Success* post-states act as mementoes to ensure that repeated invocation can be detected and results re-used.

A minimal micromapping performs exactly one model mutation to avoid inter-mapping conflict. A more pragmatic and efficient micromapping aggregates multiple non-conflicting changes.

2.2 Connections

Each micromapping typically consumes and produces one or more values each with statically declared type. Communication between producer and consumer can be managed by a connection so that connections (C*) and micromappings

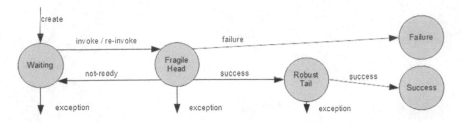

Fig. 3. Micromapping execution life cycle

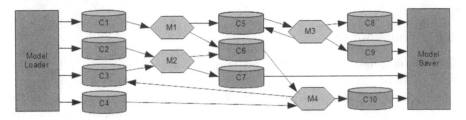

Fig. 4. Example micromapping and connection data flow graph

(M*) form a graph as shown in Fig. 4. The first layer of connections is primed by a loader, the results are drained by a saver.

The graph is directed and mostly acyclic. Acyclic parts are amenable to an efficient overall static schedule such as *for each value in C1 do M1*. Cyclic parts require dynamic run-time scheduling that is conveniently orchestrated by ensuring that each connection takes responsibility for creating each distinct invocation of each mapping. Thereafter each micromapping invocation can progress from *Waiting* to *Success/Failure* under the control of an overall dynamic scheduler.

A procedure just uses its input and returns an output. A micromapping consumes an input value from a connection and may append an output value to another connection. The connection is responsible for invoking all consuming micromappings for each available value, and for accumulating the contributions of all producing micromappings. For micromappings that consume multiple inputs, an invocation occurs for each distinct permutation of the input values.

2.3 Dependencies

The example mapping shown in Fig. 2 has a single input, but as a consequence of object navigation, it also uses three other objects. These are also inputs in so far as they must be available for execution to succeed. We should therefore augment Fig. 4 with additional nodes for each accessed object, and dependency edges for each assignment/access to each of these objects. Figure 5 shows just one such dependency where $M1$ assigns to an $O1.P1$ which is accessed by $M2$. This provides very important information for the static schedule; perform all $M1$ invocations before $M2$ invocations in order to avoid premature $M2$ invocation encountering a *not-ready* for $O1.P1$.

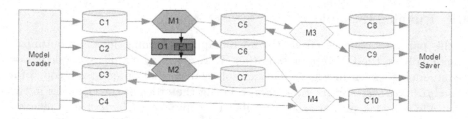

Fig. 5. Example additional object dependency

Functions provide no programming assistance to ensure that objects are accessed and updated in a sound order. This provides excellent opportunities for exciting debugging sessions as unintended concurrencies materialize in practice. Declarative mappings eliminate this major practical hazard by requiring slot accesses to wait until the slot is ready. For an OCL-based transformation language, such as QVTc or QVTr, this is possible. For a traditional non-functional programming language such as Java, it is not practical.

3   Compile-Time Analysis and Transformation Chain

The transformation chain of the Eclipse QVTd project is shown in Fig. 6.

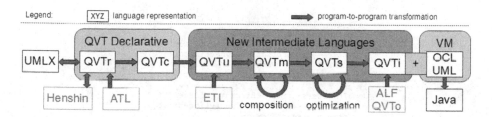

Fig. 6. Progressive transformation architecture for Declarative QVT.

– UMLX2QVTr graph patterns rewritten as tree patterns
– QVTr2QVTc rich concepts rewritten, middle model synthesized
– QVTc2QVTu (Unidirectional) irrelevant directions removed
– QVTu2QVTm (Minimal) nesting/refinement flattened
– QVTm2QVTs (Schedule) micromappings and connections identified
– QVTs2QVTi (Imperative) sequential program written
– QVTi2Java direct Java code generation

3.1   Running Example

In this paper we concentrate on the micromappings, connections and optimizations involving the QVTs representation. We use a very simple example whose metamodel is shown in Fig. 7. The example transformation creates a copy of a *DoublyLinkedList* and its *Element*s reversing the order of the elements in the copy. We will look primarily at the rule that copies one *Element* and reverses the *source/target* relationship. (The example was presented at EXE 2016 [6].)

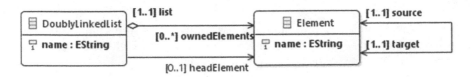

Fig. 7. Doubly-Linked List Metamodel.

The QVTr version shown in Fig. 8 demonstrates the bidirectional symmetry. Either *forward* or *reverse* may be externally selected as the output domain; the other is the input domain. Each *domain* clause has a root object and three property values, matched in the input domain, assigned in the output domain. The relationships defined by other mappings are explicit in the *when* clauses.

```
top relation element2element {
    elementName : String[1];
    domain forward forwardElement : Element {
        list = forwardList : DoublyLinkedList{},
        name = elementName,
        target = forwardTarget : Element{}
    };
    domain reverse reverseElement : Element {
        list = reverseList : DoublyLinkedList{},
        name = elementName,
        source = reverseSource : Element{}
    };
    when {
        list2list(forwardList, reverseList);
        element2element(forwardTarget, reverseSource);
    }
}
```

Fig. 8. (Manual) QVTr exposition of element2element.

The corresponding ATL [7] exposition of the example shown in Fig. 9 is much more compact but just unidirectional. The relationships established by other mappings occur invisibly as a consequence of two commented implicit invocations of the *resolveTemp* language facility.

```
rule element2element {
    from
        forwardElement : ForwardList!Element
    to
        reverseElement : ReverseList!Element (
            name <- forwardElement.name,
            list <- forwardElement.list,        -- resolveTemp
            source <- forwardElement.target     -- resolveTemp
        )
}
```

Fig. 9. (Manual) ATL exposition of element2element.

3.2 Automated Analysis

The QVTr2UMLX transformation can be used to autogenerate[3] the UMLX exposition of the example shown in Fig. 10. This again shows the symmetry of the patterns in the *forward* and *reverse* domains, together with explicit invocation of other mappings. The graphics show the patterns more clearly with many graphical decorations automatically derived from the metamodel.

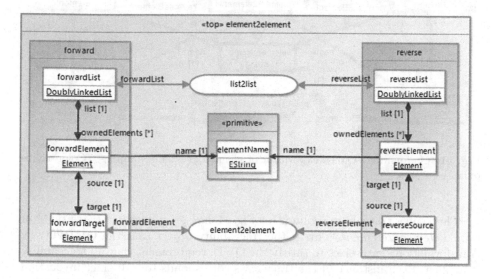

Fig. 10. (Automated) UMLX exposition of element2element. (Color figure online)

The brown elements in UMLX are internal to the mapping, whereas blue elements may interact with other mappings. Thus the outer blue box defines the *element2element* mapping with *forward, reverse* and *primitive* domains. The blue *forwardElement* and *reverseElement* are the root of each domain whose correspondence may be exploited by another mapping. For this example the *forwardTarget* and *reverseTarget* do precisely this through the use of the blue

---

[3] The layout of auto-generated diagrams has been manually improved.

rounded rectangle that is another invocation of *element2element*. Therefore on completion, the *forwardTarget* (or *reverseSource*) of each invocation of *element2element* is associated with the *forwardElement* (or *reverseElement*) of another *element2element* invocation.

The UMLX exposition demonstrates that declarative model transformations are closely related to graph transformations. It is therefore not surprising that after simplification and conversion to a unidirectional form, the residue of the QVTr AST can be analyzed to identify the object relationships. These are shown in the QVTs representation of Fig. 11. The QVTs/UMLX similarities are not surprising, so we will concentrate on the differences.

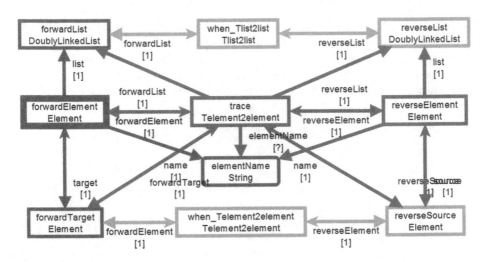

Fig. 11. (Automated) QVTs exposition of element2element Mapping. (Color figure online)

The center traceability column of Fig. 11 has an additional *trace* node of type *Telement2element*. This is the traceability object that the QVTr2QVTc transformation synthesizes to satisfy the QVTc requirement that all traceability is explicit. Each instance of the trace class corresponds to a distinct invocation of the mapping. Properties of the trace class support the use of OCL navigation expressions to explore the objects matched by a particular mapping invocation. The trace object for one mapping invocation may be referenced by another as occurs for the UMLX invocations of *list2list* and *element2element*. These are made explicit as further objects of type *Tlist2list* and *Telement2element*.

The QVTs and UMLX edges correspond to metamodel navigation paths. However whereas a UMLX arrowhead denotes navigability in OCL, a QVTs arrowhead identifies a target node that has an exactly to-one relationship with respect to its source. The significance of this becomes clear in Sect. 3.5.

The QVTs colors identify when each node becomes valid

- BLACK - model elements that are constant
- BLUE - model elements that form part of the input model
- CYAN - model elements required before mapping execution
- GREEN - model elements created by mapping execution

The colors therefore identify the dependencies on other mappings. The mapping execution must wait for any CYAN node or edge to be created by a GREEN element of another mapping, and since at compile time we cannot generally determine which particular element is required, a static schedule must wait for all possible corresponding elements. This gives the simple dependency rule; each CYAN element waits for all corresponding GREEN elements across all mappings.

3.3 Model of Computation

We have shown some graphs that are inspired by UML Class, Object, Interaction and State Machine diagrams without fully defining them. But graphs that rely on the reader's intuition are of limited utility. We must define the Model of Computation [2] that underpins QVTs and UMLX diagrams.

There is no imperative computation, rather there are many constraints that relate elements of the input and the output models. Nodes represent values, objects, slots or operations. Edges define constraints such as navigation paths. Slightly more practically, we have input models, then 'magic happens' and we have output models that satisfy all constraints to the fullest extent possible.

Our diagrams are statements of the final truth of the transformation execution. By analysing and rearranging the diagram content we are able to auto-generate an efficient executable schedule to replace the 'magic happens'.

3.4 Micromapping Partitioning

The ATL, QVTr and UMLX expositions use a programmer-friendly partitioning of the overall problem into mappings. Unfortunately this partitioning does not satisfy the atomic micromapping requirement. The problem, evidenced by the presence of a CYAN and a GREEN node of type *Telement2element* in Fig. 11, is that the *element2element* invocation of each element in the doubly linked list depends on the succeeding invocation. This cannot be resolved at compile time. A dynamic schedule must wait until the succeeding invocation has occurred Of course, since the list is circular, the dynamic schedule stalls as the first attempted invocation waits for itself.

Partitioning the mapping does not eliminate the problem, yet conventional tools execute successfully. Typically they create output nodes/objects in a first pass ignoring awkward output predicates. Then edges/relationships in a second pass. The first pass speculates that the outputs are required. Unfortunately the ignored awkward predicates may require the speculation to be reverted. This is rare in practice and so the unsound speculation may not be apparent.

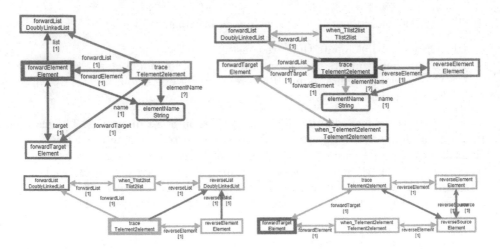

Fig. 12. (Automated) QVTs exposition of element2element with 4 Micromappings. (Color figure online)

We may exploit the trace object to speculate more accurately. Figure 12 shows a partitioning of Fig. 11 into four micromappings.

The first micromapping at top left creates the trace object provided the BLUE input pattern can be recognised, but without checking the CYAN dependencies. The speculated trace object is shown in RED to highlight the hazard that all consumers must check the residual CYAN dependencies.

The second micromapping at top right completes the dependency checks and creates the corrolaries.

A corrolary is a GREEN node that can be created without reference to other CYAN nodes once any speculation has been validated. In Fig. 10, the GREEN *reverseElement* is a corrolary of the GREEN *trace* element. The corresponding *list2list*, not shown, has its *reverseList* as a corrolary.

In Fig. 11, four CYAN nodes (and edges) must be satisfied before the GREEN elements are created. Two of the CYAN elements are corrolaries and so it is sufficient to check for successful speculation of the two non-corrolary CYAN external nodes and of the RED internal node. The three orange nodes at the top right of Fig. 12 therefore identify the nodes whose speculation must succeed before further execution is permitted.

The third and fourth mappings at the bottom join up the residual references.

In this example we have only trace nodes whose speculation is guaranteed and corrolaries that are guaranteed, allowing the troublesome micromapping step to be statically scheduled. More generally, some awkward predicates may appear at the top right of Fig. 11. These require a global run-time evaluation; if all predicates are satisfied all related speculations may proceed; if any predicate is not satisfied, no related speculation can be exploited.

The traditional 'copy all the nodes' first pass is performed by the first two micromappings. The 'copy all the edges' is performed by the last two micromappings. The traditional functionality emerges from the analysis, but without erroneously ignoring predicates that may prohibit execution.

3.5   Heads

Each micromapping must be invoked so that all possible matches are considered, so, very naively, the micromapping at the top left of Fig. 12 involving four BLUE nodes may require a four dimensional search of the elements of the input model. Consideration of the types of the BLUE nodes allows many candidates to be rejected. Consideration of the navigations allows nearly all candidates to be rejected. For each *Element* object that is considered as a match for the *forwardElement* node, we do not need to search for the other objects since they are all resolveable by to-one navigation paths from *forwardElement*. A one-dimensional search of *Element* types is therefore sufficient to find all matches.

The to-one navigation is so important to efficient scheduling that it is to-one navigation that determines the arrows in QVTs expositions. Transitive analysis of the to-one navigations identifies the minimum number of objects that have to be located to allow all other objects to be identified. These minimum objects are referred to as the heads and are drawn with thick borders in QVTs diagrams. In practice, most micromappings have a single head. Therefore most micromappings can be scheduled in linear time using a one-dimensional loop. The remainder incur often unavoidable non-linear costs.

3.6   Global Scheduling

We can join the heads, at which micromappings consume objects to the loaders/producers of all these nodes, using a connection to mediate any delays between production and consumption. This results in a graph like Fig. 4 enabling each micromapping to be invoked fairly efficiently for only sensibly typed objects. The ordering of invocations can also be quite sensible. But we can do much better by adding dependency edges from every GREEN element production to every CYAN element consumption. Just one of these is shown in Fig. 5. In practice there are a large number of such edges. Figure 13 shows about a third of our simple example. Ellipses show the connections, solid lines show the connection paths to heads, dashed lines those for the further GREEN-CYAN dependencies; orange for node-to-node dependencies, brown for edge-to-edge dependencies.

Once we have extracted the connections and dependencies, we can ignore the internals of each micromapping and use the simpler representation of Fig. 14. The loader at the top primes two elliptical connections that directly feed four micromapping rectangles which provide outputs for three other micromappings. For these simple single head micromappings the solid lines form a simple call tree with communication buffers. The dashed lines and ellipses identify further communications that do not need to be reified, since production is guaranteed

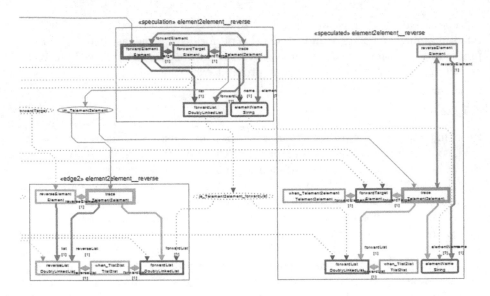

Fig. 13. (Automated) Partial overall detailed dependencies. (Color figure online)

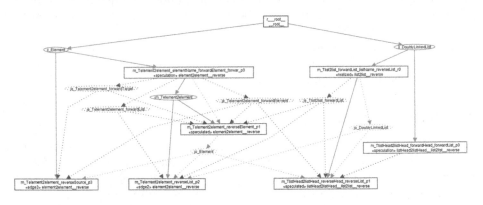

Fig. 14. (Automated) Full overall overview dependencies.

to occur before consumption. Each consuming micromapping can locate the consumed object by navigation from one if its heads.

So far the micromappings and connections have been very strongly guided by analysis of the transformation and the metamodels. Now we have a potentially NP-complete problem to solve; choose an execution order for the micromappings that minimises run-time overheads; in particular satisfy as many dependencies as possible at compile-time. In practice the graph is mostly acyclic and so there are a small number of relatively similar good solutions and large numbers of bad and truly hideous solutions that can be rejected by heuristics. The current heuristics allocate an integer index to each micromapping in a top down depth first fashion. Within a cycle micromappings have a distinct first and last indexes.

Once each micromapping has an index, or index range, and provided the run-time invokes micromappings in index order, all those dependencies that are inherently satisfied can be pruned. For the running example, all dependencies can be satisfied by the static schedule shown in Fig. 15. The indexes are shown at the bottom of each micromapping node.

Optimizations are possible, such as the merge of the micromappings at index 4 and 5. Further optimizations are future work.

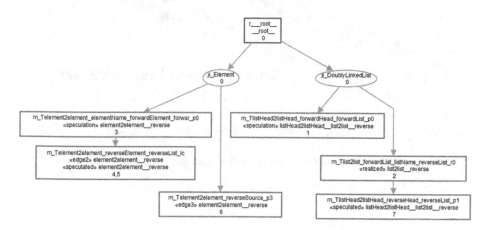

Fig. 15. (Automated) Overall schedule.

4 Results

The running example was first presented at the EXE 2016 workshop [6]. The performance of Eclipse QVTc and QVTr using interpreted execution and Java code generation was compared with alternative transformation tools. Figure 16 shows the performance on log-log scales for 100 to 10,000,000 model elements.

The two fastest results use a fully manually coded and a partially manually coded solution based on the EcoreUtil copier. The results for Eclipse QVTc and QVTr using Java Code Generation are only a little slower. The corresponding interpreted performance is about 20 times slower. These results scale fairly linear demonstrating that a good declarative schedule was identified.

The curves for ATL, EMTVM and QVTo are similar to QVTc interpreted until a quadratic effect takes over for large models. Epsilon runs out of stack for comparatively small models.

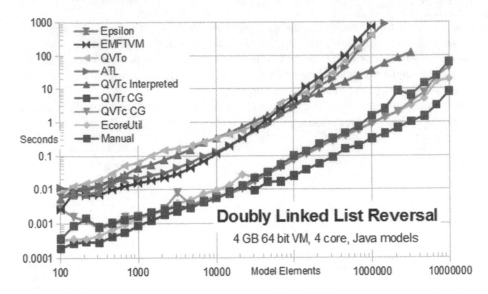

Fig. 16. Performance of the Doubly Linked List Reversal transformation.

5 Related Work

Existing model to model transformation tools such as ATL, Eclipse QVTo, Epsilon and Henshin [8] do very little if any static analysis or optimization. This work on static analysis and optimization of declarative schedules and meta-models using micromappings and connections appears to be almost completely novel.

In the Triple Graph world, a catalogue of optimizations has been proposed [1]; domain driven applicability, caching/indexing, static analysis, incremental execution. Many of these come for free in the current work.

The explicit middle model imposed by QVTc traceability reifies a trace object so that to-one navigation paths between source and target can be very cheap and optimized to avoid more expensive paths. The trace object is an inherent cache of related information. Indexing is an OCL-level further work optimization. Local and global analyses for the Micromapping Model of Computation have been described in the preceding sections.

Although not discussed in this paper, the utility of Connections shown in Fig. 4 for incremental execution is demonstrated by the Eclipse implementation.

· Detailed comparison of the approaches is quite hard, since it is very easy to provide a really bad reference implementation against almost any sensible implementation will appear fantastic.

This work diverged from an early Epsilon prototype to exploit the very strong limitations imposed by metamodels and declarative mappings. It therefore uses heuristics to produce a useful schedule relatively quickly, rather than exploring a large number of alternative schedules in an infeasible time [4].

6 Status and Further Work

The approach has evolved from an early Epsilon prototype through rewrites in Java to produce a usable tool. The next rewrite should use QVTr/UMLX as the programming language to further demonstrate their utility and to achieve the benefits of incremental code generation to enhance compilation times.

7 Conclusion

We have introduced the Micromapping Model of Computation involving Micromappings and Connections to provide local and global analyses of a declaration model transformation.

We have described optimizations that support derivation of an efficient schedule for QVTc, QVTr and UMLX.

Results of the first optimized code generated implementation show that declarative transformations can approach the performance of manually coded transformations.

Acknowledgements. Many thanks to Adolfo Sánchez-Barbudo Herrera for helpful comments on a draft, to Horacio Hoyos Rodriguez for the Epsilon prototype and to all Dimitris Kolovos' team for insightful discussions.

References

1. Leblebici, E., Anjorin, A., Schürr, A.: A catalogue of optimization techniques for triple graph grammars. In: Fill, H.G., Karagiannis, D., Reimer, U. (eds.) Modellierung 14. LNI, vol. 225, pp. 225–240. GI (2014)
2. Lee, E., Sangiovanni-Vincentelli, A.: Comparing models of computation. In: Proceedings of the 1996 IEEE/ACM International Conference on Computer-Aided Design (1996)
3. OMG. Meta Object Facility (MOF) 2.0 Query/View/Transformation Specification, Version 1.0. OMG Document Number: formal/2008-04-03, April 2008
4. Rodriguez, H.H., Kolovos, D.: Declarative model transformation execution planning. In: 15th International Workshop on OCL and Textual Modeling, Saint-Malo, October 2016
5. Willink, E.: UMLX: a graphical transformation language for MDA model driven architecture: foundations and applications. In: MDAFA 2003, 20 June 2003 (2003). http://eclipse.org/gmt/umlx/doc/MDAFA2003-4/MDAFA2003-4.pdf
6. Willink, E.: Local optimizations in eclipse QVTc and QVTr using the micromapping model of computation. In: 2nd International Workshop on Executable Modeling (Exe 2016), Saint-Malo, October 2016. http://eclipse.org/mmt/qvt/docs/EXE2016/MicroMappings.pdf
7. Eclipse ATL Project. https://projects.eclipse.org/projects/modeling.mmt.atl
8. Eclipse Henshin Project. https://projects.eclipse.org/projects/modeling.emft.henshin
9. Eclipse QVT Declarative Project. https://projects.eclipse.org/projects/modeling.mmt.qvtd

Development of Transformations

Testing Transformation Models Using Classifying Terms

Loli Burgueño[1]([⊠]), Frank Hilken[2], Antonio Vallecillo[1], and Martin Gogolla[2]

[1] Universidad de Málaga, Málaga, Spain
{loli,av}@lcc.uma.es
[2] University of Bremen, Bremen, Germany
{fhilken,gogolla}@informatik.uni-bremen.de

Abstract. Testing the correctness of the specification of a model transformation can be as hard as testing the model transformation itself. Besides, this test has to wait until at least one implementation is available. In this paper we explore the use of tracts and classifying terms to test the correctness of a model transformation specification (a transformation model) on its own, independently from any implementation. We have validated the approach using two experiments and report on the problems and achievements found concerning conceptual and tooling aspects.

1 Introduction

In general, the specification of a model transformation (as of any program) can become as complex as the program itself and thus can contain errors. Normally specifications and implementations work hand-by-hand, since they both can be considered as two complementary descriptions of the intended behavior of the system, at different levels of abstraction. Checking that the implementation conforms to the specification is one possible test for correctness of both artefacts, since they are normally developed by different people, at different times, and using different languages and approaches (e.g., declarative vs imperative). However, this process needs to wait until both the specification and the implementation are available.

Unlike other approaches, such as [2], where specifications and implementations of model transformations (MT) are tested for correctness against each other, in this paper we explore the possibility of testing the correctness of the specification of a MT on its own, independently from any possible implementation. For this we use a particular contract-based approach for MT specification [9], whereby a transformation specification is modularly given by a set of tracts, each one focusing on a particular use case of the transformation. Every tract is defined in terms of particular input and output models (those relevant to the use case) and how they should be related by the transformation. Developers are then expected to identify the transformation scenarios of interest (each one defined by one tract) and check whether the transformation behaves as expected in these scenarios.

© Springer International Publishing AG 2017
E. Guerra and M. van den Brand (Eds.): ICMT 2017, LNCS 10374, pp. 69–85, 2017.
DOI: 10.1007/978-3-319-61473-1_5

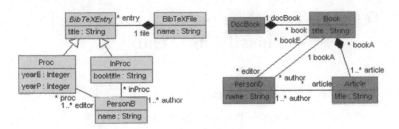

Fig. 1. BiBTeX2DocBook source and target metamodels.

To check the correctness of a MT specification (w.r.t. the intent of the specifier) the idea is to automatically simulate the behavior of any MT that conforms to that specification, and make sure that behavior is possible (satisfiability), univocally defined (functionality) and behaves as expected (given kinds of source models are transformed into the expected kinds of target models). For this we combine the use of tracts (which provide modular pieces of specification of a model transformation) and classifying terms (CT) [14] (which permit generating relevant sample models for a tract) with the completion capabilities of the USE model validator [8]. In a nutshell, the idea is to test that a tract specification of a MT is correct by generating a set of source models, use the model validator to automatically generate target models that fulfill the source-target and target constraints of the tract, and study the properties of these automatically generated models. For example, the fact that no target models can be generated means that the Tract specification is not satisfiable. If more than one target model can be obtained for the same source model, it means that the transformation is not uniquely defined. Furthermore, we can use CTs in the target domain to check that the source models are transformed according to the specifiers expectations—or that certain kinds of target models can never be generated by the transformation.

The structure of this paper is as follows. Section 2 presents the background work on which our proposal is based: tracts, CTs and the USE model validator completion capabilities. Section 3 introduces our proposal, showing how transformation models can be tested. Then, Sects. 4 and 5 describe two validation exercises we have conducted to estimate its benefits and limitations. Section 6 compares our work to similar related proposals. Finally, Sect. 7 concludes the paper and outlines some future work.

2   Preliminaries

2.1   A Running Example

In order to illustrate our proposal, let us consider a simple model transformation, `BiBTex2DocBook`, that converts the information about proceedings of conferences (in `BibTeX` format) into the corresponding information encoded in

DocBook format. This example was originally presented and discussed in [14]. The source and target metamodels that we use for the transformation are shown in Fig. 1. Associated to any metamodel there are always some constraints that define the well-formed rules for their models. The constraints for the source and target metamodels of the example are shown below.

```
-- SOURCE MM (BIBTEX) CONSTRAINTS
context Person inv uniqueName: Person.allInstances->isUnique(name)
context Proc inv uniqueTitle:  Proc.allInstances->isUnique(title)
context Proc inv withinProcUniqueTitle:
    InProc.allInstances->select(pap | pap.booktitle=title)->
        forAll(p1,p2 | p1<>p2 implies p1.title<>p2.title)
context InProc inv titleDifferentFromPrcTitle:
    Proc.allInstances->forAll(p| p.title<>title)
-- TARGET MM (DOCBOOK) CONSTRAINTS
context PersonD inv hasToBeAuthorOrEditor:
    self.article->size() + self.bookE->size() > 0
context PersonD inv uniqueName:
    PersonD.allInstances()->isUnique(name)
context Book inv uniqueTitle:
    Book.allInstances->isUnique(title)
context Book inv withinBookUniqueTitle:
    self.article->forAll(c1,c2 | c1 <> c2 implies c1.title <> c2.title)
context Book inv hasAuthorXorIsProc:
    self.author->isEmpty() xor self.editor->isEmpty()
context Book inv normalBookSectionsWrittenByAuthors:
    self.author->notEmpty() implies
        self.article->forAll(c|c.author = self.author)
```

2.2 Tracts

Tracts were introduced in [9] as a specification and black-box testing mechanism for model transformations. Tracts provide modular pieces of specification, each one focusing on a particular transformation scenario. Thus each model transformation can be specified by means of a set of tracts, each one covering a specific use case—which is defined in terms of particular input and output models and how they should be related by the transformation. In this way, tracts permit partitioning the full input space of the transformation into smaller, more focused behavioral units, and to define specific tests for them. Commonly, what developers are expected to do with tracts is to identify the scenarios of interest (each one defined by one tract) and check whether the transformation behaves as expected in these scenarios.

Tracts are specified in OCL and define the constraints on the *source* and *target* metamodels that determine the scenario of the tract, and the *source-target* constraints that provide the *specification* of the model transformation, which in our case constitutes the *Transformation Model* (TM).

Tracts constraints for the example. For the source, we will focus on BibTeX files in which all Proceedings have at least one paper, and in which all persons are either editors or authors of an entry.

```
context Person inv isAuthorOrEditor:
    inProc->size() + proc->size() > 0
context Proc inv hasAtLeastOnePaper:
    InProc.allInstances->exists(pap | pap.booktitle=title)
```

Similarly, for the target constraints we concentrate on books with at least one article, and also require that all persons participate in an entry.

```
context Book inv AtLeastOneArticle:
    self.article->size() > 0
context PersonD inv hasToBeAuthorOrEditor:
    self.bookE->size() + self.bookA->size() + self.article->size() > 0
```

Finally, the Tract source-target constraints constitute the core of the TM, and specify the relationship between the two metamodels (note that these constraints are normally direction-neutral). They make use of a class `Tract` that is added to the metamodel to store all attributes and relations of the tract itself.

```
context Tract inv Proc2Book:
    self.file.entry->selectByType(Proc)->size() =
        self.docBook.book->size() and
    self.file.entry->selectByType(Proc)->forAll(proc|
    self.docBook.book->one(book|
            proc.title = book.title and
            proc.editor->size() = book.editor->size() and
            proc.editor->forAll(editorP | book.editor->
                    one(editorB|editorP.name = editorB.name))))
context Tract inv InProc2Article:
    self.file.entry->selectByType(InProc)->size() =
        self.docBook.book.article->size() and
    self.file.entry->selectByType(InProc)->forAll(inproc|
            self.docBook.book->one(b | b.title = inproc.booktitle and
                    b.article->one(art|art.title = inproc.title and
            inproc.author->size() = art.author->size() and
            inproc.author->forAll(authP|art.author->
                    one(authA|authP.name = authA.name)))))
context t:Tract inv sameSizes:
    t.file->size() = t.docBook->size() and
    t.file->forAll(f | t.docBook->exists(db |
        f.entry->selectByType(Proc)->size() = db.book->size()))
```

2.3   Classifying Terms

Usual approaches to generate object models from a metamodel explore the state space looking for different solutions. The problem is that many of these solutions are in fact very similar, only incorporating small changes in the values of attributes and hence "equivalent" from a conceptual or structural point of view.

Classifying terms (CT) [14] constitute a technique for developing test cases for UML and OCL models. CTs are arbitrary OCL expressions on a class model that calculate a characteristic value for each object model. The expressions can either be boolean, allowing to define up to two equivalence classes, or numerical, where each resulting number defines one equivalence class. Each equivalence class is then defined by the set of object models with identical characteristic values and with one canonical representative object model. Hence, the resulting set of object models is composed from one object model per class, and therefore they represent significantly different test cases, and partition of the full input space.

For example, the following three CTs can be defined for the source metamodel of the `BiBTeX2DocBook` transformation:

```
[ yearE_EQ_yearP ]
    Proc.allInstances->forAll(yearE=yearP)
[ noManusManumLavat ]
```

```
    not PersonB.allInstances->exists(p1,p2 | p1<>p2 and
        p1.proc->exists(prc1 | p2.proc->exists(prc2 | prc1<>prc2 and
            InProc.allInstances->select(booktitle=prc1.title)->exists(
                ↪pap2 |
            pap2.author->includes(p2) and
            InProc.allInstances->select(booktitle=prc2.title)->
                exists(pap1 | pap1.author->includes(p1))))))
[ noSelfEditedPaper ]
    not Proc.allInstances->exists(prc | InProc.allInstances->
        exists(pap | pap.booktitle=prc.title and
                    prc.editor->intersection(pap.author)->notEmpty))
```

Each of the three CTs may be true or false. Together, there are thus eight ($=2^3$) equivalence classes. Each class contains those models that satisfy or not one of these properties: TTT, TTF, TFT, TFF, FTT, etc. (T if that CT evaluates to **true** and F if it evaluates to **false**). The model validator will simply return one representative of each class.

Note that we have defined some CTs for the source metamodel because we are initially interested in generating source models for the transformation. But we could have equally defined some CTs for the target metamodel in case we also want to partition the target model space. This is very useful for two main purposes. First, if we want to check that the transformation maps a certain source equivalence class of models into a given target class. And second, if we are interested in exploring some properties of the transformation or even consider the transformation in a bidirectional manner. For more details about CTs and their usages, see [14].

Also note that CTs do not always pretend to generate models that are representative of the complete metamodel, they might be used to generate models that contain interesting features w.r.t. concrete scenarios of the transformation model.

2.4 The USE Model Validator

Object models are automatically generated from a set of CTs by the USE model validator, which scrolls through all valid object models and selects one representative for each equivalence class. For this, as described in [14], each CT is assigned an integer value, and the values of the CTs are stored for each solution. Using the CTs and these values, constraints are created and given to a Kodkod solver along with the class model during the validation process. The solver prunes all object models that belong to equivalence classes for which there is already a representative element.

The validator has to be given a so-called configuration that determines how the classes, associations, datatypes and attributes are populated. In particular, for every class a mandatory upper bound for the number of objects must be stated. Both the USE tool and the model validator plugin are available for download from http://sourceforge.net/projects/useocl/.

3   A Frame for Testing Transformation Models

One central idea in this contribution is to combine CTs with a technique that
completes a partially specified and generated object diagram. The completion
technique can be applied to the source of a transformation model in order to
obtain a target. Similarly, the completion technique can be applied to the target
to obtain a source. Figure 2 show an activity diagram with the process that needs
to be followed to test the specifications in any of the directions.

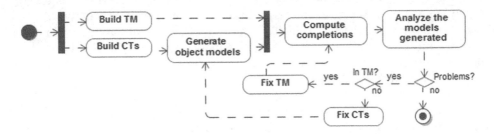

Fig. 2. Process to test the specifications.

We start building a transformation model which is constituted by a source
and a target metamodel as well as the actual transformation model in the form
of source-target constraints.

First, let us consider the direction from the source to the target. We build a
collection of source test object models determined by some source CTs. Then we
compute target completions for each source object model *som*, which is mapped
to a collection $\{tom_1, ..., tom_n\}$ of target object models. If $n = 0$ holds, this
means that the source model *som* cannot be completed. It reveals that either
the transformation model or the source CTs and with that the test object models
are inappropriately chosen.

Optionally one can now also consider the direction from the target to the
source. If target CTs are available, then we can build target test object models.
As before, we can compute source object models completions for a target object
model *tom*, which is then mapped to a collection $\{som_1, ..., som_m\}$ of source
object models. If we have $m = 0$, then this would mean that there is no source
model for the target model *tom*.

The expected result is then given as follows and can be used for test purposes
in various ways.

- We obtain a collection of (source,target) object model pairs that show to
  the developer the behavior of the transformation model in terms of concrete test cases and thus makes the transformation alive: $\{(som_1, tom_1), ...,$
  $(som_l, tom_l)\}$.
- Depending on the transformation model and the chosen CTs one will get
  witnesses for (a) non-functional behavior or (b) non-injective behavior of the
  model transformation.

(a) Non-functional behavior of the transformation model: This occurs if there is one source object model *som* connected to two different target object models tom_1 and tom_2 such that (som, tom_1) and (som, tom_2) are in the (source,target) object model set with $tom_1 \neq tom_2$.

(b) Non-injective behavior of the transformation model: This occurs if there is one target object model *tom* connected to two different source object models som_1 and som_2 such that (som_1, tom) and (som_2, tom) are in the (source,target) object model set with $som_1 \neq som_2$.

- Furthermore, a potentially existing connection between source and target CTs may be analysed. The developer may claim the source and the target CTs as being 'in correspondence': the collection of source object models generated from the source CTs must then be transformed into the collection of target object models generated from the target CTs. The developer can be supported in checking the 'in correspondence' claim. For each completion of a source object model, there must exist a target object model that shows the same behavior w.r.t. to the target CTs: A source object model *som* generated from the source CTs will be completed to a target object model *completed(som)*; and there must exist a target object model *tom* in the collection of target object models generated from the target CTs (CTS_{target}) such that the following is true (where the operation *eval* computes the value of the expression): $eval(CTS_{target}, completed(som)) = eval(CTS_{target}, tom)$. If there is no such target model, the 'in correspondence' supposition is wrong and with this the CTs are inappropriately chosen, if an 'in correspondence' relationship was desired.
- In general, one can also try to consider the direction from target to source with such a correspondence checking technique.

Developing a TM for the BIBTeX2DocBook example. In order to build the MT specification (i.e., tract source-target constraints) we gave the metamodels to one experienced developer with knowledge in OCL and the description in natural language of the transformation model. Basically, each BibTeXFile should have a direct correspondence with a DocBook; each Proc with a Book; each InProc with an Article, and each PersonB with a PersonD. Moreover, all the relationships between the source objects are kept in the target model but there exists a new relationship between a book and an article when the corresponding InProc has as booktitle the corresponding Proc.

With this, the developer provided the following four constraints (one for every pair of objects) as the transformation specification.

```
1  context Tract inv BibTeX2DocBook:
2    BibTeXFile.allInstances->forAll(file|DocBook.allInstances->exists(dB|
3      file.entry->selectByType(Proc)->forAll(proc|dB.book->
4        one(b|proc.title = b.title))))
5  context Tract inv Proc2Book:
6    Proc.allInstances->forAll(proc|Book.allInstances->exists(book|
7      proc.title = book.title and
8      proc.editor->forAll(editorP|book.editor->exists(editorB |
9        editorP.name = editorB.name and
10       book.article->forAll(art|InProc.allInstances->
11         one(inP | inP.booktitle = art.title))))))
```

```
12 context Tract inv InProc2Article:
13    InProc.allInstances->forAll(inP|Article.allInstances->exists(art|
14      inP.title = art.title and
15      art.bookA.title = inP.booktitle and
16      inP.author->forAll(authP|
17         art.author->exists(authA | authP.name = authA.name))))
18 context Tract inv PersonB2PersonD:
19    PersonB.allInstances->size() = PersonD.allInstances->size() and
20    PersonB.allInstances->forAll(p|PersonD.allInstances->exists(pd|
21      p.name=pd.name))
```

Given the transformation model and the object diagrams obtained using the CTs previously defined, the model validator could not complete any of the object diagrams. There is no possible model that fulfils all the conditions. The reason is a fault in the constraint `Proc2Book` (line 4). At the end of it, Article titles are compared to InProc booktitles, instead of InProc titles. The fix to be applied is `inP.title = art.title`.

After fixing this error, the model validator was able to complete the source object diagrams respecting the transformation model. Figure 3 shows, inside the square, one of the source object diagrams and, outside the square, the completion generated by the model validator.

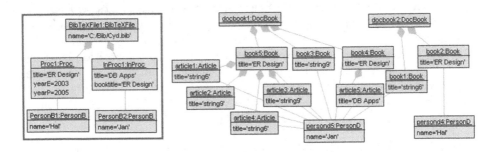

Fig. 3. Completion for the BibTeX model.

Several problems can be easily detected on this object model. First of all, there is no one-to-one correspondence between the source and target objects: the target contains more objects than it should. This problem can be solved by adding object equality to each one of the constraints to limit the number of objects generated when completing the object diagrams. For instance, for the `BibTeX2DocBook` invariant the code to add is `BibTeXFile.allInstances->size() = DocBook.allInstances->size()`.

Another observable problem is that the names were supposed to be unique (i.e., a DocBook should not have two Books with the same name and a Book should not have two Articles with the same name). In the constraints, the **one** operation, which is intended for the uniqueness, is placed inside the body of an **exists** operation. As there is one DocBook that respects the uniqueness (`docBook2`), i.e. fulfills the constraint, the overall system state is valid. In order to generate correct completions the **exists** expressions need to be replaced by **one** expressions (lines 2, 6, 13 and 20).

In summary, we have been able to follow an iterative process for the development of *transformation models*, that can be checked for correctness before any implementation is available, and independently from any of them. A transformation model was considered correct if the sample models generated from the constraints and CTs could be completed and the resulting models made sense.

4   Validation Exercise 1: Families2Persons

In order to validate our proposal with further examples and to make some estimations on the effort required by our specification development approach, we selected two representative case studies.

For each one we first defined a set of CTs, and created a set of test object models using them. Then, each author of this paper worked independently on developing the transformation models for both examples, testing them with the sample models jointly decided. This section and the next one describe the examples, the problems and issues found in each one, and some indications on the effort required to develop and test the corresponding transformation models.

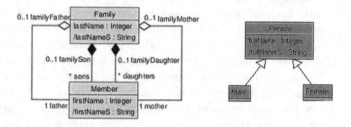

Fig. 4. Metamodels for the `Families2Persons` transformation (once corrected).

The Families2Persons model transformation. The first case study is the well-known example of the `Families2Persons` model transformation. The source and target metamodels are depicted in Fig. 4. The validation exercise consisted in developing a TM that specifies the required model transformation. For generating the sample object models we defined one tract and two CTs. The tract focused on families with less than 4 children:

```
Family.allInstances −>forAll(f|f.daughters −>size + f.sons−>size <= 3)
```

The constraint of the first CT identifies families with one son and one daughter. The second CT identifies families with at least three generations.

```
[oneDaughterOneSon]
    Family.allInstances −>forAll(f|f.daughters −>size=1 and f.sons−>size=1)
[AtLeastThreeGenerations]
    Family.allInstances ()−>exists( fstGen |
        let sndGen = (fstGen.sons.familyFather −>
                 union(fstGen.daughters.familyMother)) in
        sndGen−>exists(f|f.sons−>notEmpty() or f.daughters−>notEmpty()))
```

The combination of these two CTs determines four equivalence classes in the input model space. Using the tract and these classifying terms, we used the model validator to build the four object models (one per equivalence class) that were used to test the transformation model.

Issues found. The first problems that we all hit when developing the tract source-target constraints were due to the fact that the original metamodels were incomplete, they even contained errors (note that Fig. 4 shows the metamodel once the problems found were fixed). These issues arose when we tried to generate object models with the model validator. In particular, in the original `Families` metamodel all relationships were compositions. This bans members from belonging to two families, and therefore the existence of families with three generations. We had to change the father and mother relationships to aggregations in order to proceed.

Furthermore, as soon as we started to generate source object models we also discovered that these metamodels permitted some pathological scenarios. For example, the original source metamodel allowed a member to play the role of father and son in the same family—similarly for mother and daughters. Analogously, members' gender should be maintained: if a person is a son in a family, he cannot be the mother in another. Names cannot be empty, either.

Finally, we also had to cope with some current limitations of the model validator: for example, it cannot deal with the `concat()` operator on strings. To overcome this limitation we used integers to represent names, instead of strings. First and last names are 1-digit integers (in decimal base) and full names are 2-digit integers that can be obtained as `name*10 + lastName`. The original string attributes became derived features, for easy human interpretation of the results.

Figure 4 shows the final metamodel. The following invariants need to be added to the metamodels, to incorporate the corresponding well-formed constraints that permitted creating valid models.

```
-- FAMILIES METAMODEL
context Family
  inv nameDomain: 0 <= lastName and lastName <= 9
  inv fatherParadoxon: self.sons->excludes(father)
  inv motherParadoxon: self.daughters->excludes(mother)
  inv cycleFreeness: self.sons.familyFather->
    union(self.daughters.familyMother)->
      closure(f | f.sons.familyFather->
        union(f.daughters.familyMother))->excludes(self)
context Member
  inv nameDomain: 1 <= firstName and firstName <= 9
  inv noOrphanMember: self.familyMother->size() +
    self.familyFather->size() + self.familyDaughter->size()
    + self.familySon->size() > 0
  inv sonsBecomeFathers: self.familySon <> null implies
    self.familyMother = null
  inv daughtersBecomeMothers: self.familyDaughter <> null implies
    self.familyFather = null
  inv fatherMotherDistinct: self.familyFather = null or
    self.familyMother = null
-- PERSON METAMODEL
context Person
  inv nameDomain: 10 <= fullName and fullName <= 99
  inv nameNotEmpty: fullName <> null
```

When generating the sample test object models we also discovered that these metamodels permit other weird situations. For example, all members of a family can have the same first name. Similarly, the last name of family members in multiple families needs to be preserved and this is not controlled by the metamodel. In particular, the last name of a father or a son should be the same in all of his families.

Apart from these issues concerning the source and target metamodels, when trying to develop and test a transformation model using our approach, we also unveiled some issues related with the relationship that the transformation is trying to establish between the metamodels. For example, consider the following constraint that checks that members are transformed to persons with the proper gender (an equivalent one should be required for male members):

```
(self.familyDaughter <> null or self.familyMother <> null) implies
  Female.allInstances->exists(female |
    if self.familyMother <> null then
      female.fullName=(self.firstName*10)+self.familyMother.lastName
    else
      female.fullName=(self.firstName*10)+self.familyDaughter.lastName
    endif)
```

This approach does not work: should there be two members (left-hand side) with the same name and surname, the constraint (either with **exists** or with **one**) is fulfilled as long as there is one person (right-hand side) with the name and surname. And if we try to add another constraint that states that the number of members and persons should be the same, the model validator may create a person with a random **fullName** in order to enforce it. Therefore, apart from the constraint that checks the size, there is the need to check the exact correspondence of the names of members and persons. There are several approaches to solve this issue, and each author used one—e.g., navigating the set of all possible names and checking that the number of times they appear in the source and target models is the same; or selecting the members by gender and making sure their names appear the same number of times in both sides.

Performance analysis for the Families2Persons case study. Columns 2–5 of Table 1 show the general statistics resulting from the experiments conducted by the four paper authors (AV, FH, LB, MG) for this case study. Each author needed a number of iterations until his/her transformation model was developed and tested correct. As mentioned above, a transformation model was considered correct if the sample source models generated from the selected tract and CTs could be completed and the resulting target models were unique and made sense.

It is important to note that the tests were not really independent, particularly at the beginning of the experiment when the source and target metamodels were found inconsistent and incomplete. In order to focus on the transformation model itself, as soon as someone detected a problem in the metamodel, it was corrected and the rest of the participants were notified to avoid it.

The level of expertise of FH and MG with OCL and with the model validator was higher, and this fact had some impact when developing the TMs, as Table 1 reflects. They needed less iterations to solve the problems and they never wrote constraints that led to UNSAT states.

Table 1. Statistics for the two case studies.

	Families2Persons				Java2Graph			
	AV	FH	LB	MG	AV	FH	LB	MG
# iterations	5	2	4	2	4	2	4	2
# iterations where new problems were detected	4	1	3	1	3	1	3	1
# iterations in which a fix led to a new problem	0	0	0	0	0	0	0	0
% of time developing the OCL code (vs. % of time finding what the problem was)	40	76	20	10	40	82	20	10
% of occasions the model validator returned UNSAT (instead of generating the models)	40	0	10	0	50	0	20	0
final # of constraints developed	5	1	4	3	4	4	5	2

Although not specified in the table, note as well that in the first iterations, most of the time was spent developing the OCL code of the TM, while in the latter ones the problems were trickier and thus more time was spent identifying the problems and solving them. The total time spent running this experiment ranged between six and eight hours.

5   Validation Exercise 2: Java2Graph

The second validation experiment considered a model transformation that, starting from a model of a large Java program, transformed it into a graph (composed of nodes and edges) that has the information needed to be visualized. Graph nodes have name, shape, colour and size. Edges have a name and a label and connect nodes. Every edge is connected to one source and one target node, but you may have many different edges between two nodes.

In the transformation, every Java class is represented by a node, and every attribute whose type is another class as an edge. The label of the edge is the name of the attribute. The size of a node is the number of its outgoing edges. The shape depends on the kind of Java class: triangular if the class is abstract, square if it is final, and round (a circle) if it is a regular class. The colour depends on the number of attributes and methods: red if the class has more attributes and methods than 70% of the rest of the classes, green if it is between percentiles 30 and 70, and yellow if it has less than 30% of the rest of the classes.

The source and target metamodels for the transformation are shown in Fig. 5. Additionally, some constraints define their well-formed rules:

```
-- JAVA METAMODEL CONSTRAINTS
context NamedElement inv uniqueNames:
  not self.name.oclIsUndefined() and (self.name <> '')
  and NamedElement.allInstances->select(ne |
        self<>ne and ne.name = self.name)->size()=0
context Class inv kindNotNull:
   not self.kind.oclIsUndefined()
context Attribute inv typeNotNull:
   not self.type.oclIsUndefined()
context DataType inv noDanglingDatatypes:
   Attribute.allInstances()->exists(a | a.type = self)
```

```
-- GRAPH METAMODEL CONSTRAINTS
context Node inv validNode:
    (self.name <> null) and (self.name <> '') and (self.size>=0)
context Edge inv noNullLabel:
    (self.label <> null) and (self.label <> '')
```

To generate the sample object models used to test the transformation model we defined three CTs. They define eight equivalence classes and thus eight sample object models with different characteristics.

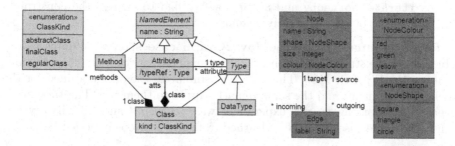

Fig. 5. Metamodels for the Java2Graph transformation.

```
[ThreeKindsOfClasses]
  Class.allInstances->exists(c1, c2, c3 | c1.kind=#abstractClass
    and c2.kind=#finalClass and c3.kind=#regularClass)
[GodObjectExists]
  Class.allInstances()->exists( c | c.atts.type->asSet()
    ->selectByKind(Class)
      ->includesAll(Class.allInstances()->excluding(c)))
[AttributeCycleLength3]
  Class.allInstances()->exists(c1,c2,c3 | Set{c1,c2,c3}->size=3 and
    c1.atts->exists(a1 | c2.atts->exists(a2 | c3.atts->exists(a3 |
      a1.type=c2 and a2.type=c3 and a3.type=c1))))
```

The first CT defines models with three kinds of classes. The second one asks models to have a class that is dependent on all others. The last one requires the existence of references between classes that form cycles of length 3.

Issues found. The nature of the issues found in this example was similar to the previous one, although the number of issues was very different.

This time we did not find any major problem with the original metamodels. The only issue found with the metamodels was not due to the metamodels themselves, but to the need to relate them by a model transformation: we found the typical example of a semantic mismatch between two metamodels when we want to relate them. In the target metamodel, we had stated in Node's `validNode` invariant that the attribute `size` should be greater than 0 with the expression "...and (self.size>0)", and hence we had to change it to allow the attribute to be 0 by replacing it with "...and (self.size>=0)". Otherwise we were not able to transform Java classes with no attributes or methods, since the size of their corresponding nodes is 0.

We also hit here the problem of imprecise specifications expressed in natural language. Namely, the problem specification (imprecisely) stated that the colour of the transformed node depended on the number of attributes and methods of "the rest of the classes." One of the authors understood that in "the rest of the classes" the class self was also included while another author excluded it. This led to slightly different results in the transformed models.

Finally, we also had to overcome some limitations of the current version of the model validator, although they were easy to address. For example, it does not support real numbers and we had to use integers instead (multiplying by 100 to get 2 decimals). Furthermore, there is no support for some OCL features such as `iterate`, `sortedby` and `Sequence`. We had to express the constraints using the subset of OCL currently available.

Performance analysis for the Java2Graph case study. Columns 6–9 of Table 1 show the statistics resulting from the experiments conducted by the four authors (AV, FH, LB, MG). They are very similar to the ones obtained for the previous experiment, and the same remarks apply to them too. The time every author spent working on this experiment was between 4 and 6 h, slightly less than before—but also because we learned from the previous experience.

Conclusions from the validation experiments. After conducting these two experiments, there are some common issues that we would like to point out. First, we were able to unveil significant problems in the specification of the source and target metamodels (even in the *a priori* very simple `Families2Persons` example). It was clear that no rigorous tests had been conducted on them, probably due to the traditional lack of tools in MDE to instantiate metamodels.

Second, we were also able to reveal semantic problems, which happen when trying to relate two (perfectly correct) independent metamodels by means of a model transformation: some of the individual metamodel integrity constraints hinder the creation of particular relations between their elements.

Third, we also suffered from the lack of precision in textual specifications, which permit multiple interpretations and hence distinct implementations.

Tool support can also represent some impediments. We hit some problems due to restricted support of model features by model validator: Java heap space when generating models with the constraint solver; lack of support for some OCL types (`Sequence`, `Real`) and operators (`iterator`, `sortedBy`).

When it comes to debugging, once the model validator finds one solution it is not easy to determine whether it is correct or not. The only thing we know is that it satisfies the imposed constraints. But then we need to interpret the results and check whether they make sense. A similar situation happens when the model validator finds more than one solution. The case is even worse when it finds no solution, because we only know that the completion is unsatisfiable.

We also learned interesting aspects of the use of the model validator. For example, using specific configurations for each test case is better than a common configuration for all cases. In this sense, a better support for model transformations and completions would be nice on the model validator side.

Finally, when we put together all the solutions independently developed by the four authors, we discovered a common schema for defining the transformation model constraints, which is the one that we show below (note that `exists` could be replaced by `one` in some cases):

```
Source->forAll(s | Target->exists(t | predicate(s,t))) -- AND --
Source->size()=Target->size()
```

Basically, in many cases the TM is composed of constraints that specify, for each source model element, how it is transformed; plus a set of constraints that determine the relations between the sizes of source and target model elements.

Note that in this paper we have focused on the validation of directional model transformations, from source to target. In general, transformation models and their associated constraints are direction neutral and thus they can be interpreted (and evaluated) from left to right and vice-versa. The validation from target to source is left for future work.

6   Related Work

In this work, we see model transformations as transformation models and focus on checking their correctness. The ideas presented in this work were first outlined in a short paper [13]. This paper contains the first complete proposal and provides some initial validation exercises that permit evaluating the advantages and shortcomings of the approach.

There are some dynamic approaches for testing MT implementations by executing them given an input model or a set of them. References [12,18] present contributions for debugging model transformations, and the work in [7] compares the generated and expected output models. The work in [1] analyses the trace model in order to find errors. In addition to Tracts, other static approaches allow the specification of contracts in a visual manner [11].

Reference [6] proposes a dynamic testing technique defining equivalence classes for the source models in a similar manner as it is done with CTs. Their proposal lacks full automation and is less expressive as they do not consider the use of OCL. Reference [10] presents a mechanism for generating test cases by analysing the OCL expressions in the source metamodel in order to partition the input model space. This is a systematic approach similar to ours, but focusing on the original source model constraints. Our proposal allows the developer partitioning the source (and target) model space independently from these constraints, in a more flexible manner. Sen et al. [16] considered the completion of partial models to satisfy a set of constraints.

The work in [15] proves the correctness of specifications by making use of algebras. Our approach can be seen as a first step and as an easier and cheaper way that does not require the developer to have any extra knowledge or create any other software artifact. Similarly, in [5], Alloy is used to validate models while the UML/OCL model under test is translated to and from Alloy before and after the validation, respectively. This works for Alloy experts, but might be difficult for other modelers. Our approach works on the UML/OCL and hides the transformation details between the languages.

Finally, the work in [3] is similar to ours but uses refinement between specifications and/or implementations to check whether one can safely replace another. OCL is used as a base language where specifications and MT implementations are mapped to, and then SAT solvers look for counterexamples. As part of future work we would like to evaluate if our proposal is simpler (and more effective) than writing a reference implementation in parallel and checking if the implementation is a refinement of the specification. Refinement of MT specifications has also been studied in [17] in the context of tracts.

7   Conclusions and Future Work

Even the simplest model transformations, not to mention their specifications, may contain faults [4]. In this paper we have proposed a method that uses tracts and classifying terms to test the correctness of a model transformation specification (i.e., a transformation model), independently from any possible implementation. We have validated the approach using two experiments and report on the problems and achievements found concerning conceptual and tooling aspects.

There are several lines of work that we plan to address next. First, we want to take into account the fact that TM constraints are direction-neutral, being able to analyze further properties of the MT under development. Second, we would like to validate our proposal with more transformations, in order to gain a better understanding of its advantages and limitations. Third, we plan to improve the tool support to further automate all tests, so human intervention is kept to the minimum. Finally, we need to define a systematic approach of defining classifying term and transformation model testing using the ideas outlined in this paper.

References

1. Aranega, V., Mottu, J.M., Etien, A., Dekeyser, J.L.: Traceability mechanism for error localization in model transformation. In: Proceedings of ICSOFT 2009 (2009)
2. Burgueño, L., Troya, J., Wimmer, M., Vallecillo, A.: Static fault localization in model transformations. IEEE Trans. Softw. Eng. **41**(5), 490–506 (2015)
3. Büttner, F., Egea, M., Guerra, E., Lara, J.: Checking model transformation refinement. In: Duddy, K., Kappel, G. (eds.) ICMT 2013. LNCS, vol. 7909, pp. 158–173. Springer, Heidelberg (2013). doi:10.1007/978-3-642-38883-5_15
4. Cuadrado, J.S., Guerra, E., de Lara, J.: Static analysis of model transformations. IEEE Trans. Softw. Eng. **1**, 1–32 (2016)
5. Cunha, A., Garis, A.G., Riesco, D.: Translating between alloy specifications and UML class diagrams annotated with OCL. SoSym **14**(1), 5–25 (2015)
6. Fleurey, F., Baudry, B., Muller, P.A., Traon, Y.L.: Qualifying input test data for model transformations. Softw. Syst. Model. **8**(2), 185–203 (2009)
7. García-Domínguez, A., Kolovos, D.S., Rose, L.M., Paige, R.F., Medina-Bulo, I.: EUnit: a unit testing framework for model management tasks. In: Whittle, J., Clark, T., Kühne, T. (eds.) MODELS 2011. LNCS, vol. 6981, pp. 395–409. Springer, Heidelberg (2011). doi:10.1007/978-3-642-24485-8_29

8. Gogolla, M., Hamann, L., Hilken, F.: On static and dynamic analysis of UML and OCL transformation models. In: Proceedings of AMT 2014, CEUR Workshop Proceedings, pp. 24–33 (2014). http://ceur-ws.org/Vol-1277/3.pdf
9. Gogolla, M., Vallecillo, A.: *Tract*able model transformation testing. In: France, R.B., Kuester, J.M., Bordbar, B., Paige, R.F. (eds.) ECMFA 2011. LNCS, vol. 6698, pp. 221–235. Springer, Heidelberg (2011). doi:10.1007/978-3-642-21470-7_16
10. González, C.A., Cabot, J.: Test data generation for model transformations combining partition and constraint analysis. In: Ruscio, D., Varró, D. (eds.) ICMT 2014. LNCS, vol. 8568, pp. 25–41. Springer, Cham (2014). doi:10.1007/978-3-319-08789-4_3
11. Guerra, E., de Lara, J., Wimmer, M., Kappel, G., Kusel, A., Retschitzegger, W., Schönböck, J., Schwinger, W.: Automated verification of model transformations based on visual contracts. Autom. Softw. Eng. **20**(1), 5–46 (2013)
12. Hibberd, M., Lawley, M., Raymond, K.: Forensic debugging of model transformations. In: Engels, G., Opdyke, B., Schmidt, D.C., Weil, F. (eds.) MODELS 2007. LNCS, vol. 4735, pp. 589–604. Springer, Heidelberg (2007). doi:10.1007/978-3-540-75209-7_40
13. Hilken, F., Burgueño, L., Gogolla, M., Vallecillo, A.: Iterative development of transformation models by using classifying terms. In: Proceedings of AMT 2015, CEUR Workshop Proceedings, pp. 1–6 (2015). http://ceur-ws.org/Vol-1500/paper2.pdf
14. Hilken, F., Gogolla, M., Burgueño, L., Vallecillo, A.: Testing models and model transformations using classifying terms. Softw. Syst. Model. (2016). http://link.springer.com/article/10.1007%2Fs10270-016-0568-3
15. Orejas, F., Wirsing, M.: On the specification and verification of model transformations. In: Palsberg, J. (ed.) Semantics and Algebraic Specification. LNCS, vol. 5700, pp. 140–161. Springer, Heidelberg (2009). doi:10.1007/978-3-642-04164-8_8
16. Sen, S., Mottu, J.-M., Tisi, M., Cabot, J.: Using models of partial knowledge to test model transformations. In: Hu, Z., Lara, J. (eds.) ICMT 2012. LNCS, vol. 7307, pp. 24–39. Springer, Heidelberg (2012). doi:10.1007/978-3-642-30476-7_2
17. Vallecillo, A., Gogolla, M.: Typing model transformations using tracts. In: Hu, Z., Lara, J. (eds.) ICMT 2012. LNCS, vol. 7307, pp. 56–71. Springer, Heidelberg (2012). doi:10.1007/978-3-642-30476-7_4
18. Wimmer, M., Kappel, G., et al.: A Petri Net based debugging environment for QVT Relations. In: Proceedings of ASE 2009, pp. 3–14. IEEE Computer Society, Washington, DC (2009). doi:10.1109/ASE.2009.99

Differencing of Model Transformation Rules: Towards Versioning Support in the Development and Maintenance of Model Transformations

Timo Kehrer[1]([⊠]), Christopher Pietsch[2], and Daniel Strüber[3]

[1] Humboldt-Universität zu Berlin, Berlin, Germany
`timo.kehrer@informatik.hu-berlin.de`
[2] Universität Siegen, Siegen, Germany
`cpietsch@informatik.uni-siegen.de`
[3] Universität Koblenz-Landau, Koblenz, Germany
`strueber@uni-koblenz.de`

Abstract. With model transformations arising as primary development artifacts in Model-driven Engineering, dedicated tools supporting the development and maintenance of model transformations are strongly required. Calculating differences between versions of transformations is an essential service for effectively managing their evolution. In this tool demonstration paper, we present support for this task which is tailored for the differencing of graph-based model transformation rules. Our implementation is based on the model differencing framework SiLift which we adapt to the Henshin model transformation language. We demonstrate the usefulness of this feature using a running example.

1 Introduction

Model-driven engineering (MDE) emphasizes model transformation as a central activity in all stages of software construction. Many model transformation approaches have emerged to address a multitude of transformation scenarios [1]. However, less effort has been spent in providing dedicated tools supporting transformation developers in a variety of development and maintenance tasks. With model transformations arising as primary development artifacts, such tools are strongly required to fully turn the MDE vision into reality. Tools supporting some development tasks, such as clone detection for model transformations [2], have been addressed by the model transformation research community recently. In general, however, developers are not nearly as broadly supported as they are used to from traditional development environments, which is still a major obstacle to a more widespread adoption of MDE [3].

In this tool demonstration paper, we address the problem of managing transformations evolving into several versions, which must be supported by a differencing service for comparing two versions of a transformation. Providing a high-quality differencing service is challenging in the case of visual model transformation languages, particularly when the language's abstract syntax substantially

© Springer International Publishing AG 2017
E. Guerra and M. van den Brand (Eds.): ICMT 2017, LNCS 10374, pp. 86–91, 2017.
DOI: 10.1007/978-3-319-61473-1_6

differs from the graphical syntax tool users are familiar with. This is the case for graphical transformation rules developed in Henshin [4,5], a transformation language and framework based on graph transformation concepts targeting models defined in the Eclipse Modeling Framework (EMF). Here, differences obtained from off-the-shelf comparison tools are often too low-level and hard to understand for tool users, since they report fine-grained changes based on Henshin's abstract syntax maintained in the background of the Henshin diagram editor. To mitigate this problem, modern model differencing frameworks such as EMF Compare [6] or SiLift [7] can be adapted to a given (visual) language. In this paper, we present our adaptation of SiLift to the Henshin model transformation language and environment. This way, we obtain more user-friendly descriptions of changes reflecting the way how transformation rules are edited in the Henshin diagram editor. We demonstrate the usefulness of this feature using an example. Further information, including a tool demo as well as download and installation instructions, are provided at http://pi.informatik.uni-siegen.de/projects/SiLift/icmt2017.php.

2   Motivating Example

Consider the transformation rules *startColumn* and *extendColumn* on the right-hand side of Fig. 3, which are part of a Henshin transformation constructing a *sparse grid* as described in the "Comb benchmark" by Varró et al. [8]. Both rules are shown in the graphical syntax of the Henshin diagram editor, where left- and right-hand sides (LHS, RHS) of a rule are combined into a single graph with annotations, e.g. «create» indicating RHS graph elements without a LHS counterpart. The syntactic sugar @Grid specifies the presence of a *Grid* node to be used as container for all created nodes.

Assume that we obtained the rule *extendColumn* from the rule *startColumn* using the Henshin diagram editor. This can be achieved in a seemingly simple way in six edit steps: (1) renaming the rule from *"startColumn"* to *"extendColumn"*, (2) changing the kind of the rule parameter *next* from *out* to *inout*, (3)

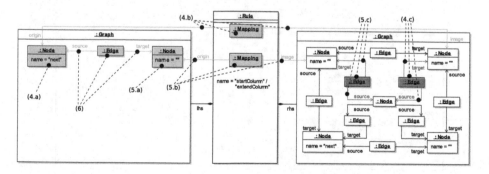

Fig. 1. ASG changes caused by editing the rule *startColumn* to become the revised rule *extendColumn*.

setting the identifier of the upper left node to *"next"*, (4) converting the upper
left node into a node to be preserved, (5) doing the same conversion for the
upper right node, and (6) converting the edge connecting these nodes into an
edge which is to be preserved.

Following the basic MDE principle "everything is a model" [9], Henshin transformation rules are represented as models, thus model differencing tools can be
used for comparing two versions of a rule. However, available tools deliver change
descriptions on the abstract syntax level which are often hard to understand. For
example, the generic differencing facility of EMF Compare [6], without being
adapted to the Henshin transformation language, describes the effect of edit
step (4) in terms of three low-level changes: (4.a) the creation of a LHS node
of type *Node*, (4.b) the creation of a *Mapping* associating that node with an
already existing one in the RHS, and (4.c) the deletion of a containment edge
connecting the RHS node with the container node of type *Grid*. Note the syntactic sugar `@Grid`, which causes change (4.c). Analogously, three low-level changes
are reported for edit step (5), in the sequel referred to as (5.a), (5.b) and (5.c).
Finally, step (6) is reported as introducing a new edge in the RHS instead of a
conversion of the existing edge into an edge to be preserved. Figure 1 illustrates
these low-level ASG changes using the well-known UML object diagram notation (some containment edges are represented by nesting nodes); ASG elements
colored in red are deleted, while elements colored in green are created.

3   Differencing of Transformation Rules Using SiLift

Structural differencing tools basically calculate a difference between two model
versions, say v_1 and v_2, in two steps: First, a model-matching algorithm [10] identifies corresponding nodes and edges in both ASGs. Subsequently, a difference
is derived from a matching: Elements of v_1 which do not have a corresponding
element in v_2 are considered to be deleted, while elements of v_2 not having a
corresponding element in v_1 are considered to be created. In Sect. 2, we have
seen that using such primitive graph operations on the ASG typically impairs
the readability of the resulting differences.

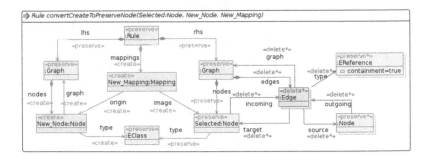

Fig. 2. Edit operation *convertCreateNodeToPreserveNode* specified in Henshin.

The model differencing framework SiLift [7] is a suitable basis for semantically lifting low-level changes to the level of edit operations, based on the approach presented in [11]. SiLift needs to be configured for a specific modeling language by specifying the edit operations available in this language. These edit operations need to be provided as Henshin rules. To support the differencing of Henshin transformations, we produced two sets of edit operations. First, we generated a complete set of *elementary* edit operations from the Henshin meta-model using the approach and supporting tool presented in [12,13]. In addition, we manually specified 15 complex edit operations available in the Henshin diagram editor, including the operations *convertCreateNodeToPreserveNode* covering edit steps (3) and (4) as well as *convertCreateEdgeToPreserveEdge* covering edit step (6) of our example. The Henshin specification of edit operation *convertCreateNodeTo-PreserveNode* is shown in Fig. 2, aggregating all change actions causing the low-level changes (4.a), (4.b), (4.c) and (5.a), (5.b), (5.c), respectively. Note that the multi-rule parts, indicated by the * symbol, are used to indicate optional rule actions; they are not applied when a root node of an EMF model is converted.

To present calculated differences in a user-friendly way, we integrated the Henshin diagram editor with SiLift's difference presentation UI. Figure 3 shows how the difference obtained from comparing the rules *startColumn* and *extendColumn* is presented. The control window on the left displays the edit steps; selecting an edit step causes that its arguments are highlighted in the Henshin diagram(s) on the right.

Currently, a technical limitation when working with Henshin is that structural elements of a transformation rule must be equipped with UUIDs. These are used to (i) establish correspondences between elements in two versions of a rule and (ii) to identify graphical elements in Henshin diagrams.

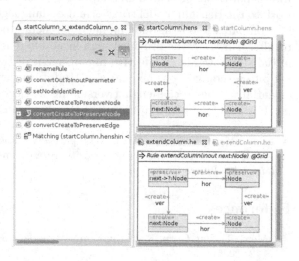

Fig. 3. Difference obtained from comparing Henshin transformation rules *startColumn* and *extendColumn* using SiLift.

4   Related Work

Many model differencing techniques were proposed in the last 15 years. The approaches surveyed in [10] focus on the matching step of the difference calculation. All of them suffer from the problem that only low-level changes are derived from a matching. More recently, the customization of the generic differencing engine has been addressed in EMF Compare [6], and adaptable techniques for lifting low-level changes to the level of edit operations have been proposed [14,15]. However, to the best of our knowledge, none of these approaches has yet been adapted to a graphical rule-based model transformation language. Moreover, edit operations for Henshin transformation rules can be quite complex, and their specification needs a sophisticated language. Instead of defining a custom configuration language, SiLift uses Henshin for this purpose, a dedicated transformation language supporting in-place transformations in an expressive way. Finally, the set of available complex edit operations can be easily extended by Henshin tool users since they do not need to learn an additional configuration language.

5   Conclusion and Future Work

In this paper, we presented an adaptation of the SiLift model differencing framework to the Henshin model transformation language, and demonstrated its benefits compared to off-the-shelf model differencing tools producing rather low-level results. However, the provided high-level differencing support only serves as an initial step towards an effective management of Henshin transformations evolving into several versions and variants. In future work, we want to address further essential yet highly challenging versioning services on top of differencing, particularly the patching and updating of Henshin transformations.

Acknowledgments. This work was partially supported by the DFG (German Research Foundation) under the Priority Programme SPP1593: Design For Future - Managed Software Evolution.

References

1. Mens, T., Van Gorp, P.: A taxonomy of model transformation. ENTCS **152**, 125–142 (2006)
2. Strüber, D., Plöger, J., Acreţoaie, V.: Clone detection for graph-based model transformation languages. In: Van Gorp, P., Engels, G. (eds.) ICMT 2016. LNCS, vol. 9765, pp. 191–206. Springer, Cham (2016). doi:10.1007/978-3-319-42064-6_13
3. Whittle, J., Hutchinson, J., Rouncefield, M., Burden, H., Heldal, R.: Industrial adoption of model-driven engineering: are the tools really the problem? In: Moreira, A., Schätz, B., Gray, J., Vallecillo, A., Clarke, P. (eds.) MODELS 2013. LNCS, vol. 8107, pp. 1–17. Springer, Heidelberg (2013). doi:10.1007/978-3-642-41533-3_1
4. Arendt, T., Biermann, E., Jurack, S., Krause, C., Taentzer, G.: Henshin: advanced concepts and tools for in-place EMF model transformations. In: Petriu, D.C., Rouquette, N., Haugen, Ø. (eds.) MODELS 2010. LNCS, vol. 6394, pp. 121–135. Springer, Heidelberg (2010). doi:10.1007/978-3-642-16145-2_9
5. Strüber, D., Born, K., Gill, K.D., Groner, R., Kehrer, T., Ohrndorf, M., Tichy, M.: Henshin: a usability-focused framework for EMF model transformation development. In: de Lara, J., Plump, D. (eds.) ICGT 2017. LNCS, vol. 10373, pp. 196–208. Springer, Heidelberg (2017). doi:10.1007/978-3-319-61470-0_12

6. Brun, C., Pierantonio, A.: Model differences in the eclipse modeling framework. UPGRADE **9**(2), 29–34 (2008)
7. Kehrer, T., Kelter, U., Ohrndorf, M., Sollbach, T.: Understanding model evolution through semantically lifting model differences with SiLift. In: ICSM (2012)
8. Varró, G., Schurr, A., Varró, D.: Benchmarking for graph transformation. In: Symposium on Visual Languages and Human-Centric Computing (2005)
9. Bézivin, J.: On the unification power of models. SoSym **4**(2), 171–188 (2005)
10. Kolovos, D.S., Di Ruscio, D., Pierantonio, A., Paige, R.F.: Different models for model matching: an analysis of approaches to support model differencing. In: CVSM@ICSE (2009)
11. Kehrer, T., Kelter, U., Taentzer, G.: A rule-based approach to the semantic lifting of model differences in the context of model versioning. In: ASE (2011)
12. Kehrer, T., Taentzer, G., Rindt, M., Kelter, U.: Automatically deriving the specification of model editing operations from meta-models. In: Van Gorp, P., Engels, G. (eds.) ICMT 2016. LNCS, vol. 9765, pp. 173–188. Springer, Cham (2016). doi:10. 1007/978-3-319-42064-6_12
13. Rindt, M., Kehrer, T., Kelter, U.: Automatic generation of consistency-preserving edit operations for MDE tools. In: Demos@MoDELS (2014)
14. Langer, P., Wimmer, M., Brosch, P., Herrmannsdörfer, M., Seidl, M., Wieland, K., Kappel, G.: A posteriori operation detection in evolving software models. J. Syst. Softw. **86**(2), 551–566 (2013)
15. Khelladi, D.E., Hebig, R., Bendraou, R., Robin, J., Gervais, M.-P.: Detecting complex changes and refactorings during (meta) model evolution. Inform.Syst. **62**, 220–241 (2016)

Automatic Inference of Rule-Based Specifications of Complex In-place Model Transformations

Timo Kehrer[1]($\boxtimes$), Abdullah Alshanqiti[2], and Reiko Heckel[2]

[1] Humboldt-Universität zu Berlin, Berlin, Germany
timo.kehrer@informatik.hu-berlin.de
[2] University of Leicester, Leicester, UK
amma2@leicester.ac.uk, reiko@mcs.le.ac.uk

Abstract. Optimal support for continuous evolution in model-based software development requires tool environments to be customisable to domain-specific modelling languages. An important aspect is the set of change operations available to modify models. In-place model transformations are well-suited for that purpose. However, the specification of transformation rules requires a deep understanding of the language metamodel, limiting it to expert tool developers and language designers. This is at odds with the aim of domain-specific visual modelling environments, which should be customisable by domain experts.

We follow a model transformation by-example approach to mitigate that problem: Users generate transformation rules by creating examples of transformations using standard visual editors as macro recorders. Our ambition is to stick entirely to the concrete visual notation domain experts are familiar with, using rule inference to generalise a set of transformation examples. In contrast to previous approaches to the same problem, our approach supports the inference of complex rule features such as negative application conditions, multi-object patterns and global invariants. We illustrate the functioning of our approach by the inference of a complex and widely used refactoring operation on UML class diagrams.

Keywords: Model-driven development · Model evolution · In-place model transformation · Transformation rules · Model transformation by-example · Graph transformation

1 Introduction

Model-driven engineering (MDE) [10] raises the level of abstraction in software engineering by using models as primary artefacts. In particular, domain-specific modelling languages (DSMLs) can ease the transition between informally sketched requirements or designs and implementations by supporting high-level yet formal representations as a starting point for automation. With models becoming an integral part of the software throughout its lifecycle, the effectiveness of tools managing model evolution is particularly important and has to be

© Springer International Publishing AG 2017
E. Guerra and M. van den Brand (Eds.): ICMT 2017, LNCS 10374, pp. 92–107, 2017.
DOI: 10.1007/978-3-319-61473-1_7

customised to the DSML and project- or domain-specific settings. This includes the set of change operations available to modify models of a particular DSML. In-place model transformations have shown to be well-suited to define model refactorings, see e.g. [24], and other kinds of complex change operations such as recurring and highly schematic editing patterns [28]. That means, language- or project-specific change operations can be specified by model transformation rules which can be used to adapt a variety of MDE tools supporting model evolution; advanced model editors [28], modern refactoring tools, high-level differencing [20] and merging tools [21], or evolution analysis tools [16] being examples of this.

However, generic model transformation techniques and tools supporting in-place transformations are commonly based on the abstract syntax of modelling languages, Henshin [5] and VIATRA2 [7] being examples of this. Thus, the specification of transformation rules requires a deep understanding of the language meta-model and its relation to the visual representation, which makes dedicated model transformation techniques only accessible to expert tool developers and language designers [2,19]. This is at odds with the aim of domain-specific visual modelling environments, which should be designed and customised with the help of domain experts. We believe that the customisation of generic model management tools by complex change operations for creating, manipulating and refactoring domain-specific models can multiply the benefits of visual DSMLs. Our aim is to enable such a customisation by the users of the tool, i.e., strictly at the level of the visual notation without requiring an understanding of the meta-model and without the need for learning a model transformation language.

We follow the general methodology known as *model transformation by-example* (MTBE) [19], where users can describe model transformations using a standard visual editor as a macro recorder. The examples, recorded in their concrete syntax, are internally mapped to their abstract syntax which in turn is generalised into a model transformation rule. In previous MTBE approaches targeting in-place transformations [11,27], this generalisation was not fully automated but required manual post-processing at the level of the abstract syntax, mainly because the initial version of a transformation rule was derived from only a single example. This causes several problems which will be analysed in more detail in Sect. 2. Our ambition is to stick entirely to the concrete visual notation domain experts are familiar with, using inference techniques to automatically generalise a set of examples. Provided enough examples are specified, there is no need to resort to manual adaptations of inferred transformation rules.

In this paper, we focus on the technical problem of inferring general in-place transformation rules from specific examples. Our approach builds upon previous work [3] on the extraction of graph transformation rules describing Java operations from program execution logs, specifically the generalisation from instance-level towards general rules, but extends this solution in a number of ways: (A) The notion of a simple type graph is extended to a type graph with inheritance, along with an adaptation of the graph matching algorithms used for inference to the notion of graph morphism with inheritance. This enables further generalisation of rules, especially for meta-models with deep inheritance hierarchies as, e.g., in the case of the UML. (B) We add support for inferring multi-object patterns to support universally quantified operations over complex structures. (C) The inference of model transformation rules also requires the creation of negative application conditions as part of the preconditions of these rules, so we support inference from negative examples. (D) We add a further generalisation step for identifying and eventually abstracting from global invariants, i.e., context universally present in all rules. (E) From a tooling point of view, graph transformation rules in our approach describe model transformations rather than object dynamics, so our solution is integrated with the Eclipse Modeling Framework and the model transformation tool Henshin [5].

The paper is structured as follows: Sect. 2 motivates our approach introducing a complex and widely used refactoring operation on UML class diagrams as a running example. Our approach to inferring complex in-place transformation rules is presented in Sect. 3, its integration with an MDE environment is briefly outlined in Sect. 4. We demonstrate the functioning of our approach by showcasing the inference of a transformation rule for our running example in Sect. 5. Related work is discussed in Sects. 6 and 7 concludes the paper.

2   Problem Analysis and Motivating Example

In this section, we analyse the main reasons which demand manual post-processing if transformation rules are derived from a single example. These problems apply to all in-place MTBE approaches proposed in the literature (see Sect. 6).

Consider the well-known object-oriented refactoring operation pullUpAttribute as a running example. It replaces all common attributes, i.e. attributes having the same name and type, in a set of subclasses by a single attribute of this name and type in the superclass. This refactoring operation has been adopted for UML class diagrams and formally specified using in-place model transformation

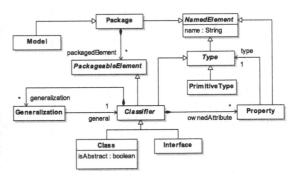

Fig. 1. Excerpt of the UML meta-model.

techniques [5]. It may be demonstrated by providing an original and a changed UML class diagram like the ones shown on top of Fig. 2. The corresponding abstract syntax representations of these models, basically attributed graphs typed over the UML meta-model [26], are shown at the bottom of Fig. 2. The relevant yet slightly simplified excerpt of the UML meta-model is shown in Fig. 1. Provided there is a proper strategy for identifying the corresponding elements in the model versions before and after the sample transformation, the graphs shown in Fig. 2 can be considered as pre- and postconditions which may be conveyed in a model transformation rule following graph transformation concepts. Pre- and post graphs represent the left-hand side (LHS) and the right-hand side (RHS) of this rule, respectively. In Fig. 2, correspondences between LHS and RHS nodes are indicated by node identifiers. Corresponding edges are given implicitly if they have the same type and their source and target nodes are corresponding.

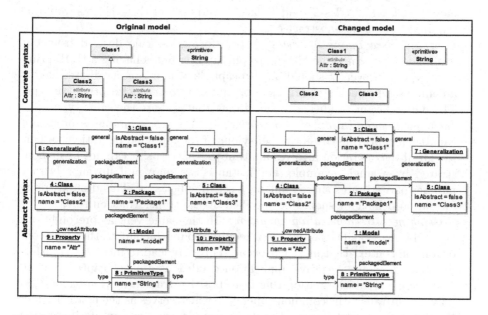

Fig. 2. Transformation pullUpAttribute demonstrated by a single example: Original (left) and changed model (right) demonstrating the transformation; concrete syntax (top) and abstract syntax (bottom).

In general, transformation rules derived from a single example are neither *correct*, i.e. they may allow transformation behaviour which leads to a wrong result, nor *complete*, i.e. there may be situations in which the derived rule achieves only a partial effect or is not applicable at all. In particular, preconditions derived from a single example are usually too restrictive, while the postconditions are typically too weak. In the remainder of this section, we discuss the main issues in more detail, illustrating them by means of our running example of Fig. 2. Issues (1), (2), (3) and (4) refer to completeness, while issue (5) pertains correctness.

(1) *Overspecified structural context.* Transformation rules derived from a single example are typically affected by overspecified structural context. In our example, the UML classes *"Class1"*, *"Class2"* and *"Class3"* as well as the definition of the UML primitive type called *"String"* do not necessarily have to be contained in the same package. Moreover, a derived rule would contain context which does not prevent a more general usage of the rule but which can be considered as unnecessary context which might affect the performance

of a model transformation. In the UML, for example, a node of type *Model* is always the top-most container of a model. This node will show up as unnecessary context in every transformation rule obtained from an example.

(2) *Literal interpretation of attribute values.* Attribute values derived from a single example are interpreted in a strictly literal way. For instance, a transformation rule derived from our example would be only applicable to classes named *"Class1"*, *"Class2"* and *"Class3"*, and each of these classes would be required to be a non-abstract class.

(3) *Overspecialised typing of nodes.* A transformation rule derived from our example of Fig. 2 may be applied to pull up attributes having a UML primitive type. However, it should be also capable of handling attributes having a complex type such as UML class or interface instead of a primitive type. The only relevant condition is that all attributes share the same type.

(4) *Incomplete specification of transformation.* A single example is often not capable of capturing the entire behaviour of the intended operation. In particular, if the operation involves multi-object patterns, it can not be demonstrated by a single example. For instance, we may pull up an arbitrary number of attributes shared among a set of subclasses. This desired transformation behaviour should be specified by the transformation rule.

(5) *Missing negative application conditions.* In the same vein as preconditions derived from a single example often require too much context, they lack conditions on context that must not occur. This may lead to incorrect transformation behaviour. Negative application conditions are not captured at all if we derive a transformation rule from positive transformation example(s) only. For instance, the common superclass which serves as the new container for the attributes to be pulled up must not already have an attribute with the same name.

3   Inference of Transformation Rules

We work with model transformation rules based on graph transformation concepts following the DPO approach [13], supporting typed attributed directed multi graphs with node-type inheritance. An attributed type graph TG, visually represented as a class diagram, defines the DSML meta-model. An *object graph* over TG is a graph G equipped with a homomorphism (a structure-preserving mapping) $G \to TG$ that assigns every element in G its type in TG. In accordance with the notion of E-graph [13], data occurring in graphs are represented by value nodes linked to objects by attribute edges. Apart from simple equations and assignments over attributes, variables and constants we do not infer complex data conditions or operations. Therefore we do not require access to the full algebraic structure (operations and axioms) of the data types used for attribution, limiting ourselves to equalities between two variables, and between variables and constants.

Our aim is to derive rules of the form $L \Rightarrow R$ (formally spans of graph inclusions $L \leftarrow K \to R$) with graphs L and R, called the *left-* and *right-hand side* of the rule, expressing its pre- and postconditions and thus its effect in a declarative way: $L\backslash R$, $L \cap R$ $(= K)$ and $R\backslash L$ represent the elements to be deleted, preserved and created by the rule. In addition, a basic rule r may be equipped with a set NAC_r of negative application conditions of the form $NAC(x)$, where $x : L \rightarrow X$ is a typed monomorphism [13]. The left-hand side of a rule r can have several matches ("occurrences") in a graph G, a match m being a typed monomorphism $m : L \rightarrow G$. Given a graph G, a rule is applicable at a match m if all negative application conditions are satisfied, i.e. for all $NAC(x_i) \in NAC_r$ with $x_i : L \rightarrow X_i$, there does not exist a graph monomorphism $p : X_i \rightarrow G$ with $p \circ x_i = m$. This means that there is no NAC graph to which the occurrence $m(L)$ of the left-hand side can be extended. Finally, we use the concepts of rule schemes and amalgamation as a concise way to specify transformations of recurring model patterns. A rule scheme $RS = (r_k, M)$ consists of a kernel rule r_k and a set $M = \{r_i \mid 1 \leq i \leq n\}$ of multi-rules with $r_k \subseteq r_i$ for all $1 \leq i \leq n$. The idea is that each multi-rule specifies one multi-object pattern and its transformation. A rule scheme is applied as follows: The kernel rule is applied once, just like a "normal" rule. The match of this application is used as a common partial match for all multi-rules, which are matched as often as possible. We will refer to rule schemes as *rules with multi-object patterns*. Such a rule distinguishes a set $MOP = \{P_i \mid 1 \leq i \leq n\}$ with $P_i = r_i\backslash r_k$ $(L_i\backslash L_k, K_i\backslash K_k$ and $R_i\backslash R_k)$ representing the specification of a multi-object pattern transformation. Note that, in general, multi-object patterns are just graph fragments and not graphs.

Figure 3 describes our inference process starting from a set of instance-level transformations, i.e. positive and negative examples demonstrating a dedicated transformation. Positive examples are pairs of pre and post graphs of transformations, so-called *rule instances*. Negative examples are individual graphs, referred to as *NAC graph instances*, to which the rules to be derived shall not be applicable. From sets of rule instances and NAC graph instances, general rules with negative application conditions and multi-object patterns can be inferred as follows. First, we combine the given instances into higher-level rules by (1) classifying them by effect and (2) abstracting from non-essential context. Then, we (3) derive negative application conditions using NAC graph instances. Next, we (4) further generalise by identifying complex object structures being treated in a uniform way by a set of generalised rules, but with different cardinalities. The result is a set of generalised rules with NACs and multi-object structures. Taking this set of generalised rules as input, we (5) further raise the level of abstraction by extracting context universally present as global invariant (not shown in Fig. 3). Each of the above mentioned steps will be discussed in the remainder of this section.

Classification by Effect and Derivation of Shared Context. For each rule instance, we generate a *minimal rule* that is able to perform the rule instance's effect in a minimal context. It is obtained from an instance by cutting all context not needed to achieve the observed changes. The result is a classification of rule instances by effect: All instances with the same minimal rule have the same effect, but possibly different preconditions. Minimal rule construction has been formalised in [9] and implemented (without considering node-type inheritance) in [4]. Formally, given a rule instance $i : G \Rightarrow H$, its minimal rule is the smallest rule $L \Rightarrow R$ such that $L \subseteq G$, $R \subseteq H$ with $G \backslash H = L \backslash R$ and $H \backslash G = R \backslash L$.

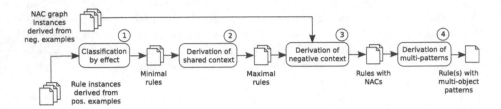

Fig. 3. Overview of the rule inference process.

Here, we extend the minimal rule construction by exploiting node-type inheritance. Two minimal rules may be merged if they only differ in the types of their context nodes and these types share a common super type. More formally, given two minimal rules $r_1 : L_1 \Rightarrow R_1$ and $r_2 : L_2 \Rightarrow R_2$, they may be merged to a single rule $r : L \Rightarrow R$ if there are typed morphisms $L_1 \to L, L_2 \to L$ and $R_1 \to R, R_2 \to R$ such that $L \backslash R = L_1 \backslash R_1 = L_2 \backslash R_2$ and $R \backslash L = R_1 \backslash L_1 = R_2 \backslash L_2$. That means r, r_1 and r_2 specify the same effect while the types of context nodes in $L \cap R$ may be more general than those in $L_1 \cap R_1$ and $L_2 \cap R_2$, respectively.

Sets of rule instances classified by a minimal rule are generalised by one so called *maximal rule* which extends the minimal rule by all the context that is present in all instances, essentially the intersection of all its instances' preconditions [3].

For a rule instance obtained from our example shown in Fig. 2, a minimal rule would contain only the nodes of type *Class* and *Property* along with their connecting edges. All other graph elements are context elements not required to achieve the transformation effect. Since there is only one rule instance, they would be part of the maximal rule. Note that if we provide another example in which we replace the primitive type of the attribute being pulled up by a complex type such as *Class* or *Interface*, we still obtain a single minimal (and maximal) rule, however, with the *Property* node representing the attribute typed over the more general type *Type*.

Derivation of Negative Context. Providing negative examples enables the derivation of negative application conditions for maximal rules. The idea is to associate a negative example to a positive one, thereby implying which model elements prevent a transformation rule from being applicable. In other words, we assume a NAC graph instance to be a supergraph of a rule instance's pre graph.

More formally, for each positive example yielding a rule instance $i : G \Rightarrow H$, we may add several sets of negative examples, say NEG_x. Each negative example represents a NAC graph instance $N \supseteq G$, i.e., an extension of the rule instance's left-hand side by forbidden context. A NAC graph X is obtained from each of the sets NEG_x as the intersection of all NAC graphs $N_i \in NEG_x$, analogously to the construction of maximal rules. The obtained condition is $NAC(x)$ with $x : G \to X$. It is translated into a condition $NAC(x')$ over the maximal rule $r_{max} : L_{max} \Rightarrow R_{max}$ generalising rule instance i, where $x' : L_{max} \to X'$ is obtained by restricting x to $L_{max} \subseteq G$. After inferring all negative application conditions for the same maximal rule, duplicate NACs are eliminated.

Please note that, since we treat attributes and their values as attribute edges and value nodes, the NAC inference procedure includes the derivation of negative conditions over attributes. For our example of Fig. 2, e.g., we may add a negative example in which the superclass already contains an attribute named "Attr".

Derivation of Multi-object Patterns. To derive rules with multi-object patterns from generalised rules, we have to discover sets of rule patterns that have the same structure and transformation behaviour, and thus can be represented by a single multi-object pattern. To that end, we first introduce a notion of *rule pattern* and their *equivalence*. Let $r_{max} : L_{max} \Rightarrow R_{max}$ be a maximal rule derived in step (2). Let further $P = (FL, FR)$ be a pair of graph fragments with $FL \subseteq L_{max}$ and $FR \subseteq R_{max}$, and let $BL \subseteq L_{max}$ and $BR \subseteq R_{max}$ be the smallest graphs completing FL and FR to graphs; we refer to BL and BP as boundary graphs of FL and FR, respectively. P is a rule pattern in r_{max} if $BL \Rightarrow BR$ is a subrule of r_{max}. Two rule patterns P_1 and P_2 in r_{max} are equivalent if (i) their boundary graphs are isomorphic, i.e. there are type-preserving isomorphisms $BL_1 \to BL_2$ and $BR_1 \to BR_2$; and (ii) they overlap in the completing nodes of their boundary graphs, i.e. $(BL_1 \backslash FL_1) = (BL_2 \backslash FL_2)$ and $(BR_1 \backslash FR_1) = (BR_2 \backslash FR_2)$.

Assume that we extend our example of Fig. 2 such that we have three subclasses with a common UML attribute being pulled up. Figure 4 illustrates the maximal rule derived from this example, omitting nodes of types *Package* and *Model*, edge types and attributes. It contains two equivalent patterns, the respective graph fragments are completed to boundary graphs by the same nodes.

We derive rules with multi-object patterns in two steps. First, we merge equivalent rule patterns in maximal rules: For each maximal rule m in a set of maximal rules, and each non-trivial equivalence class of rule patterns in m, one pattern is chosen as the representative for that class and added to the set MOP of multi-object patterns for m, while all other patterns of that class are deleted. The resulting set of rules with multi-object patterns is MOR. Second, we combine isomorphic rules: A maximal set of structurally equivalent rules in MOR forms an isomorphism class. For each such class we derive a single rule by selecting a representative one.

Derivation of Universal Context. To extract and cut context universally present in all generalised rules, we employ a similar proceeding as for the derivation of maximal rules. That is, we compare the preconditions of all maximal rules to identify structures that are universally present. Universal context presented as global invariant can reduce the size of rules, make them more concise and

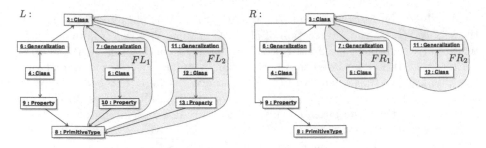

Fig. 4. Maximal rule illustrating the occurrence of two equivalent rule patterns $P_1 = (FL_1, FR_1)$ and $P_2 = (FL_2, FR_2)$.

readable. In case of the UML, for instance, we could spot the universal presence of a *Model* node serving as a container for all model elements.

4   Integration with an MDE Development Environment

Our approach is open to be used in the context of any modelling environment or visual editor that can be used for specifying example transformations, and any model transformation engine for executing the inferred transformation rules.

As a proof of concept, we implemented the inference approach presented in Sect. 3 based on the Eclipse Modeling Framework (EMF) and the rule-based model transformation language and tool Henshin, available from the accompanying website for this paper [1]. Since EMF and Henshin employ the usual object-oriented representation with attributes being inlined as properties of objects, attributes are transformed into our conceptual representation based on attribute edges and value nodes. The general idea of exporting attribute edges and value nodes occurring in generalised rules is to derive equations over attributes from attribute edges, e.g., if two attributes a, b point to the same value node, an equation $a = b$ is added. In Henshin, an internal variable, say x, has to be defined and assigned to attributes, i.e., we have $a = x$ and $b = x$ for the attributes a and b in the example above.

To be independent of the visual editor being used to specify example transformations, we follow a state-based approach to transformation recording [19]. To reliably identify the corresponding model elements in the original and the changed model of an example, we assume a model matcher [22] for a given DSML to be readily available.

5   Case-Based Evaluation

In this section, we illustrate the applicability of our approach by means of the example of Sect. 2. We show how a suitable rule can be inferred using our approach and tool. For depicting transformations, we use the visual UML editor Papyrus (v. 1.0.2), which is based on an EMF-based implementation of the

UML Superstructure Specification (v. 2.5) [26]. We generally ignore meta-model elements defined by the UML Superstructure for which there is no visual representation in the diagram notation supported by Papyrus. Since Papyrus attaches universally unique identifiers (UUIDs) to model elements, we employ the UUID-based matching facility of the model comparison tool EMF Compare for deriving corresponding elements in the original and the changed model of an example.

Section 5.1 outlines the examples defined for demonstrating the refactoring operation pullUpAttribute. We concentrate on the rationale of each of the examples w.r.t. the desired effect on the generalised rule(s), thereby emphasising the issues presented in Sect. 2. We discuss threats to validity in Sect. 5.2.

5.1 Solving the Motivating Example

To infer a general transformation rule for the refactoring pullUpAttribute, we start by providing an initial example ($Example_1$) corresponding to the one presented in Fig. 2. W.r.t. to the state-of-the-art in generating in-place transformation rules by-example (cf. Sect. 6), the rule derived from this example serves as a baseline for a qualitative evaluation of our approach. To infer a general transformation rule, we proceed by adding further examples, each of them addressing one of the issues discussed in Sect. 2.

(1) *Overspecified structural context.* We add another transformation example ($Example_2$) to avoid overspecified structural context, where we abstain from using a dedicated container of type *Package*, which thus gets eliminated during maximal rule construction. Moreover, the element of type *Model* is identified as universal context over all examples and gets eliminated, too. The resulting Henshin rule is shown in Fig. 5 (left). In the Henshin notation, the LHS and RHS of a rule are merged into a single graph. The LHS comprises

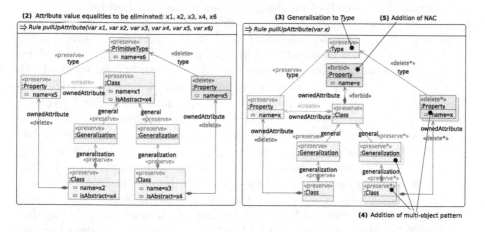

Fig. 5. Inferred Henshin rules after providing additional examples of step 1 (left), and steps 2 to 5 (right).

all elements stereotyped by delete and preserve, while the RHS contains all elements annotated by preserve and create. Due to space limitations, we present only a subset of the generated Henshin rule comprising those rule elements being typed over the visible excerpt of the UML meta-model shown in Fig. 1. The complete rule can be found on the supplementary website for this paper [1].

(2) *Interpretation of attribute values.* As a side-effect of providing a second example, rule variables $x1$ to $x6$ are inferred denoting equalities of attribute values. For instance, all classes occurring in the transformation rule inferred from $Example_1$ and $Example_2$ have to be abstract, indicated by variable $x4$ (see Fig. 5 (left)). To handle attributes properly, we add a third transformation example ($Example_3$) in which attributes irrelevant for the transformation are assigned values differing from the ones used in $Example_1$. We rename all classes, turn these classes into concrete classes, and change the primitive type from *"String"* to *"int"*. As indicated by annotation (2) in Fig. 5, we get rid of all variables except of $x5$, which denotes equality of names of the *Property* to be pulled up. This is on purpose, i.e., we learn that all attributes to be pulled up must have the same name.

(3) *Overspecialized typing of nodes.* The transformation rule pullUpAttribute shall also be applicable to attributes having a complex type instead of a primitive type. Thus, we add another example ($Example_4$) which slightly modifies our first one such that the primitive type called *"String"* of all attributes *"Attr"* is exchanged by a UML class representing a complex type. The minimal rule which results from $Example_1$ to $Example_3$ may be merged with the minimal rule obtained for $Example_4$ since (i) the UML node types *Class* and *PrimitiveType* share the same supertype *Type* (cf. Fig. 1), and (ii) the supertype replacement is permitted in this context. The effect of adding $Example_4$ is illustrated in the inferred rule shown in Fig. 5 (right). Note that $Example_2$ to $Example_4$ could be combined to a single example achieving the same effect on the generalised transformation rule.

(4) *Incomplete specification of transformation.* Since, in general, arbitrarily many attributes may be pulled up to a common superclass, we give another example ($Example_5$) which differs from $Example_1$ of Fig. 2 in that we have three subclasses containing an attribute named *"Attr"* typed by the UML primitive type called *"String"*. In the inferred rule, we get the specification of the transformation of a multi-object pattern as shown in Fig. 5 (right).

(5) *Missing negative application conditions.* Attributes may only be pulled up if the superclass does not already contain an attribute of the same name. To that end, we provide two negative examples ($Negative_1$ and $Negative_2$) referring to $Example_1$. The basic idea is to copy the original model of the positive example $Example_1$ and to add an attribute named *"Attr1"* to the common superclass *"Class1"*. To demonstrate that it is only the name of this additional attribute which prevents the refactoring from being applied successfully while we do not care about its type, we provide two negative examples in which the additional name attribute has different types. As a result, the inferred rule is equipped with a negative application condition

as shown in Fig. 5, indicated by the stereotype forbid in the Henshin notation. This rule represents the final result of our example-driven process to
specifying and inferring a general rule for refactoring pullUpAttribute. It
corresponds to the transformation rule PUAExecuteRule presented in [5] for
the same refactoring operation but a slightly simplified variant of the UML
meta-model.

5.2 Threats to Validity

In this section, we evaluated the applicability of the proposed approach by investigating a complex in-place transformation rule whose inference from a set of
examples is faced with several challenges. Although our study shows very promising results, we are aware of some threats to validity giving rise to a critical
discussion.

As every case-based evaluation, our experiment suffers from a lack of compre-
hensiveness, which affects the external validity of our results. We only considered
one meta-model and a single transformation rule typed over this meta-model. We
mitigate this threat by choosing a comprehensive meta-model exposing several
pitfalls for the specification of transformation, and a non-trivial transformation
rule which can be considered as representative for a considerable amount of refactoring operations. However, there may be change operations which can only be
expressed using more sophisticated model transformation features than those
supported by our approach. The most severe limitation pertains the handling
of complex constraints on attributes. Ignoring the algebraic structure of data
types used for graph attribution limits our approach to the inference of simple
equations and assignments over attributes, variables and constants.

Another threat to validity is that we defined the transformation examples
ourselves. We are familiar with the UML meta-model, the inference process for
learning transformation rules, and the fact that we exploit persistent identifiers
attached by Papyrus to identify corresponding model elements. These internal
details are typically not known by domain experts who would use our approach.
Thus, they might produce examples leading to transformation rules which are
both incorrect and incomplete, examples that are inconsistent or contradict each
other, or they might simply need significantly more examples to eventually infer
proper transformation rules. Such issues and requirements for future research
must be analysed in an empirical user study, which we leave for future work.

6 Related Work

The main objective of our work is to provide a technique supporting domain
experts in the specification of complex change operations for creating, manipulating and refactoring domain-specific models. In the model transformation
community, there are two main lines of research which basically pursue the same
goal, *model-transformation by-example* and *model transformation based on concrete syntax*, which we will review in that order as our approach falls into the former category. Finally, we briefly review related *approaches from other domains*.

Model Transformation By-example. Since specifying model transformations from scratch using the abstract syntax of a DSML is a difficult and error-prone task, learning them from existing transformation examples is highly desirable and has motivated a plethora of work in this field, see the pre-2012 approaches surveyed in [19] and, more recently, in [6].

The majority of existing approaches, e.g. [6,8,15,23], target model-to-model transformations, often referred to as exogenous transformations [25] since source and target models typically correspond to different meta-models. Such transformations are well-suited to capture vertical translations, which build the basis for model refinement and code generation, and horizontal translations, which are of specific importance in model-based integration and migration scenarios. Model-to-model transformation scenarios are inherently different from the model evolution scenarios addressed by our approach. Their main problem is to adequately infer semantically equivalent modelling concepts in the source and target domain of a transformation, e.g., in UML class models and Entity Relationship models. This is not an issue at all in case of in-place transformations which are inherently endogenous [25].

To the best of our knowledge, which is in accordance with the surveys presented in [6,19], only two dedicated approaches addressing the specification of in-place transformations by-example have been proposed in the literature [11,27]. They have in common with our approach the idea of using standard visual editors to demonstrate model transformations. However, transformation rules are derived from a single example, which merely corresponds to the first step of our inference process. They do not support to generalise a set of examples including advanced features such as the inference of multi-object patterns, negative application conditions, abstraction from universal context and super type generalisation as offered by our approach.

Model Transformation Based on Concrete Syntax. An alternative approach to improve the usability of transformation languages is to enable modellers to specify model transformations based on the concrete syntax of a DSML.

One class of approaches is based on the idea of turning a DSML into a domain-specific *transformation* language. Hölldobler et al. [18] assume a DSML to be specified using a context-free grammar and present a generative approach to systematically derive a textual domain-specific transformation language from that grammar. Consequently, the approach is limited to textual DSMLs.

In contrast, Grønmo [17] and Acreţoaie et al. [2] address concrete syntax-based transformation of graphical models. Similar to [18], the approach presented in [17] is generative in the sense that transformation rule editors are generated from the DSML meta-model which must be equipped with a mapping to the set of symbols of the DSML concrete syntax. However, this means domain experts cannot define the transformation rules using their favourite editor. This problem is avoided in [2] which follows a generic approach in which transformation rules are specified using a readily available host language model editor. The only assumption is that this editor provides a mechanism to annotate models with certain transformation actions. The approach is similar to ours in the sense that it aims at achieving transparency w.r.t. the DSML, the modelling environment and the underlying transformation language at the same time. However, domain experts still have to learn a dedicated transformation language called VMTL to be used for annotating transformation actions.

Approaches From Other Domains. In other areas, rule inference approaches have been suggested to address problems of mining business processes [12] and learning (bio-)chemical reaction rules [14,29]. Although related in the aim of discovering rules, the challenges vary based on the nature of the graphs considered, e.g., directed, attributed or undirected graphs, the availability of typing or identity information, as well as in the scalability requirements in terms of the size and number of the examples to be considered.

7 Conclusion

In this paper, we presented a novel approach to model transformation by-example which enables the inference of transformation rules which are formally considered as graph transformation rules and obtained by generalising over a set of rule instances. Our approach supports the inference of complex rule features such as negative application conditions, multi-object patterns and global invariants. The approach is supported by a tool integrated with the Eclipse Modeling Framework and the model transformation tool and language Henshin. Our case-based evaluation illustrates the applicability of our approach and shows that, in principle, the inference of complex transformation rules is possible by providing only a few example transformations. In this paper we focused on the technical approach to rule inference. We leave a wider empirical evaluation, e.g., of the manual effort to provide examples for a larger set of transformations for future work.

Acknowledgments. The work of the first author was partially supported by the DFG (German Research Foundation) under the Priority Programme SPP1593: Design For Future – Managed Software Evolution.

References

1. Accompanying material for this paper (2017). http://icmt.mtrproject.uk
2. Acreţoaie, V., Störrle, H., Strüber, D.: VMTL: a language for end-user model transformation. Softw. Syst. Model., 1–29 (2016)
3. Alshanqiti, A., Heckel, R.: Extracting visual contracts from Java programs. In: ASE (2015)
4. Alshanqiti, A., Heckel, R., Khan, T.: Learning minimal and maximal rules from observations of graph transformations. In: ECEASST, vol. 58 (2013)
5. Arendt, T., Biermann, E., Jurack, S., Krause, C., Taentzer, G.: Henshin: advanced concepts and tools for in-place EMF model transformations. In: Petriu, D.C., Rouquette, N., Haugen, Ø. (eds.) MODELS 2010. LNCS, vol. 6394, pp. 121–135. Springer, Heidelberg (2010). doi:10.1007/978-3-642-16145-2_9

6. Baki, I., Sahraoui, H.: Multi-step learning and adaptive search for learning complex model transformations from examples. TOSEM **25**(3), 20 (2016)
7. Balogh, A., Varró, D.: Advanced model transformation language constructs in the VIATRA2 framework. In: ACM Symposium on Applied Computing (2006)
8. Balogh, Z., Varró, D.: Model transformation by example using inductive logic programming. SoSym **8**(3), 347–364 (2009)
9. Bisztray, D., Heckel, R., Ehrig, H.: Verification of architectural refactorings: rule extraction and tool support. In: ECEASST, vol. 16 (2009)
10. Brambilla, M., Cabot, J., Wimmer, M.: Model-Driven Software Engineering in Practice. Morgan & Claypool Publishers, San Rafael (2012)
11. Brosch, P., Langer, P., Seidl, M., Wieland, K., Wimmer, M., Kappel, G., Retschitzegger, W., Schwinger, W.: An example is worth a thousand words: composite operation modeling by-example. In: Schürr, A., Selic, B. (eds.) MODELS 2009. LNCS, vol. 5795, pp. 271–285. Springer, Heidelberg (2009). doi:10.1007/978-3-642-04425-0_20
12. Bruggink, H.J.S.: Towards process mining with graph transformation systems. In: Giese, H., König, B. (eds.) ICGT 2014. LNCS, vol. 8571, pp. 253–268. Springer, Cham (2014). doi:10.1007/978-3-319-09108-2_17
13. Ehrig, H., Ehrig, K., Prange, U., Taentzer, G.: Fundamentals of Algebraic Graph Transformation. Springer, Heidelberg (2006)
14. Flamm, C., Merkle, D., Stadler, P.F., Thorsen, U.: Automatic inference of graph transformation rules using the cyclic nature of chemical reactions. In: Echahed, R., Minas, M. (eds.) ICGT 2016. LNCS, vol. 9761, pp. 206–222. Springer, Cham (2016). doi:10.1007/978-3-319-40530-8_13
15. García-Magariño, I., Gómez-Sanz, J.J., Fuentes-Fernández, R.: Model transformation by-example: an algorithm for generating many-to-many transformation rules in several model transformation languages. In: Paige, R.F. (ed.) ICMT 2009. LNCS, vol. 5563, pp. 52–66. Springer, Heidelberg (2009). doi:10.1007/978-3-642-02408-5_5
16. Getir, S., Rindt, M., Kehrer, T.: A generic framework for analyzing model co-evolution. In: ME@MoDELS (2014)
17. Grønmo, R.: Using concrete syntax in graph-based model transformations. Ph.D. thesis, University of Oslo (2009)
18. Hölldobler, K., Rumpe, B., Weisemoller, I.: Systematically deriving domain-specific transformation languages. In: MoDELS (2015)
19. Kappel, G., Langer, P., Retschitzegger, W., Schwinger, W., Wimmer, M.: Model transformation by-example: a survey of the first wave. In: Düsterhöft, A., Klettke, M., Schewe, K.-D. (eds.) Conceptual Modelling and Its Theoretical Foundations. LNCS, vol. 7260, pp. 197–215. Springer, Heidelberg (2012). doi:10.1007/978-3-642-28279-9_15
20. Kehrer, T., Kelter, U., Ohrndorf, M., Sollbach, T.: Understanding model evolution through semantically lifting model differences with silift. In: ICSM (2012)
21. Kehrer, T., Kelter, U., Reuling, D.: Workspace updates of visual models. In: ASE (2014)
22. Kolovos, D.S., Di Ruscio, D., Pierantonio, A., Paige, R.F.: Different models for model matching: An analysis of approaches to support model differencing. In: CVSM@ICSE (2009)
23. Kühne, T., Hamann, H., Arifulina, S., Engels, G.: Patterns for constructing mutation operators: limiting the search space in a software engineering application. In: European Conference on Genetic Programming (2016)

24. Mens, T.: On the use of graph transformations for model refactoring. In: Lämmel, R., Saraiva, J., Visser, J. (eds.) GTTSE 2005. LNCS, vol. 4143, pp. 219–257. Springer, Heidelberg (2006). doi:10.1007/11877028_7

25. Mens, T., Van Gorp, P.: A taxonomy of model transformation. In: ENTCS, vol. 152 (2006)

26. Object Management Group: UML 2.5 superstructure specification. OMG Document Number: formal/15-03-01 (2015)

27. Sun, Y., White, J., Gray, J.: Model transformation by demonstration. In: Schürr, A., Selic, B. (eds.) MODELS 2009. LNCS, vol. 5795, pp. 712–726. Springer, Heidelberg (2009). doi:10.1007/978-3-642-04425-0_58

28. Taentzer, G., Crema, A., Schmutzler, R., Ermel, C.: Generating domain-specific model editors with complex editing commands. In: Schürr, A., Nagl, M., Zündorf, A. (eds.) AGTIVE 2007. LNCS, vol. 5088, pp. 98–103. Springer, Heidelberg (2008). doi:10.1007/978-3-540-89020-1_8

29. You, C.h., Holder, L.B., Cook, D.J.: Learning patterns in the dynamics of biological networks. In: International Conference on Knowledge Discovery and Data Mining (2009)

A Survey of Model Transformation Design Pattern Usage

Kevin Lano[1]([✉]), Shekoufeh Kolahdouz-Rahimi[2], Sobhan Yassipour-Tehrani[1], and Mohammadreza Sharbaf[2]

[1] Department of Informatics, King's College London, London, UK
{kevin.lano,sobhan.yassipour_tehrani}@kcl.ac.uk
[2] Department of Software Engineering, University of Isfahan, Isfahan, Iran
{sh.rahimi,m.sharbaf}@eng.ui.ac.ir

Abstract. Model transformation design patterns have been proposed by a number of authors, but their usage appears to be sporadic and sometimes patterns are applied without recognition of the pattern. In this paper we provide a literature review of transformation design pattern applications, with regard to their effectiveness and range of use, and consider how pattern usage can be made more effective.

1 Introduction

Design patterns have become a widely-used technique for software engineering, to support systematic software construction and the reuse of design solutions. Mainstream patterns, such as those defined in [9], have become part of standard programming knowledge, and have been incorporated into programming languages and environments. In the model transformations (MT) domain, patterns have also been identified and formalised [4,13,21]. We carried out a survey to discover how widely MT patterns have been used in practice, and if patterns are of clear benefit for MT development.

2 Research Questions

The research questions we asked were:

Q1. Design pattern usage: How often are model transformation design patterns used in practice in MT development? Which categories of patterns and which individual patterns are used? Is the use explicit (recognised as a pattern application) or not?

Q2. Design patterns benefits: What perceived benefits were obtained from using patterns? Is there evidence for these benefits?

Q3. Gaps: Are there cases where patterns should have been applied? Are there necessary patterns which have not yet been formalised?

Q4. Trends: Has there been a change in the adoption of MT patterns over time?

Q5. MT languages: Do different MT languages differ in their capabilities for expressing and using MT patterns?

© Springer International Publishing AG 2017
E. Guerra and M. van den Brand (Eds.): ICMT 2017, LNCS 10374, pp. 108–118, 2017.
DOI: 10.1007/978-3-319-61473-1_8

3   Sources and Selection Criteria

We surveyed papers from specific sources: The SoSyM journal; the Transformation Tool Contest (TTC); the ICMT and MODELS conferences. In addition, we performed an online search using the search string "Model transformation". Only papers which included some transformation specifications or designs from transformation developments, industrial or academic, were then selected for further consideration. Purely theoretical papers or papers with insufficient details were excluded. A list of papers included in our survey is given at https://nms.kcl.ac.uk/kevin.lano/mtdp/dpslr.pdf. Patterns were identified according to the criteria given at https://nms.kcl.ac.uk/kevin.lano/mtdp/criteria.pdf.

4   Results

Concerning research question 1, from the initial search results we identified 210 papers that described MT developments. Of these, 86 (41%) contained some use of MT patterns. In most of these cases, an explicit design decision was made to use the pattern (59 cases, 28%), however only a small number of cases named or identified the pattern being used (19 cases, 9%).

Table 1 identifies the categories of patterns that were used in the surveyed cases. We use the following categories from [21]:

1. **Architectural patterns** – organise systems of transformations to improve modularity or processing capabilities.
2. **Rule modularisation patterns** – concerned with the structuring and organisation of rules within a transformation.
3. **Optimisation patterns** – concerned with increasing the efficiency of transformation execution at the rule/individual transformation level.
4. **Model-to-text** – concerned with aspects specific to code or text generation from models.
5. **Bidirectional** – concerned with aspects specific to bidirectional transformations (bx) and model synchronisation.
6. **Expressiveness** – patterns concerned with providing extended capabilities for a transformation language.
7. **Classical** – patterns from the GoF book [9] or from the patterns community external to MT.

Architectural and rule modularisation patterns were the most widely used, constituting over 70% of the total number of pattern applications.

4.1   The Extent of Pattern Usage

Tables 2, 3 and 4 show the applications of specific MT design patterns in the surveyed papers.

The most frequently used patterns are: (i) Entity Splitting, 16 uses; (ii) Auxiliary Metamodel, 10 uses; (iii) Auxiliary Correspondence Model, 8 uses;

Table 1. MT design patterns categories in surveyed papers

Papers	Category	Total	Percentage
S2, S12, S18, S19, S25 S28, [10], [19], S33, [6] S34, S44, S48, S49, [8] [11], S50, S55, S60, S68 S71, S75, S76	Architectural	23	27%
[18], S1, S4, S7, S8, S9, S10, S11, S13, S15, S16, [23], S17, S20, S22, [25], S25, S26, S31, S35, S36, [26], S38, S39, S41, S46 S47, S51, S52, S53, [24] S54, S56, S61, S62, S63 S64, S65, S66, S68, S69 S72, S73, S75, S78, [12]	Rule Modularisation	46	53%
S30, [19], S40, S41, S43 S52, [7], S57, S58	Optimisation	9	10.5%
S6, S33, [10], S45, [27] S49, S71	Model-to-text	7	8%
S5, S23, S67, S70, S72 [25]	Expressiveness	6	7%
S3, S21, S24, S29, S37 [12], S74	Bidirectional	7	8%
S14, S32, S59	Classical (GoF, etc.)	3	3.5%

Table 2. Applications of rule modularisation design patterns in surveyed papers

Papers	Pattern	Benefits/motivation
S1, S16, S17, S22 S35, S51, S61, S64 S73, S75	Auxiliary Metamodel	Flexibility, optimisation, tracing, execution control
S7, S9, [18], S11 S38, S66, S69	Structure Preservation	Modularisation
S13, [18]	Phased Construction	Modularisation
S11, S13, S25, [23] S51	Entity Splitting	Modularisation
	Entity Merging	Modularisation
S10, S20, S36, [18], S38 S47, S65, S69, [12]	Entity Splitting	Modularisation
S53, S56, S63	Entity Splitting	Modularisation
	Phased Construction	Modularisation
S4, [24], [26]	Map Objects Before Links	Modularisation
S39, S46, S52, S68	Introduce Rule Inheritance	Modularisation
S62, [23], S68	Recursive Descent	Modularisation
S31	Unique Instantiation	Correctness
[25], [11], S54, S69	Sequential Composition	Modularisation

Table 3. Applications of optimisation and architectural MT design patterns in surveyed papers

Papers	Pattern	Benefits/motivation
S40	Restrict Input Ranges,	Efficiency
	Remove Duplicated Expr. Eval	Efficiency
S41	Map Objects Before Links	Modularisation
	Construction and Cleanup	Modularisation
	Omit Negative Application Conditions	Efficiency
S30	Remove Duplicated Expr. Eval	Efficiency
[19]	Restrict Input Ranges	Efficiency
	Replace Fixed-point by Bounded Iter	Efficiency
	Filter	Scalability
S43	Replace Fixed-point by Bounded Iter	Efficiency
S57, S58	Implicit Copy	Efficiency, conciseness
S55, [6]	Generic Transformations	Reuse
S12, S25, S28, S33 S44, S75, S76	Transformation Chain	De/Composition
S34	Filter	Scalability

(iv) Transformation Chain, Structure Preservation (7 uses); (v) Entity Merging, Phased Construction (5 uses). Overall, 29 different (previously-documented) patterns and 21 of the 29 patterns described in [21] occur in transformation development cases. Different patterns tend to be used for different categories of transformation, with Entity Merging/Splitting and Map Objects before Links more common in cases of migration and refinement transformations, rather than in refactorings. Structure Preservation occurs in relatively simple migration or refinement cases, such as [18]. Auxiliary Metamodel is a fundamental pattern which is used within several other patterns.

Although applications of patterns are quite common, particularly of rule modularisation patterns, it is unusual for the patterns to be explicitly quoted or formally described (as, for example, using the pattern template of [9]). The term 'transformation design pattern' is rarely used.

The terminology of patterns differs between authors, and especially between the model transformation and graph transformation communities. For example, phasing is termed *layering* in graph transformation languages [25]. Some patterns could be subdivided into distinct subpatterns, for example, Entity Splitting has both a 'horizontal' version, where different instances of one source entity type are mapped to different target entity types (as in the mapping of Pseudostates in [18], or family members in [12]), or a 'vertical' version (Structure Elaboration)

Table 4. Applications of specialised MT design patterns in surveyed papers

Papers	Pattern	Benefits/motivation
S6, [27], S33, S45	Text Templates	Simplify text generation
S14	Proxy, Sliding Window	Manage model elements from streamed data
S59	Visitor	Organise processing
S32	State	Express statemachine in code
S3, S8, S21, S24 S26, [12], S29, S37	Auxiliary Correspondence Model	Bx properties, incrementality, synchronisation
S5, S22, S23	Collection Matching	Expressiveness
S67, S70	Simulate Universal Quantification	Expressiveness
S27	Simulate Collection Matching	Expressiveness

where each source instance is mapped to multiple target objects. The former variant is more suited to migration cases, and the latter to refinements.

We consider that it would be beneficial if there was wider awareness of MT patterns, and an agreed terminology, to make the use of such solutions to specification/design problems more systematic. A library of pattern application examples would help MT developers in this respect. Further research is needed to refine and improve the definitions of known patterns, to fit these more closely to actual practice.

4.2   Benefits of MT Pattern Use

Concerning research question 2, precise evaluation of the benefits of pattern applications is unusual. Improved execution times from the application of optimisation patterns are reported in [21], and improved scalability is shown in quantitative terms in [19]. Quantitative comparisons of transformations with and without patterns are given in [27]. Positive results for the customisability achieved by the Factor Code Generation pattern are described in [8]. Efficiency improvements from Sequential Composition/layering are shown in [11]. Quantitative evaluation of different transformation styles and languages is carried out in [1], including evaluation of the effect on performance of the removal of duplicated expression evaluations by caching. Generally, where evaluation has been carried out, pattern use does show the expected benefits.

4.3   Occurrences of Novel Patterns

Concerning research question 3, Tables 5 and 6 describe new patterns that were introduced in surveyed papers.

Table 5. New MT architectural patterns

Papers	New pattern	Summary	Benefits
S18	Localised Model Transformations	Decompose complex transformations into chains of cohesive small transformations operating on metamodel subsets. Related to Implicit Copy	Modularity, verifiability, changeability, flexibility
S19	Adapter Transformations	Use pre/post processing to adapt transformation to evolved metamodels	Supports evolution.
S49, S68 [10], S71 [8]	Factor Code Generation into Model-to-Model and Model-to-Text	Map to metamodel of target text language, and define text generation from this	Modularisation, flexibility
S2, S25 S28, S48 S50	Pre-Normalisation	Pre-process source model to simplify main transformation processing	Modularisation, efficiency
S15	Post-Normalisation	Normalise/simplify transformation result	Modularisation, separates mapping and refactoring
S72	Migrate along Domain Partitions	Migrate largely independent domain model parts separately	Modularisation
S60	Data Cleansing	Clean legacy/source data before transforming it. Related to Filter, Pre-Normalisation	Simplify main transformation by pre-processing.
S74	Three-way Merge	Consistently combine 2 independent updates of a model	Model synchronisation

Table 6. New MT optimisation/modularisation patterns

Papers	New pattern	Summary	Benefits
S40	Replace Collection Matching	Replace $s : Set(T)$ input range by $x : T$ & $s = f(x)$	Efficiency
S52	Rule Caching	Cache rule result to avoid re-execution. Cf.: ATL *unique lazy* rules	Efficiency
[7]	Fixed-point Iteration	Pattern for computing result using incremental approximation steps	Organises processing
[27]	Transformation Inheritance	Reuse/adapt a transformation by specialisation/superposition	Avoids duplication

4.4 Trends and Influences

Concerning research question 4, Fig. 1 identifies the changing usage of MT patterns over time. As expected, both the absolute numbers of papers per year using patterns, and the percentage numbers, have tended to increase.

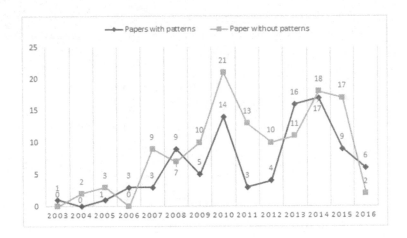

Fig. 1. MT pattern usages per year

The most-cited papers on MT patterns (papers with more than 15 citations as of February 2017) are: (i) Iaco et al. [13] (57 citations); (ii) Kurtev et al. [15] (47); (iii) Lano et al. [20] (33); (iv) Bezivin et al. [4] (32); (v) Lano and Kolahdouz-Rahimi [21] (22); (vi) Johannes et al. [14] (20); (v) Cuadrado et al. [5] (16). Despite the high number of citations for the top two of these papers, it is still unusual to find explicit reference in MT cases to the patterns that they define.

Tool support for MT design patterns is in its early stages. The UML-RSDS tool incorporates optimisation patterns into its design synthesis algorithm [22]. The work of [24] describes a language and tool to recognise occurrences of MT design patterns.

4.5 Patterns in Different MT Languages

Concerning research question 5, a wide range of MT languages were used in the surveyed papers, including custom languages and programming languages: ATL (15 cases); Graph Transformations (14 cases); QVT-R (13 cases); UML-RSDS (11 cases); TGG (11 cases); ETL (6 cases).

ATL provides good support for Entity Splitting. Standard mode ATL already has inbuilt a Map Objects Before Links execution strategy. Rule inheritance is only partly supported [17]. Unique lazy rules can be used for rule caching. Helper functions can be used to factor out duplicated expressions. There is no implicit copying facility. It is a unidirectional language, and external mechanisms are needed to support bx capabilities, as in [23]. Likewise, genericity [6] and composition of transformations [26] are facilities external to the core ATL language. It has a limited update-in-place mode, so that its application for refactoring transformations is limited. Table 7 shows patterns used in the first 24 of the ATL Zoo transformations [2].

Table 7. MT design patterns in the ATL zoo

Pattern	Used in ATL Zoo cases
Remove Dup. Exp. Eval.	1, 2, 4, 6, 7, 9–14, 17–23, 25, 26
Struc. Pres.	1, 2, 3, 6, 9, 10, 12–14, 17, 20, 22–25
Entity Split (vertical)	1, 3, 5, 6, 9–13, 20, 22, 25
Restrict Input Ranges	3, 6, 7, 9, 11–13, 20, 22
Map Obj. Before Links	1, 3, 5, 6, 9–13
Entity Split (horizontal)	1, 9, 11–13, 20, 22
Trans. Chain	1, 7, 9, 10, 13, 22
Rule Caching	2, 11, 12, 25
Entity Merging	4, 6, 10
Recursive Descent	12
Object Indexing	24

QVT-R is a bidirectional MT language. Entity Splitting and Entity Merging are both directly supported, and QVT-R supports rule and transformation inheritance. A common style of QVT-R specification is Recursive Descent, with top-level rules calling non-top rules, which may then in turn call other rules.

UML-RSDS is a hybrid MT language which supports rule ordering, and has inbuilt support for Object Indexing and other optimisation patterns. If rules are specified as operations, then operation inheritance can be used to provide rule inheritance. UML-RSDS has direct support for update-in-place transformations, and transformations may be composed within the language. The tools support Implicit Copy. ETL is a MT language similar to ATL, but with stronger support for update-in-place transformations, and a more procedural orientation.

We can conclude that the choice of MT language does have a significant effect on the application of MT patterns. Whilst simple patterns, such as Structure Preservation, can be used in any MT language, more complex patterns may be difficult to use in some MT languages.

The lack of consistency between different MT languages impairs reuse to the extent that language-independent transformation designs using patterns cannot necessarily be equivalently expressed in different MT languages.

5 Threats to Validity

A threat to the validity of the study is the omission of relevant cases through incorrect selection procedures. We have tried to avoid this by initially considering a general selection of all published case studies of MT, from both specialised MDE conferences and journals, and from the general scientific research domain. We have also checked all of the 82 papers of the large-scale survey [3] of MT cases. It is possible that mistakes have been made in recognising patterns in the selected papers, we have tried to minimise this problem by having two independent reviewers for each paper, with conflicting views resolved by discussion. In many published transformation cases there were insufficient details provided to determine if patterns had been used, so it is possible that some positive examples have been overlooked.

6 Related Work

To our knowledge, there is no other survey of MT design patterns in practice. In [21], some examples of applications of the proposed patterns are cited, to provide evidence for existence of the patterns. Kusel et al. [16,17] survey MT reuse mechanisms, including generic and higher-order transformations, but do not explicitly consider patterns. They conclude that reuse mechanisms in MT languages lack consistency, and that reuse in practice in MT developments is still quite low. Regarding ATL, they also note the low use of rule and transformation inheritance in the ATL zoo [17], and the high use of functions for factorisation. A study of MT developments in general is given in [3], this identified 82 MT cases, which we have also included in our survey. This study also identified a lack of validation in the surveyed cases.

7 Conclusions and Future Work

We have shown that MT design pattern use is quite widespread, however this use is often unconscious and unsystematic. We identified also a trend towards increasing use of patterns, with very few explicit uses of transformation patterns before 2005. We identified some new patterns which had not previously been formally recognised as MT patterns.

Overall, we can conclude that although MT patterns represent a useful tool for the construction of high quality transformations, awareness of existing patterns needs to be raised, together with improved tool support, guidance and documentation for MT patterns.

References

1. Amstel, M., Bosems, S., Kurtev, I., Ferreira Pires, L.: Performance in model transformations: experiments with ATL and QVT. In: Cabot, J., Visser, E. (eds.) ICMT 2011. LNCS, vol. 6707, pp. 198–212. Springer, Heidelberg (2011). doi:10.1007/978-3-642-21732-6_14

2. ATL Zoo, 30 November 2016. www.eclipse.org/atl/atlTransformations
3. Batot, E., Sahraoui, H., Syriani, E., Molins, P., Sboui, W.: Systematic mapping study of model transformations for concrete problems. In: Modelsward 2016, pp. 176–183 (2016)
4. Bezivin, J., Jouault, F., Palies, J.: Towards Model Transformation Design Patterns. ATLAS group, University of Nantes (2003)
5. Sánchez Cuadrado, J., Jouault, F., García Molina, J., Bézivin, J.: Optimization patterns for OCL-based model transformations. In: Chaudron, M.R.V. (ed.) MODELS 2008. LNCS, vol. 5421, pp. 273–284. Springer, Heidelberg (2009). doi:10.1007/978-3-642-01648-6_29
6. Cuadrado, J., Guerra, E., de Lara, J.: A component model for model transformations. IEEE TSE **7**(7) (2013)
7. Ergin, H., Syriani, E.: Identification and application of a model transformation design pattern. In: ACMSE 2013 (2013)
8. Funk, M., Nysen, A., Lichter, H.: From UML to ANSI-C: an Eclipse-based code generation framework. In: RWTH (2007)
9. Gamma, E., Helm, R., Johnson, R., Vlissides, J.: Design Patterns: Elements of Reusable Object-Oriented Software. Addison-Wesley, Reading (1994)
10. Hemel, Z., Kats, L., Groenewegen, D., Visser, E.: Code generation by model transformation: a case study in transformation modularity. SoSyM **9**, 375–402 (2010)
11. Hermann, F., Nachtigall, N., Braatz, B., Gottmann, S., Engel, T.: Solving the FIXML2Code case study with HenshinTGG. In: TTC 2014 (2014)
12. Hidaka, S., Tisi, M., Cabot, J., Hu, Z.: Feature-based classification of bidirectional transformation approaches. SoSyM **15**, 907–928 (2016)
13. Iacob, M.E., Steen, M.W.A., Heerink, L.: Reusable model transformation patterns. In: Enterprise Distributed Object Computing Conference Workshops, 2008, pp. 1–10 (2008). doi:10.1109/EDOCW.2008.51
14. Johannes, J., Zschaler, S., Fernández, M.A., Castillo, A., Kolovos, D.S., Paige, R.F.: Abstracting complex languages through transformation and composition. In: Schürr, A., Selic, B. (eds.) MODELS 2009. LNCS, vol. 5795, pp. 546–550. Springer, Heidelberg (2009). doi:10.1007/978-3-642-04425-0_41
15. Kurtev, I., Van den Berg, K., Joualt, F.: Rule-based modularisation in model transformation languages illustrated with ATL. In: Proceedings 2006 ACM Symposium on Applied Computing (SAC 2006), pp. 1202–1209. ACM Press (2006)
16. Kusel, A., Schonbock, J., Wimmer, M., Kappel, G., Retschitzegger, W., Schwinger, W.: Reuse in model-to-model transformation languages: are there yet? SoSyM **14**(2), 537–572 (2015)
17. Kusel, A., Schonbock, J., Wimmer, M., Retschitzegger, W., Schwinger, W., Kappel, G.: Reality check for MT reuse: the ATL transformation zoo case study. In: AMT 2013 (2013)
18. Lano, K., Kolahdouz-Rahimi, S.: Model migration transformation specification in UML-RSDS. In: TTC 2010 (2010)
19. Lano, K., Yassipour-Tehrani, S.: Solving the TTC 2014 Movie Database Case with UML-RSDS. In: TTC 2014 (2014)
20. Lano, K., Kolahdouz-Rahimi, S.: Constraint-based specification of model transformations. J. Syst. Software **88**(2), 412–436 (2013)
21. Lano, K., Kolahdouz-Rahimi, S.: Model-transformation design patterns. IEEE Trans. Software Eng. **40**, 1224–1259 (2014)
22. Lano, K.: Agile model-based development using UML-RSDS. CRC Press, Boca Raton (2016)

23. Macedo, N., Cunha, A.: Least-change bidirectional model transformation with QVT-R and ATL. SoSyM **15**, 783–810 (2016)
24. Mokaddem, C., Sahraoui, H., Syriani, E.: Towards rule-based detection of design patterns in model transformations. In: Grabowski, J., Herbold, S. (eds.) SAM 2016. LNCS, vol. 9959, pp. 211–225. Springer, Cham (2016). doi:10.1007/978-3-319-46613-2_14
25. Natschlager, C.: Deontic BPMN: a powerful extension of BPMN with a trusted model transformation. SoSyM **14**, 765–793 (2015)
26. Tisi, M., Cabot, J.: Combining transformation steps in ATL chains (2010)
27. Tisi, M., Cabot, J., Jouault, F.: Improving higher-order transformations support in ATL. In: Tratt, L., Gogolla, M. (eds.) ICMT 2010. LNCS, vol. 6142, pp. 215–229. Springer, Heidelberg (2010). doi:10.1007/978-3-642-13688-7_15

Applications and Case Studies

Generating Efficient Mutation Operators
for Search-Based Model-Driven Engineering

Daniel Strüber[✉]

University of Koblenz and Landau, Koblenz, Germany
strueber@informatik.uni-marburg.de

Abstract. Software engineers are frequently faced with tasks that can be
expressed as optimization problems. To support them with automation,
search-based model-driven engineering combines the abstraction power of
models with the versatility of meta-heuristic search algorithms. While current approaches in this area use genetic algorithms with fixed mutation
operators to explore the solution space, the efficiency of these operators
may heavily depend on the problem at hand. In this work, we propose *FitnessStudio*, a technique for generating efficient problem-tailored mutation
operators automatically based on a two-tier framework. The lower tier is a
regular meta-heuristic search whose mutation operator is "trained" by an
upper-tier search using a higher-order model transformation. We implemented this framework using the Henshin transformation language and
evaluated it in a benchmark case, where the generated mutation operators
enabled an improvement to the state of the art in terms of result quality,
without sacrificing performance.

1 Introduction

Optimization lies at the heart of many software engineering tasks, including the
definition of system architectures, the scheduling of test cases, and the analysis
of quality trade-offs. Search-based software engineering (SBSE, [1]) studies the
application of meta-heuristic techniques to such tasks. In this area, genetic algorithms have shown to be a particularly versatile foundation: the considered problem is represented as a search over solution candidates that are modified using
mutation and crossover operators and evaluated using fitness criteria.

Combining SBSE with model-driven engineering (MDE), which aims to
improve the productivity during software engineering via the use of models, is a
promising research avenue: SBSE techniques can be directly applied to existing
MDE solutions, mitigating the cost of devising problem representations from
scratch. Success stories for transformation orchestration [2], version management [3], and remodularization [4] indicate the potential impact of such efforts.

In this context, we focus on a scenario where the task is to optimize a given
model towards a fitness function. The state of the art supports this task with two
classes of techniques: those involving a dedicated encoding of models [5,6], and
those using models directly as solution candidates [7]. In both cases, applications
typically involve a minimal set of transformation rules that is sufficient to modify

© Springer International Publishing AG 2017
E. Guerra and M. van den Brand (Eds.): ICMT 2017, LNCS 10374, pp. 121–137, 2017.
DOI: 10.1007/978-3-319-61473-1_9

the solution candidates systematically, so that optima in the solution space can eventually be located. Yet, such modification does not put an emphasis on *efficiency* in the sense that improved solutions are located fast and reliably.

Example. This example is inspired by the 2016 Transformation Tool Contest (TTC) case [8]. We consider the problem of modularizing a system design, given as a class model, so that coherence and coupling are optimized. Class models contain a set of *packages*, where each package includes a set of *classes*. Classes are related via *associations*. The following modifications are allowed: classes may be moved between packages, and empty packages may be deleted and created. Classes and associations may not be deleted or created. Optimality of models is measured using a metric called *HCLC*, indicating high cohesion and low coupling, based on the intra- and inter-package associations of the contained packages:

$$HCLC(\underline{M}) = \sum_{P \in \underline{M}} \frac{\#intraPackageAs(P)}{\#classes(P)^2} - \sum_{P_1, P_2 \in \underline{M}} \frac{\#interPackageAs(P_1, P_2)}{\#classes(P_1) * \#classes(P_2)}$$

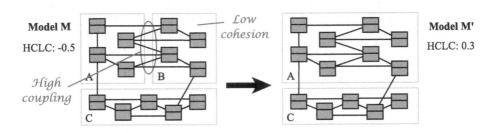

Fig. 1. Solution candidates: class models M and M'.

Consider an instance of this problem where models M and M' in Fig. 1 are solution candidates. Packages are denoted using light-gray boxes; classes and associations are denoted using filled squares with black lines between them. The HCLC score of M is -0.5: Packages A and B have few intra-package associations (low cohesion), and numerous inter-package associations (high coupling). M' improves this situation: after merging packages A and B, their inter-package associations have become intra-package ones, reflected in a HCLC score of 0.3.

To identify improved solution candidates such as M' automatically, we can use a genetic algorithm, employing the HCLC metric as the fitness function. Using class models directly as solution candidates, we need to provide mutation and crossover operators. In the following, we focus on the mutation operator, which can be specified as an in-place model transformation. Figure 2 shows three possible candidate rules for this purpose, specified using Henshin [9]. In these rules, nodes represent model elements, edges represent links, and all elements have a type and one of the actions «create», «delete», «preserve», and «forbid». Rule moveClass moves a class between two packages by deleting its

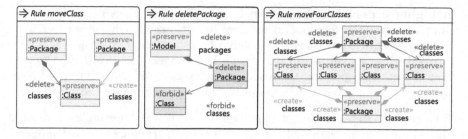

Fig. 2. Henshin rules used to define a mutation operator.

containment edge and creating a new one. Rule deletePackage deletes a package from the model. The «forbid» part in this rule ensures that the package to be deleted is empty, which is necessary to comply with the constraint that classes may not be deleted. Rule moveFourClasses moves *four* classes between particular packages.

To pinpoint the drawback of the existing minimal mutation operators, assume a mutation operator based on the rules moveClass, deletePackage and a third rule createPackage for creating packages, based on the rationale that these rules have all the ingredients to enumerate all possible solution candidates. Indeed, model M' can be obtained from M by applying moveClass repeatedly to move all classes in B to A, and deleting B via deletePackage. However, in a genetic algorithm, the bottleneck of this process is getting the order of rule applications right: as we apply moveClass at randomly selected places, we often move classes from A and C to B, including classes that we earlier moved away from B. We may eventually discover M', but the road is long and paved with meritless candidates.

An alternative mutation operator can be defined by adding moveFourClasses to the rule set. This additional rule gives us a shortcut that allows us to identify M' at a minimum of two rule applications instead of five. Therefore, it is clearly tempting to assume that this mutation strategy is more efficient. However, while the manual effort to define this particular mutation operator is low, we only have an intuition, but no evidence that this operator is more efficient in the overall problem class. Worse, there is no guarantee that we did not miss yet another, even more efficient mutation operator. A systematic strategy to design efficient mutation operators for a particular problem class is generally lacking.

To address these issues, in this paper, we introduce *FitnessStudio*, a technique for generating efficient, problem-tailored mutation operators automatically. Specifically, we make the following contributions:

– A **two-tier framework** of nested genetic algorithms: In the lower tier, we consider a regular search over concrete solution candidates. In the upper tier, we "train" the mutation operator of the lower tier (Sect. 2).

- A **higher-order transformation** for mutating the rules of the lower-tier mutation operator, focusing on the goal to optimize its efficiency (Sect. 3).
- An **implementation** using the Henshin transformation language (Sect. 4).
- A **preliminary evaluation** based on a benchmark scenario. Using the generated mutation operator, the result quality was significantly improved compared to previous solutions, without sacrificing performance (Sect. 5).

The key idea to train the mutation operator on concrete examples is inspired by the notion of *meta-learning* [10], that refers to the tuning of mutation operations in the context of genetic programming. Our technique is the first to generate mutation operators for search-based MDE. We discuss the specific requirements of this use-case in Sect. 3, and survey related work in Sect. 6.

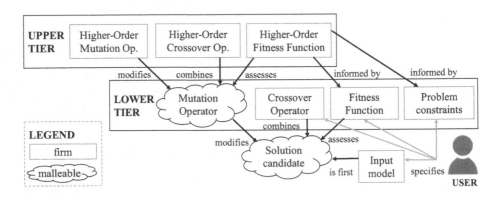

Fig. 3. Overview.

2   Framework Overview

Given a search problem in which solution candidates are expressed as models, the goal of our technique is to generate an efficient mutation operator. To this end, we introduce a two-tier framework of nested genetic algorithms. As illustrated in Fig. 3, the upper tier optimizes the mutation operator of the lower tier. An interesting feature is that the mutation operator of the lower tier is *malleable*, in the same sense that the solution candidates are. In other words, the upper tier allows us to consider a *family* of genetic algorithms in the lower tier.

- As **solution candidates**, we consider models directly, i.e., we do not use a dedicated encoding. This setting allows us to modify the solution candidates using transformation rules that can be modified using higher-order rules.
- The **lower tier** of our framework includes several components that are customized by the user to the problem at hand: the fitness function, the crossover operator, and problem constraints (e.g., in our example, the constraint that classes may not be deleted). This manual customization effort is the same as in state-of-the-art search-based MDE approaches. In contrast

to these approaches, the mutation operator is generated fully automatically. The mutation operator comprises a set of transformation rules that are orchestrated by a simple algorithm as described later.

– The **upper tier** is generic in the sense that it remains constant over arbitrary problems. Its most sophisticated feature is the mutation operator that uses a higher-order transformation to modify the lower-tier mutation operator. The crossover operator combines two randomly selected subsets of the rule sets of the two considered mutation operators. The higher-order fitness function assesses fitness in terms of the fitness of the fittest solution candidate produced in a sample run on a given input model. More sophisticated fitness functions as supported by multi-objective genetic algorithms are generally possible in this framework, although we did not explore this option in our implementation. Constraints imposed on the lower-tier mutation operator are checked directly after upper-tier mutations.

3   Upper-Tier and Lower-Tier Mutation Operators

This section is dedicated to our main technical contribution, the upper- and lower-tier mutation operators. We revisit necessary preliminaries, fix requirements based on our particular goals, and show the rules and their orchestration included in both levels.

3.1   Preliminaries

First, we revisit Henshin's meta-model, which defines an abstract syntax of rules. This meta-model acts in two ways as the foundation of our technique, as we transform rules using higher-order transformation rules. For clarity, we use the term **domain rules** for rules that are applied to domain models (in the example, class models), and **HOT rules** for rules that are applied to domain rules.

Figure 4 shows the relevant excerpt of the meta-model, and an example domain rule `deletePackage` created using the meta-model. The domain rule is the same one as shown in Fig. 2, but, to illustrate the meta-model, shown in a tree-based concrete syntax, rather than the more concise graphical concrete syntax.

A *rule* has a left-hand and a right-hand side *graph*, in short, LHS and RHS. A graph contains a set of *nodes* and a set of *edges*, so that each edge runs between a pair of nodes. Nodes can have *attributes*. Nodes from different graphs can be declared as identical using *mappings*. A mapping between an LHS and a RHS graph specifies that the respective node is a «preserve» node, i.e., it will be not be affected by the application of the rule. Nodes, edges, and attributes have types, which are references to suitable EClasses, EReferences, and EAttributes from the domain model's meta-model. The example rule includes as types the EClasses `Model`, `Package`, `Class`, and the EReferences `packages` and `classes`.

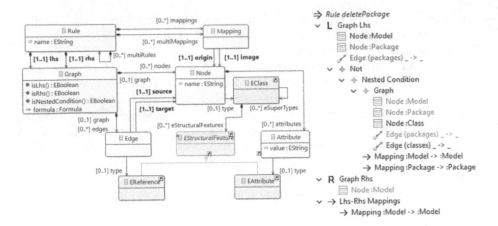

Fig. 4. Henshin meta-model and example domain rule.

In the example rule, the «delete» and «preserve» elements from the graphical syntax correspond to distinct ways of including these elements in the containment tree: The `Package` node and its incoming containment edge are to be deleted by the application of the rule and, thus, only appear in the LHS. The `Model` node is to be preserved by applications of the rule, and therefore appears in the LHS and the RHS, with a dedicated mapping to specify identity.

A further concept of rules are negative application conditions (NACs), which can be nested using a Boolean formula. For simplicity, we omit a large portion of the meta-model describing NACs.[1] At this time, it's sufficient to know that each NAC specifies a distinct graph, and its meaning is to «forbid» the existence of this graph in the input model. In the example rule, to represent the connection to the LHS, this graph contains some *context nodes and edges* to represent elements from the LHS, as specified via mappings. The forbidden part, highlighted in blue, includes all non-context-elements, here, the `Class` node and `classes` edge.

Rules can contain further rules, which are then referred to as *multi-rules*. During the application of a rule with multi-rules, the actual rule or *kernel rule* is applied first, and afterwards each multi-rule is applied as often as possible to the same matching site. Mappings running between a multi-rule and its containing rule are called *multi-mappings*.

3.2   Requirements

As a basis for design decisions influencing our higher-order transformation, we stipulate the following requirements.

---

[1] Details are found at https://wiki.eclipse.org/Henshin_Transformation_Meta-Model.

R1: Plausibility. It is tempting to design a completely unconstrained rule mutation mechanism that can produce all possible domain rules. Yet, a large class of domain rules is actually undesirable and can be avoided for better efficiency: *disconnected domain rules*, where the graphs in the rule are composed of multiple connected components of nodes and edges, may lead to the creation and deletion of elements outside of the containment tree. Therefore, domain rules shall be altered in such a way that the result rule represents a connected graph.

R2: Size variation. Generally, it cannot be determined in advance how many rules an efficient mutation operator will consist of. Therefore, in addition to mutating the involved rules, the higher-order mutation operator needs to ensure that different sizes of the mutation rule set are explored.

R3: Validity. Problem constraints as specified by the user can be violated by specific domain rules, e.g., in the running example, a rule that deletes classes. To avoid such offending rules without losing the generality of the HOT, we can discard them directly after a mutation. Moreover, the output models of the framework must be valid concerning well-formedness and problem constraints. To ensure that our mutation operators contribute to this goal, we check the validity of the produced models during the upper-tier fitness evaluation.

R4: Performance. The mutation operators on both meta-levels involve a step where a rule is matched to an input model, an NP-hard task [11] that is applied many times during the identification of solution candidates. Since we generally only need to identify a single match, rather than all possible ones, many rules are simple enough to avoid notable performance drawbacks. To deal with occasional problematic ones, a timeout can be applied.

3.3   Upper-Tier Mutation Operator

Our upper-tier mutation operator includes a set of HOT rules and a simple algorithm to orchestrate their application. We first walk through the rules, starting with simple HOT rules addressing basic features of domain rules, and then move to HOT rules for advanced rule features and, finally, rule orchestration.

The initial input of our HOT is an empty domain rule, called `initial`. Figure 5 shows this rule plus three selected HOT rules. Since our aim is to produce connected rules (**R1**), nodes are generally added together with an edge that relates them to the rest of the graph. The only exception is rule `createFirstNodeMapped`, which is only applied to the initial rule, so that it adds a node of the same type to the LHS and RHS. Both nodes are related via a mapping, yielding a «preserve» node in total. From there, we can extend the graph with additional nodes and edges. Rule `createRHSorLHSNodeWithContainmentEdge` adds a node with its incoming containment edge to the LHS or the RHS, i.e., a «delete» or «create» node. Modeling the containment edge is important, since creating or deleting a model element requires the addition or removal of this element in the containment tree. Rule `createRHSorLHSEdge` adds further «delete» or «create» edges; the «forbid» part avoids the creation of multiple edges of the same type between the same nodes, which is illegal. Variants of these rules exist for the addition and removal of «preserve» nodes and edges. In all rules, types of newly created nodes and edges are chosen arbitrarily based on the provided meta-model.

HOT rules for introducing the advanced concepts of NACs and multi-rules are shown in Fig. 6. Based on the requirement to create connected rules, the goal of HOT rule `createNACWithNodeAndContext` is to create a NAC whose elements are related to elements of the containing rule, which reflects the notion of *context elements* as explained in Sect. 3.1. The HOT rule assumes a domain rule where the LHS contains a node, so that a reference between the node's type `EClass` and some other `EClass` exists, allowing us create an edge between these nodes. Given such a rule, the NAC is added by creating a negated application condition (called *NestedCondition*, since Henshin allows nesting them) to the LHS. The conclusion of the NAC is a graph which is populated with two nodes and an edge relating the nodes. One of the nodes is mapped to the existing LHS node, and thus becomes the context node. The non-context node and the edge are «forbid» elements. For completeness, a dual opposite of this rule exists, where the direction of the edge running between the nodes is inverted.

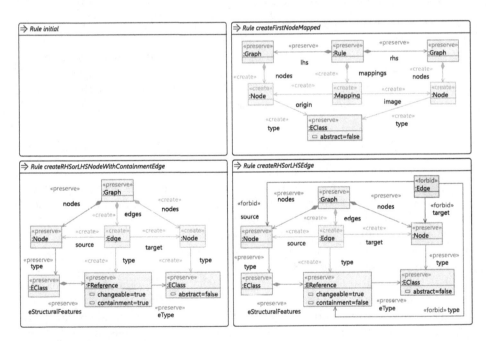

Fig. 5. Empty domain rule *initial* and three selected higher-order-transformation rules for creating basic rule elements.

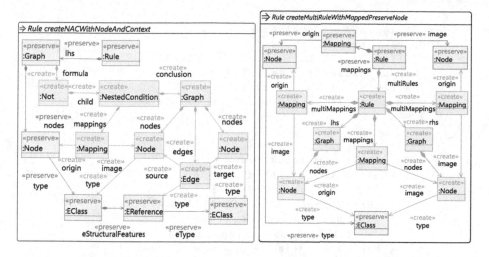

Fig. 6. Higher-order mutation rules for creating advanced rule elements.

Similarly, rule `createMultiRuleWithMappedPreserveNode` aims to create a multi-rule which contains a context part from the original rule. We use a «preserve» node from the original rule as context, i.e., a pair of LHS and RHS nodes with a mapping. The multi-rule is created so that its LHS and RHS contained a «preserve» node as well, which is mapped to the original rule using multi-mappings. The multi-rules and NACs created using these rules can be further populated using the simple HOT rules as introduced above.

The algorithm for orchestrating the HOT rules is introduced in Fig. 7. Lines 1–9 address the requirement to achieve variability in the size of the rule set: we initially start with a fixed number of domain rules (stored in a constant INIT, not shown). However, since a more efficient mutation operator might require additional or fewer rules, we change the size of the set dynamically by removing or rules in case a certain probability threshold, DIE or REPLICATE, is reached (**R2**). In lines 10–21, we iterate over pairs of domain rules and HOT rules, applying the latter to the former in case another probability threshold MUTATE_HOT is met. To perform the mutation, we wrap the domain rule into an EGraph, which encapsulates the input model in a Henshin transformation for a RuleApplication of the HOT rule. Constraints imposed on domain rules (e.g., in our running example, classes may not be deleted or created) are checked in line 19, leading to an undo of the mutation if a constraint is violated (**R3**). Specific mutated rules might be affected by performance bad smells [12] that will not become obvious until the higher-order fitness evaluation. To keep these inefficient rules from spoiling the overall performance, we support a user-specified timeout duration that is applied to the complete evolution iteration (**R4**).

```
 1 // Achieve variability in the rule set size
 2 for (Rule rule : domainRules) {
 3     double fate = Math.random();
 4     if (fate < DIE && domainRules.size() > 2) {
 5         domainRules.remove(rule);
 6     } else if (fate > REPLICATE) {
 7         domainRules.add(domainRule.createCopy());
 8     }
 9 }
10 // Randomly apply HOT rules to domain rules
11 for (Rule rule : domainRules) {
12     for (Rule hotRule : hotRules) {
13         if (Math.random() > MUTATE_HOT) {
14             EGraph graph = new EGraphImpl(rule);
15             RuleApplication app = new
                    RuleApplicationImpl(graph, hotRule);
16             boolean applied = app.execute(null);
17             if (applied && violatesConstraint(domainRule))
18                 app.undo(null);
19         }
20     }
21 }
```

Fig. 7. Orchestration of higher-order mutation operator.

3.4   Lower-Tier Mutation Operator

The lower-tier mutation operator in our framework consists of the domain rules generated by the upper tier, and a short algorithm for orchestrating these rules. The algorithm, shown in Fig. 8, copies the current solution candidate to mutate it. The mutation rules to be applied are selected using a static threshold, MUTATE_DOM, to specify the mutation probability.

```
1 EObject mutated =
       EcoreUtil.copy(mutated);
2 EGraph graph = new
       EGraphImpl(mutated);
3 for (Rule rule : domainRules) {
4     if (Math.random() > MUTATE_DOM)
5         new RuleApplicationImpl(graph,
               rule).execute(null);
6 }
```

Fig. 8. Orchestration of domain rules.

4   Implementation

We implemented FitnessStudio based on Henshin and a genetic algorithm, providing the implementation at https://github.com/dstrueber/fitnessstudio. The genetic algorithm, available at https://github.com/lagodiuk/genetic-algorithm, is a simple single-objective one. The rationale for choosing this algorithm was its convenient application to our technique, and positive experience made with a solution to the TTC 2016 case [13].

As illustrated in Fig. 9, in each iteration, the algorithm takes each chromosome of the parent population, mutates it, and performs a crossover with a randomly chosen chromosome from the parent population. The results are merged with the parent population and trimmed to obtain the same number of chromosomes again.

```
for (Chromosome c1 :
    parentPopulation) {
  Chromosome c2 = c1.mutate();
  Chromosome c3 =
      parentPopulation.rand();
  population.addAll(c2.crossover(c3));
}
population.addAll(parentPopulation);
population.sortByFitness();
population.trim(populationSize);
```

Fig. 9. Evolution iteration in the used algorithm.

We assigned the thresholds introduced in Sects. 3.3 and 3.4 as follows, based on the rationale to have a "balanced" amount of mutation: $\{INIT = 4, DIE = 0.33, REPLICATE = 0.8, MUTATION\_HOT = 0.8, MUTATION\_DOM = 0.4\}$. Further experimentation with dynamic thresholds may lead to improved results.

5   Preliminary Evaluation

To evaluate the efficiency of the generated mutation operators, we investigated two research questions: (**RQ1**) What is the quality of the solutions produced by the generated mutation operators? (**RQ2**) How do the generated mutation operators affect performance? We evaluated these questions using the "Class Responsibility Assignment" (CRA) case of the Transformation Tool Contest 2016 [8], a case that qualifies as a first benchmark for search-based model driven engineering, in which ten existing solutions are available.

Scenario. In the CRA case, the task is to create a high-quality decomposition of a given class model. The input model comprises a set of *features*, i.e., methods and attributes with functional and data dependencies between them. Features can be assigned arbitrarily to classes, so that a combined coherence and coupling score, called *CRA index*, is maximized.

Table 1. Input models (from [8]).

Models	A	B	C	D	E
Attributes	5	10	20	40	80
Methods	4	8	15	40	80
Data dep.	8	15	50	150	300
Function dep.	6	15	50	150	300

In our evaluation, we used five input models of varying size that were provided with the case description, since they allow a direct comparison of our technique and the existing solutions. Detailed information on these models is provided in Table 1. To discuss the efficiency of our technique, we consider two baselines: the best-performing and a median solution the TTC case study, allowing a detailed comparison to the state of the art. The best-performing solution was based on the Viatra-DSE framework [5]. For our comparison, we used the values reported in the final proceedings version [14], which were obtained on a system comparable to the one used in this paper. The information about median solutions – we considered median scores and times separately for all input models – was obtained from a publicly available overview spreadsheet[2]. Where available, we used the scores of the improved post-workshop versions. In this table, it is not specified if the best or average solution is reported, and the execution times were measured on different systems. Both aspects threaten the accuracy of comparisons based on these data, but arguably not to a disqualifying extent (as discussed later).

Set-up. Our technique has an initial cost for deriving the mutation operator. To mitigate this cost, we aimed to ensure that the same mutation operator can be reused over problems in the same problem class, i.e., is not overfitted. To this end, we worked with training and evaluation sets, so that the actual benchmark was the evaluation set. As the training set, we used model C, since it enabled a compromise between representative size and training duration. In the provided input model, we encapsulated each given function and attribute in a singleton class. The crossover operator was based on combining randomly selected classes from both considered models. We evaluated quality in terms of the CRA index of the produced models, as well as performance in terms of execution time. All rules, models and data produced during our experiments are available at https:// github.com/dstrueber/fitnessstudio.

Preparation: generation of the mutation operator. We applied FitnessStudio to input model C, configuring the upper tier to a population size of 40 and 20 iterations, and the lower tier to population size 2 and 40 iterations. We repeated the generation 10 times; the median run took 8:50 min. The best-performing mutation operator produced by FitnessStudio contained nine rules that each reassigned between one and three features. Interestingly, all rules shared a common pattern, where the specified target class of a feature F contains another feature F' so that a dependency between F and F' exists, thus contributing to cohesion. Each rule had one NAC; no rule had a multi-rule.

Benchmark measurement. We applied the genetic algorithm together with the top-scoring generated mutation operator to models A–E. To study the variability of the produced results, we repeated the experiment 30 times, using a population size of 40 and 400 iterations. All experiments were performed on a Windows 10 system (Intel Core i7-5600U, 2.6 GHz; 8 GB of RAM, Java 1.8 with 2 GB maximum memory size).

Results. Table 2 and Fig. 10 show the results of our experiments.

RQ1: Result quality. In all cases, fitness of our best identified solution candidates, as measured in terms of CRA, was equal to (A–B) or greater than (C–E)

---

[2] For the original spreadsheet, see http://tinyurl.com/z75n7fc – for the computation of medians, see our spreadsheet at https://git.io/vyGpJ.

Table 2. Results, times being denoted in terms of mm:ss.xxx.

Input model	Median TTC solution		Viatra-DSE			FitnessStudio		
	CRA	Time	CRA best	CRA median	Time median	CRA best	CRA median	Time median
A	3.0	00:02.284	3.0	3.0	00:04.729	3.0	3.0	00:05.260
B	3.3	00:04.151	4.0	3.8	00:13.891	4.0	3.2	00:11.511
C	1.8	00:24.407	3.0	2.0	00:17.707	4.0	3.3	00:24.837
D	0.4	01:42.685	5.1	2.9	01:19.136	8.1	6.5	01:30.799
E	0.2	11:04.802	8.1	5.0	09:14.769	17.2	12.8	05:09.194

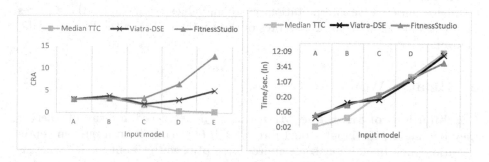

Fig. 10. Median CRA scores and execution times.

both baseline solutions. Strikingly, the delta between the best found solution of Viatra-DSE and FitnessStudio increased with the size of the model, ranging from no improvement in the case of A and B, to a strong improvement in the case of E. The median CRA improved in a similar manner, except for model B, where our mutation operator was too coarse-grained to yield the optimal solution as consistently as ViatraDSE. Altogether, our observations indicate an improved quality in particular for larger models.

RQ2: Performance. The time required to produce solutions using the mutation operator from FitnessStudio was in the same order of magnitude as Viatra-DSE. For the largest considered model E, we actually achieved a speed-up by factor 1.8, although a general trend towards better scalability is not obvious.

The results demonstrate that the mutation operators produced by our technique can produce better solution candidates than the state of the art, without sacrificing performance. We still need to evaluate our technique in a larger benchmark set of cases to confirm the generality of this conclusion.

Limitations and Threats to Validity. A limitation is that the mutation operator generation adds an initial performance overhead to applications of our technique. The severity of this limitation depends on the use-case: the overhead is less important if the search is to be ran repeatedly, either on different instances of the problem or changed versions of the same instance. As a lesson learned from our experiments, generation time can be reduced by training the mutation operator on a representative, but not overly large model.

External validity of our results is threatened by use of a single benchmark case. Particularly, the low complexity of the involved meta-model is a caveat against generalization to more complicated cases. In fact, we might need additional HOT rules to support meta-models where generalization plays a more important rule, to capture different combinations of relating EClasses (and supertypes thereof) via EReferences. To avoid pattern duplication during the creation of these variants, a promising strategy is to express them using variability-based rules [15,16]. Reliability of our comparison is threatened by the variability of baseline data for the median TTC solution. Still, even if we assume a conservative interpretation where all values are medians, these scores would still be below the median scores of the Viatra-DSE and the FitnessStudio solutions.

6   Related Work

Combinations of SBSE and MDE can be distinguished in terms of whether they operate on the input model directly [7], or encode it to a custom representation [5,6]. In addition, some approaches optimize the input model, whereas others optimize the orchestration of rules applied to the model. In all cases that we are aware of, including the solutions submitted to the TTC case [8], the mutation operators for the considered problem are defined manually. In fact, the Henshin solution [13] experimented with a selection of different manually defined mutation rules. The authors observed a drastic impact of the chosen mutation strategy, an observation that inspired the present work. Remarkably, those manually defined mutation operators are outperformed by our generated one. Finally, Mkaouer and Kessentini [17] haved used a genetic algorithm for optimizing transformation rules; yet, the baseline scenario of this approach is a regular transformation, rather than a genetic operator in an optimization process.

Rule generation for arbitrary meta-models is supported by an approach of Kehrer et al. [18] for the generation of consistency-preserving editing rules. A benefit of this approach is that the produced rule set is complete in the sense that it can produce all valid models. However, our example in Sect. 1 illustrates why such a rule set may not be most effective for our specialized usecase. Since rules are a particular type of model, their generation can also be enabled by using a model generator. In this context, Popoola et al. [19] provide a DSL for specifying a model generation strategy. In contrast, our approach aims to discover efficient mutation operators automatically, without relying on user input.

Model mutation is also an important concept in other contexts than SBSE. Focusing on testing, Troya et al. [20] and Alhwikem et al. [21] have proposed approaches for the systematic design of mutation operators for ATL and arbitrary domain-specific languages, respectively. Both approaches involve the definition of generic or abstract mutation operators that are instantiated to obtain concrete ones. In addition, the approach by Troya et al. uses an ATL higher-order transformation to manipulate the generated operators. Similarly to Kehrer's approach, the generation strategies in these works are complementary to ours, since they aim at completeness, while ours aims at fitness, leading to a different set of requirements. Wodel [22] is an expressive domain-specific language for model mutation, providing high-level mutation primitives so that users can specify purpose-specific mutation strategies. In contrast, our higher-order-transformation does not rely on a user specification of the mutation strategy, as it aims to discover efficient mutation operators automatically.

Mutation operator improvement has attracted the attention of the genetic programming community. A group of approaches based on *self-adaptive mutation* [23] modifies the probability of performing a mutation over the course of the genetic algorithm's application, rather than the mutation structure itself. Philosophically most similar to ours is the work by Woodward and Swan [10], which is based on the notion of meta-learning, and modifies mutation operators encoded in general-purpose-language using a notion of register machines. The work by Martin and Tauritz [24] expands on that idea as it aims to optimize the algorithm *structure*, rather than the involved genetic operators.

7   Conclusion and Future Work

The goal of this work is to provide a more systematic alternative to the current ad-hoc development style of mutation operators for search-based model-driven engineering. Our fundamental contribution is a higher-order transformation that generates and optimizes domain-specific mutation operators, as inspired by the notion of meta-learning. The early results obtained based on the TTC case indicate the generated mutation operators can be used to produce improved results compared to the state of the art, without sacrificing performance.

The present work opens up several exciting directions for future work. A fascinating problem concerns the self applicability of our technique: Our higher-order mutation was developed in an ad-hoc fashion, not unlike the domain-specific mutation operators we aim to improve on. Can we obtain further improvements if we optimize the higher-order mutation as well, using a second-level higher-order-transformation, as would lead to *meta-meta-learning*? Moreover, the principles considered in this work could also inform the generation of cross-over operators. Finally, we aim to apply the approach to a broader variety of use-cases, including the refactoring of transformation rules [25], the prioritization of clones during quality assurance [26], and trade-off management in model-based privacy analysis [27]. In these scenarios, we also intend to study the impact of the used genetic algorithm, and the use of our technique for multi-objective optimization.

Acknowledgement. This research was partially supported by the research project Visual Privacy Management in User Centric Open Environments (supported by the EU's Horizon 2020 programme, Proposal number: 653642).

References

1. Harman, M., Jones, B.F.: Search-based software engineering. Inf. Softw. Technol. **43**(14), 833–839 (2001)
2. Fleck, M., Troya, J., Wimmer, M.: Search-based model transformations. Softw. Evol. Process **28**, 1081–1117 (2016)
3. Debreceni, C., Ráth, I., Varró, D., Carlos, X., Mendialdua, X., Trujillo, S.: Automated model merge by design space exploration. In: Stevens, P., Wąsowski, A. (eds.) FASE 2016. LNCS, vol. 9633, pp. 104–121. Springer, Heidelberg (2016). doi:10.1007/978-3-662-49665-7_7
4. Fleck, M., Troya, J., Kessentini, M., Wimmer, M., Alkhazi, B.: Model transformation modularization as a many-objective optimization problem. IEEE Trans. Softw. Eng. (2017)
5. Abdeen, H., Varró, D., Sahraoui, H., Nagy, A.S., Debreceni, C., Hegedüs, Á., Horváth, Á.: Multi-objective optimization in rule-based design space exploration. In: ASE, pp. 289–300. ACM (2014)
6. Fleck, M., Troya, J., Wimmer, M.: Search-based model transformations with MOMoT. In: Van Gorp, P., Engels, G. (eds.) ICMT 2016. LNCS, vol. 9765, pp. 79–87. Springer, Cham (2016). doi:10.1007/978-3-319-42064-6_6
7. Zschaler, S., Mandow, L.: Towards model-based optimisation: using domain knowledge explicitly. In: Milazzo, P., Varró, D., Wimmer, M. (eds.) STAF 2016. LNCS, vol. 9946, pp. 317–329. Springer, Cham (2016). doi:10.1007/978-3-319-50230-4_24
8. Fleck, M., Troya, J., Wimmer, M.: The class responsibility assignment case. In: TTC, pp. 1–8 (2016)
9. Arendt, T., Biermann, E., Jurack, S., Krause, C., Taentzer, G.: Henshin: advanced concepts and tools for in-place EMF model transformations. In: Petriu, D.C., Rouquette, N., Haugen, Ø. (eds.) MODELS 2010. LNCS, vol. 6394, pp. 121–135. Springer, Heidelberg (2010). doi:10.1007/978-3-642-16145-2_9
10. Woodward, J.R., Swan, J.: The automatic generation of mutation operators for genetic algorithms. In: GECCO, pp. 67–74 (2012)
11. Mehlhorn, K.: Graph Algorithms and NP-Completeness. Springer, New York (1984)
12. Tichy, M., Krause, C., Liebel, G.: Detecting performance bad smells for Henshin model transformations. In: AMT (2013)
13. Born, K., Schulz, S., Strüber, D., John, S.: Solving the class responsibility assignment case with Henshin and a genetic algorithm. In: TTC, pp. 45–54 (2016)
14. Nagy, A.S., Szárnyas, G.: Class responsiblity assignment case: a Viatra-DSE solution. In: TTC, pp. 39–44 (2016)
15. Strüber, D., Schulz, S.: A tool environment for managing families of model transformation rules. In: Echahed, R., Minas, M. (eds.) ICGT 2016. LNCS, vol. 9761, pp. 89–101. Springer, Cham (2016). doi:10.1007/978-3-319-40530-8_6
16. Strüber, D.: Model-driven engineering in the large: refactoring techniques for models and model transformation systems. Ph.D. thesis, Philipps-Universität Marburg (2016)
17. Mkaouer, M.W., Kessentini, M.: Model transformation using multiobjective optimization. Adv. Comput. **92**, 161–202 (2014)
18. Kehrer, T., Taentzer, G., Rindt, M., Kelter, U.: Automatically deriving the specification of model editing operations from meta-models. In: Van Gorp, P., Engels, G. (eds.) ICMT 2016. LNCS, vol. 9765, pp. 173–188. Springer, Cham (2016). doi:10.1007/978-3-319-42064-6_12

19. Popoola, S., Kolovos, D.S., Rodriguez, H.H.: EMG: a domain-specific transformation language for synthetic model generation. In: Van Gorp, P., Engels, G. (eds.) ICMT 2016. LNCS, vol. 9765, pp. 36–51. Springer, Cham (2016). doi:10.1007/978-3-319-42064-6_3

20. Troya, J., Bergmayr, A., Burgueño, L., Wimmer, M.: Towards systematic mutations for and with ATL model transformations. In: Workshop on Mutation Analysis, pp. 1–10 (2015)

21. Alhwikem, F., Paige, R.F., Rose, L., Alexander, R.: A systematic approach for designing mutation operators for MDE languages. In: MoDEVVa, pp. 54–59 (2016)

22. Gómez-Abajo, P., Guerra, E., de Lara, J.: A domain-specific language for model mutation and its application to the automated generation of exercises. In: Computer Languages, Systems & Structures (2016)

23. Smullen, D., Gillett, J., Heron, J., Rahnamayan, S.: Genetic algorithm with self-adaptive mutation controlled by chromosome similarity. In: CEC, pp. 504–511. IEEE (2014)

24. Martin, M.A., Tauritz, D.R.: Evolving black-box search algorithms employing genetic programming. In: GECCO, companion volume, pp. 1497–1504. ACM (2013)

25. Strüber, D., Rubin, J., Arendt, T., Chechik, M., Taentzer, G., Plöger, J.: *Rule-Merger*: automatic construction of variability-based model transformation rules. In: Stevens, P., Wąsowski, A. (eds.) FASE 2016. LNCS, vol. 9633, pp. 122–140. Springer, Heidelberg (2016). doi:10.1007/978-3-662-49665-7_8

26. Strüber, D., Plöger, J., Acreţoaie, V.: Clone detection for graph-based model transformation languages. In: Van Gorp, P., Engels, G. (eds.) ICMT 2016. LNCS, vol. 9765, pp. 191–206. Springer, Cham (2016). doi:10.1007/978-3-319-42064-6_13

27. Ahmadian, A.S., Strüber, D., Riediger, V., Jürjens, J.: Model-based privacy analysis in industrial ecosystems. In: ECMFA. Springer (2017)

Graph Constraint Evaluation over Partial Models by Constraint Rewriting

Oszkár Semeráth[1,2](✉) and Dániel Varró[1,2](✉)

[1] MTA-BME Lendület Research Group on Cyber-Physical Systems,
Budapest University of Technology and Economics, Budapest, Hungary
{semerath,varro}@mit.bme.hu
[2] Department of Electrical and Computer Engineering,
McGill University, Montreal, Canada

Abstract. In the early stages of model driven development, models are frequently incomplete and partial. Partial models represent multiple possible concrete models, and thus, they are able to capture uncertainty and possible design decisions. When using models of a complex modeling language, several well-formedness constraints need to be continuously checked to highlight conceptual design flaws for the engineers in an early phase. While well-formedness constraints can be efficiently checked for (fully specified) concrete models, checking the same constraints over partial models is more challenging since, for instance, a currently valid constraint may be violated (or an invalid constraint may be respected) when refining a partial model into a concrete model.

In this paper we propose a novel technique to evaluate well-formedness constraints on partial models in order to detect if (i) a concretization may potentially violate or (ii) any concretization will surely violate a well-formedness constraint to help engineers gradually to resolve uncertainty without violating well-formedness. For that purpose, we map the problem of constraint evaluation over partial models into a regular graph pattern matching problem over complete models by semantically equivalent rewrites of graph queries.

1 Introduction

Model-Driven Engineering (MDE) is a widely used technique in many application domains such as automotive, avionics or other cyber-physical systems [37]. MDE facilitates the use of models in different phases of design and on various levels of abstraction. These models enable the automated synthesis of various design artifacts (such as source code, configuration files, documentation) and help catch design flaws early by model validation techniques. Model validation highly depends on repeatedly checking multiple design rules and well-formedness constraints captured in the form of graph constraints [3,17,21] over large (graph) models to highlight violating model elements to systems engineers.

During the early phase of development as well as in case of software product line engineering, the level of uncertainty represented in the models is still

E. Guerra and M. van den Brand (Eds.): ICMT 2017, LNCS 10374, pp. 138–154, 2017.
DOI: 10.1007/978-3-319-61473-1_10

high, which gradually decreases as more and more design decisions are made. To support uncertainty during modeling, a rich formalism of partial models has been proposed in [10] which marks model elements with four special annotations (namely, may, set, variable and open) with well defined semantics. During the design, these partial models can then be concretized into possible design candidates [28,31].

However, evaluating well-formedness constraints over partial models is a challenging task. While existing graph pattern matching techniques provide efficient support for checking well-formedness constraints over regular model instances [7,17,20,35], SMT/SAT solvers have been needed so far to evaluate the same constraints over partial models, which have major scalability problems [31].

Our objective is to evaluate well-formedness constraints over partial models by graph pattern matching instead of SAT/SMT solving, which poses several conceptual challenges. First, a single node in a graph constraint may be matched to zero or more nodes in a concretization of a partial model. Moreover, graph constraints need to be evaluated over partial models with open world semantics as new elements may be added to the model during concretization.

In the paper, we propose (i) a new partial modeling formalism based on 3-valued logic [16], (ii) a mapping of a popular partial modelling technique called MAVO [10] into 3-valued partial models, and (iii) and novel technique that rewrites the original graph constraints (to be matched over partial models) into two graph constraints to be matched on 3-valued partial models. One constraint will identify matches that *must* exist in all concretizations of the partial model while the other constraint will identify matches that *may* exist. Although the complexity of the pattern increases by the proposed rewrite, we can still rely upon efficient existing graph pattern matching techniques for evaluating the constraints, which is a major practical benefit. As a result, engineers can detect if concretizations of a partial model will (surely) violate or may (potentially) violate a well-formedness constraint which helps them gradually to resolve uncertainty. Our approach is built on top of mainstream modeling technologies: Partial models are represented in Eclipse Modeling Framework [34] annotated in accordance with [10], well-formedness constraints are captured as graph queries [3].

The rest of the paper is structured as follows: Sect. 2 summarizes core modeling concepts of partial models and queries in the context of a motivating example. Section 3 provides an overview on 3-valued partial models with a graph constraint evaluation technique. Section 4 provides initial scalability evaluation of the approach, Sect. 5 overviews related approaches available in the literature. Finally, Sect. 6 concludes the paper.

2   Preliminaries

2.1   Motivating Example: Validation of Partial Yakindu Statecharts

Yakindu Statechart Tools [38] is an industrial integrated development environment (IDE) for developing reactive, event-driven systems captured by statecharts using a combined graphical and textual syntax.

Partial Model   Example Concretization

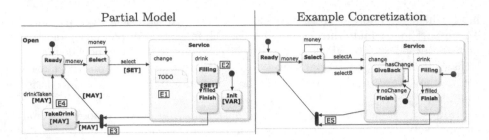

Fig. 1. A partial statechart model and a sample concretization.

A partial model of a coffee machine is illustrated on the left part of Fig. 1 together with a sample concrete model on the right. Initially, the machine starts in state `Ready` and after inserting coins by `money` events, a drink can be selected in state `Select`. While multiple concrete drink options may be available in the concrete model (like `selectA` and `selectB`), but in the partial model each one is represented by a generic `select` event. After the selection, the machine starts filling coffee, and gives back the change in state `Service`. The `change` management region is missing in the partial model, while a `drink` preparation region already contains some details. As the developer is uncertain about the initial state in this region, a placeholder state `Init` is created. In the partial model, it is undecided if it is required to wait until the previous drink is taken (in state `TakeDrink`), or the machine can enter its initial `Ready` state immediately.

These uncertainties are captured by special annotations introduced in [10] such as `may` (elements can be omitted), `var` (elements that can be merged), `set` (representing sets of elements) or `open` (new elements can be added).

The Yakindu IDE checks several well-formedness rules on the statecharts:

C_1 Each region shall have exactly one entry, which has a transition to a state in the same region.

C_2 The target and source states of a synchronization shall be contained in the same parent state.

Both constraints can be defined (e.g. in OCL [21] or graph constraints [3]) and checked over complete models, but our paper focuses on detecting (potential and certain) conceptual errors (marked by `E1-4` in Fig. 1) in partial models.

`E1` marks that an entry state is missing from region `change`, thus violating C_1. However, as the model is under construction, it can be repaired in a later stage. The other region (marked by `E2`) already contains an entry state, thus the WF constraint is currently satisfied, but it can potentially be violated in a future refinement by connecting it to a state located in a different region. `E3` shows evidence of an invalid synchronization of parallel states `Finish` and its parent `Service` violating C_2. This error will be present in *all possible concretizations* (or completions) of the partial model, e.g. as `E5` in Fig. 1. Finally, `E4` marks a possible error for synchronizing two target states that are not parallel (`TakeDrink` and `Ready` if all `may` elements are preserved).

2.2   Metamodels and Instance Models

A domain-specific (modeling) language (DSL) is typically defined by a *metamodel* and several *well-formedness constraints*. A metamodel defines the main concepts and relations in a domain, and specifies the basic graph structure of the models. In this paper, domain models are captured by the Eclipse Modeling Framework (EMF) [34], which is widely used in industrial modeling tools including Yakindu statecharts.

A metamodel defines a vocabulary $\Sigma = \{C_1, \ldots, C_n, exist, R_1, \ldots, R_m, \sim\}$ where a unary predicate symbol C_i $(1 \leq i \leq n)$ is defined for each *EClass*, and a binary predicate symbol R_j $(1 \leq j \leq m)$ is derived for each *EReference*. Moreover, we define a unary *exist* predicate to denote the existence of an object in a given model, while $\sim$ denotes an equivalence relation over objects. For a set of unique *Id* constants, $id_1, \ldots, id_k$, $k \in \mathbb{Z}^+$ well-formed terms can be constructed as $C(id_i)$, $exist(id_i)$, $R(id_i, id_j)$ and $id_i \sim id_j$, where $1 \leq i, j \leq k$. For space considerations, we omit the precise handling of attributes from this paper, which could be introduced accordingly.

An *instance model* can formally be represented as a logic structure $M = \langle Obj_M, \mathcal{I}_M \rangle$ where Obj_M is the finite, nonempty set of individuals in the model (i.e. the objects), and $\mathcal{I}_M$ provides interpretation for all constants in *Id* and predicate symbols in Σ as follows:

- the interpretation of a constant id_i (denoted as $\mathcal{I}_M(\text{id}) : Id \rightarrow Obj_M$) is an element from Obj_M;
- the 2-valued interpretation of a unary predicate symbol C_i (and similarly *exist*) is defined in accordance with the existence of objects in the EMF model and denoted as $\mathcal{I}_M(C_i) : Obj_M \rightarrow \{1, 0\}$;
- the 2-valued interpretation of a binary predicate symbol R_j (and also $\sim$) is defined in accordance with the links in the EMF model and denoted as $\mathcal{I}_M(R_j) : Obj_M \times Obj_M \rightarrow \{1, 0\}$;

For a notational shortcut, we will use $exist_M(x)$ instead of $\mathcal{I}_M(exist)(x)$ and $x \sim_M y$ in place of $\mathcal{I}_M(\sim)(x, y)$ (where x and y could be variables or constants). For a *simple* instance model M we assume the following S1-4 properties:

S1 $\forall o \in Obj_M$: $(o \sim_M o) > 0$ (reflexive).
S2 $\forall o \in o_1, o_2 \in Obj_M$: $(o_1 \sim_M o_2) = (o_2 \sim_M o_1)$ (symmetric)
S3 $\forall o_1, o_2 \in Obj_M$: $(o_1 \neq o_2) \Rightarrow (o_1 \sim_M o_2 < 1)$ (unique objects)
S4 $\forall o \in Obj_M$: $exist_M(o) > 0$ (model does not contain not existing objects)

Which means that in a simple instance model M, $\sim$ is the same as $=$, and for all objects o existence predicate is always evaluated to true: $exist_M(o) = 1$.

2.3   Graph Patterns as Logic Formulae

In many industrial modeling tools, WF constraints are captured either by standard OCL constraints [21] or alternatively, by graph patterns (GP) [3,17,20], which provide an expressive formalism. A graph pattern (or constraint) captures structural conditions over an instance model as paths in a graph. In order to have a unified and semantically precise handling of evaluating graph patterns for regular and partial models, we use a tool-independent logic representation (which was influenced by [25,36]) that covers the key features of several concrete graph pattern languages.

Syntax. Syntactically, a graph pattern is a first order predicate $\varphi(v_1, \ldots, v_n)$ over (object) variables. A graph formula φ can be inductively constructed (see Fig. 2) by using class and relation predicates $C(v)$ and $R(v_1, v_2)$, equivalence check $=$, standard first order logic connectives $\neg$, $\vee$, $\wedge$, and quantifiers $\exists$ and $\forall$.

Semantics. A predicate $\varphi(v_1, \ldots, v_n)$ can be evaluated on model M along a variable binding Z, which is a mapping $Z : \{v_1, \ldots, v_n\} \to Obj_M$ from variables to objects in M. The truth value of φ can be evaluated over model M and Z (denoted by $[\![\varphi(v_1, \ldots, v_n)]\!]_Z^M$) in accordance with the semantic rules defined in Fig. 2. Note that min and max takes the numeric minimum and maximum values of 0 and 1, and the rules follow the construction of standard first order logic formulae as used in [25,36].

$$
\begin{aligned}
&[\![C(v)]\!]_Z^M := \mathcal{I}_M(C)(Z(v)) & &[\![R(v_1, v_2)]\!]_Z^M := \mathcal{I}_M(R)(Z(v_1), Z(v_2)) \\
&[\![exist(v)]\!]_Z^M := \mathcal{I}_M(exist)(Z(v)) & &[\![v_1 \sim v_2]\!]_Z^M := \mathcal{I}_M(\sim)(Z(v_1), Z(v_2)) \\
&[\![\varphi_1 \wedge \varphi_2]\!]_Z^M := min([\![\varphi_1]\!]_Z^M, [\![\varphi_2]\!]_Z^M) & &[\![\varphi_1 \vee \varphi_2]\!]_Z^M := max([\![\varphi_1]\!]_Z^M, [\![\varphi_2]\!]_Z^M) \\
&[\![\neg\varphi]\!]_Z^M := 1 - [\![\varphi]\!]_Z^M \\
&\quad [\![\exists v : \varphi]\!]_Z^M := max\{[\![exist(x) \wedge \varphi]\!]_{Z, v \mapsto x}^M : x \in Obj_M\} \\
&\quad [\![\forall v : \varphi]\!]_Z^M := min\{[\![\neg exist(x) \vee \varphi]\!]_{Z, v \mapsto x}^M : x \in Obj_M\}
\end{aligned}
$$

Fig. 2. Semantics of graph logic expressions (defined inductively)

A variable binding Z where the predicate φ is evaluated to 1 over M is often called a *pattern match*, formally $[\![\varphi]\!]_Z^M = 1$. Otherwise, if there are no bindings Z to satisfy a predicate, i.e. $[\![\varphi]\!]_Z^M = 0$ for all Z, then the predicate φ is evaluated to 0 over M. Graph query engines like [3,5] can retrieve (one or all) matches of a pattern over a model. When using graph patterns for validating WF constraints, a match of a pattern usually denotes a violation, thus the corresponding graph formula needs to capture the erroneous case.

Example. To capture the erroneous case as a pattern match, the WF constraints C_1 and C_2 from the Yakindu documentation need to be reformulated as follows:

φ_{1a} There is an entry state without an outgoing transition.
φ_{1b} There is an entry state with a transition to a vertex in a different region.
φ_2 The target and source states of a synchronization are contained in different regions of the same parent state.

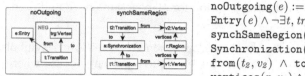

$$noOutgoing(e) :=$$
$$Entry(e) \land \neg \exists t, trg : from(t, e) \land to(t, trg)$$
$$synchSameRegion(s) \quad := \quad \exists t_1, t_2, v_1, v_2, r \quad :$$
$$Synchronization(s) \land from(t_1, v_1) \land to(t_1, s) \land$$
$$from(t_2, v_2) \land to(t_2, s) \land vertices(r, v_1) \land$$
$$vertices(r, v_2) \land \neg t_1 \sim t_2$$

Fig. 3. Sample graph patterns for statecharts with their equivalent logic formula

Graph patterns and the corresponding logic formulae for φ_{1a} and φ_2 are depicted in Fig. 3. With a negative condition (marked by NEG) in noOutgoing, Entry states can be detected without any outgoing transitions. Moreover pattern synchSameRegion searches for synchronizations between vertices v_1 and v_2 which are in the same region.

3   Formalism of 3-Valued Partial Models

Partial modeling [10,15,29] is a generic technique to introduce uncertainty into instance models. Semantically, one abstract partial model represents a range of possible instance models, which are called *concretizations*. During the development, the level of uncertainty can be gradually reduced by *refinements*, which results in partial model with less concretizations. In the following we present a novel 3-valued partial modeling formalism, and give a method to evaluate graph patterns on it.

3.1   Properties of 3-Valued Logic

In this paper 3-valued logic [10,25] is used to explicitly represent unspecified or unknown properties of the models with a third $1/2$ logic value (beside 1 and 0 which means a value must be true or false). During a refinement, $1/2$ properties are gradually refined to either 0 or 1. This refinement is defined by an information ordering relation $X \sqsubseteq Y$, which specifies that either $X = 1/2$ and Y refined to a more specific 1 or 0, or $X = Y$.

$$X \sqsubseteq Y := (X = 1/2) \lor (X = Y)$$

Information ordering $X \sqsubseteq Y$ has two important properties: first, if we know that $X = 1$ then it can be deduced that Y must be 1, and secondly, if $Y = 1$ then $X \geq 1/2$ (i.e. 1 or $1/2$). Those two properties will be used to approximate possible values of a concrete model by checking the property on a partial model.

3.2   Partial Models Based on 3-Valued Logic

In this paper we propose a generic, 3-valued partial modeling formalism. A partial model of the same vocabulary $\Sigma = \{C_1, \dots, C_n, exist, R_1 \dots R_m, \sim\}$ is a 3-valued logic structure $P = \langle Obj_P, \mathcal{I}_P \rangle$, where Obj_P is the finite set of symbolic objects, and $\mathcal{I}_P$ provides 3-valued interpretation for all constants in Id and predicate symbols in Σ.

Uncertain Types. $\mathcal{I}_P$ gives a 3-valued interpretation to each *EClass* symbol C_i in Σ: $\mathcal{I}_P(C_i)$: $Obj_P \to \{1, 0, 1/2\}$, where an $1/2$ value represents a case where it is unknown if an object has a type C or not.

Uncertain References. $\mathcal{I}_P$ gives a 3-valued interpretation to each *EReference* symbol R_j in Σ: $\mathcal{I}_P(R_j)$: $Obj_P \times Obj_P \to \{1, 0, 1/2\}$. An uncertain $1/2$ value represent possible references.

Uncertain Equivalence. $\mathcal{I}_P$ gives a 3-valued interpretation for the equivalence relation $\mathcal{I}_P(\sim)$: $Obj_P \times Obj_P \to \{1, 0, 1/2\}$. An uncertain $1/2$ value relation between two objects means that the object might be equals and they can be potentially merged. For an object o where $o \sim_P o = 1/2$ it means that the object may represent multiple different objects, and can be split later on.

Uncertain Existence. $\mathcal{I}_P$ gives a 3-valued interpretation for the existence relation $\mathcal{I}_P(exist)$: $Obj_P \to \{1, 0, 1/2\}$, where an $1/2$ value represents objects that may be removed from the model.

The simplicity requirements S1-4 defined on page 4 are also assumed on partial models, which, in this case, allow uncertain $1/2$ equivalences and existence.

Figure 4 illustrates three partial models, where P_1 shows a submodel of the coffee machine from Fig. 1. The objects are represented with nodes labelled with a unique name of its class. Solid and dashed lines represent references with 1 value and $1/2$ references respectively, and missing edges represent 0 values. For example, in $P1$ state *Init* must be the `target` of transition $t1$, and *Filling* and *Finish* are potential targets. Uncertain $1/2$ equivalences are also marked by dashed line with an $=$ symbol. In $P1$ this means that state *Init* may be merged to states *Filling* and *Finish*, or $t2$ may be split into multiple objects between *Filling* and *Finish*.

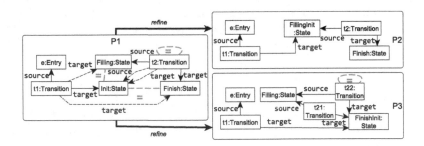

Fig. 4. Example 3-valued partial model with refinements

3.3 Refinement and Concretization

By resolving some uncertain parts, a partial model P can be refined to a more concrete partial model Q (denoted as $P \rightsquigarrow Q$). A refinement is defined by a function $refine : Obj_P \rightarrow 2^{Obj_Q}$, which maps each object of P to a set of objects in the refined partial model Q. A valid refinement $refine$ respects the information order of type, reference, equivalence and existence predicates:

- for each class C and for each $p \in Obj_P$ and $q \in refine(p)$: $[\![\mathtt{C}(p)]\!]^P \sqsubseteq [\![\mathtt{C}(q)]\!]^Q$.
- for each reference R and for each $p_1, p_2 \in Obj_P, q_1 \in refine(p_1), q_2 \in refine(p_2)$: $[\![\mathtt{R}(p_1, p_2)]\!]^P \sqsubseteq [\![\mathtt{R}(q_1, q_2)]\!]^Q$
- for each $p_1, p_2 \in P, q_1 \in refine(p_1), q_2 \in refine(p_2)$: $[\![p_1 \sim p_2]\!]^P \sqsubseteq [\![q_1 \sim q_2]\!]^Q$
- for each $p \in Obj_P$ and $q \in refine(p)$: $[\![exist(p)]\!]^P \sqsubseteq [\![exist(q)]\!]^Q$
- for each $p \in Obj_P$ if $[\![exist(p)]\!]^P = 1$ then $refine(p)$ is not empty

Figure 4 illustrates two partial models $P2$ and $P3$ as possible refinements of $P1$. $P2$ represents a refinement scenario where $Init$ and $Filling$ are mapped to the same objects $FillingInit$, and the equivalence between the two objects are refined to 1 from $1/2$. Simultaneously, the possible equivalence between $FillingInit$ and $Finish$ must be refined to 0 to satisfy the information order, because $[\![Filling \sim Finish]\!]^{P1}$ was 0. In $P2$ the equivalence on Transition $t2$ is refined to 1 from $1/2$, and mapped to a single object. $P3$ represents another valid refinement, where the $Init$ and $Finish$ are merged, and $t2$ is refined into two different objects $t21$ and $t22$, where $t22$ still represents a set of objects.

If a refinement resolves all uncertainty, and there are no $1/2$ values in a partial model $P = \langle Obj_P, \mathcal{I}_P \rangle$, and P is simple, then P represents a concrete (simple) instance model $M = \langle Obj_M, \mathcal{I}_M \rangle$ where $Obj_M = Obj_P$ and $\mathcal{I}_M = \mathcal{I}_P$, which is called concretization and also marked with $P \rightsquigarrow M$. As $P2$ in Fig. 4 does not contain any $1/2$ values, it can be interpreted as concretization of $P1$.

3.4 Evaluating Predicates on 3-Valued Partial Models

The main goal of this paper is to evaluate graph patterns on partial models in order to check possible matches on all possible concretizations. Evaluating a graph query over a partial model may have multiple outcomes: a pattern *may* ($1/2$), *must* (1) or *cannot* (0) have a match depending on whether the partial model can possibly be concretized in a way to fulfill the condition of the pattern.

Syntax. The same syntax is used for defining predicates on partial models as for concrete models, therefore the same well-formedness constraints can be used to check the correctness of partial models as for instance models.

Semantics. The predicates are evaluated in two steps: first, some expression rewriting is required to resolve *implicit equivalence checks*, then the rewritten pattern can be *directly evaluated* on the partial model. Implicit equivalence means that a match has to substitute the same value for each occurrence of a single pattern variable. For example in predicate noOutgoing(e) in Fig. 3 the expression $\text{from}(t,e) \wedge \text{to}(t,trg)$ implicitly states that the value of the two t is the same. Our technique requires the explicit notation of equivalences, which can be achieved by rewriting each variable occurrence (except for those in equality constraints) to a new variable, and explicitly defining the equivalence between the new variables, by creating a logically equivalent expression. For example, the previous expression is changed to $\text{from}(t_1,e) \wedge \text{to}(t_2,trg) \wedge t_1 \sim t_2$.

We have constructed the semantic derivation rules of 2-valued logic in Fig. 2 to evaluate 3-valued logic by using a numeric value of the unknown symbol $1/2$, resulting in a 3-valued logic (similar to [16,25]). Therefore the same derivation rules can be used to evaluate the rewritten (but logically equivalent) rules on partial model. Additionally, the truth value of the expression follows the $\sqsubseteq$ information ordering, which has two important consequences:

Theorem 1 (Forward concretization). *If* $[\![\varphi]\!]^P = 1$ *in a partial model* P, *then* $[\![\varphi]\!]^Q = 1$ *in each partial model* Q *where* $P \rightsquigarrow Q$, *and* $[\![\varphi]\!]^M = 1$ *in a each* M *concretization where* $P \rightsquigarrow M$. *Similarly, if* $[\![\varphi]\!]^P = 0$, *then* $[\![\varphi]\!]^Q = [\![\varphi]\!]^M = 0$.

Theorem 2 (Backward concretization). *If* $[\![\varphi]\!]^M = 1$ *in a concrete model* M, *then* $[\![\varphi]\!]^P \geq 1/2$ *in a partial model* P *where* $P \rightsquigarrow M$. *Similarly, if* $[\![\varphi]\!]^M = 0$ *then* $[\![\varphi]\!]^P \leq 1/2$.

Therefore, if an error predicate evaluates to 1, then it identifies an invalid partial model that cannot be repaired in any concretization. If it evaluates to $1/2$ it highlights possible ways to inject errors. And finally, a 0 value can prove that an error cannot occur in the concretizations.

This approach provides a conservative approximation for 1 and 0 values, where inaccurate cases are considered as $1/2$. In other words, the match result is approximated in the direction of $1/2$, which also includes the unknown cases. That is a safe compromise in many application areas such as model validation.

3.5   Rewriting Predicates to Must and May Predicates

In the previous section we defined the resolution rules for evaluating a graph predicate over a 3-valued partial model, which can result in three possible values: 1, $1/2$, or 0. However, traditional query engines support only 2-valued pattern evaluation on 2-valued models. Therefore, to utilise efficient graph pattern matching engines like introduced in [3], we introduce a predicate rewriting technique to calculate 3-valued predicate using two 2-valued predicates called *must* and *may* predicates, and combining the into 3 logic value. A predicate $must(\varphi)$ is a must predicate of φ, if $[\![must(\varphi)]\!]_Z^P = 1$ when $[\![\varphi]\!]_Z^P = 1$, otherwise $[\![\varphi_{must}]\!]_Z^P = 0$. Similarly a predicate $may(\varphi)$ is a may predicate of φ, if $[\![may(\varphi)]\!]_Z^P = 1$ when $[\![\varphi]\!]_Z^P \geq 1/2$, otherwise $[\![\varphi_{may}]\!]_Z^P = 0$.

In the following, we give expression rewriting rules (illustrated in Fig. 5) to create may and must predicates from a predicate. First, atomic expressions $C(v)$, $R(v_1, v_2)$, $exist(v)$ and $v_1 \sim v_2$ are replaced by $(\varphi \geq 1/2)$ and $(\varphi = 1)$ 2-valued

May and Must rewriting of atomic expressions

$may(\mathtt{C}(v)):=(\mathtt{C}(v) \geq 1/2)$	$must(\mathtt{C}(v)):=(\mathtt{C}(v) = 1)$
$may(\mathtt{R}(v_1,v_2)):=(\mathtt{R}(v_1,v_2) \geq 1/2)$	$must(\mathtt{R}(v_1,v_2)):=(\mathtt{R}(v_1,v_2) = 1)$
$may(exist(v)):=(exist(v) \geq 1/2)$	$must(exist(v)):=(exist(v) = 1)$
$may(v_1 \sim v_2):=(v_1 \sim v_2 \geq 1/2)$	$must(v_1 \sim v_2):=(v_1 \sim v_2 = 1)$

May and Must rewriting of complex predicates

$may(\varphi_1 \wedge \varphi_2):=may(\varphi_1) \wedge may(\varphi_2)$	$must(\varphi_1 \wedge \varphi_2):=must(\varphi_1) \wedge must(\varphi_2)$
$may(\varphi_1 \vee \varphi_2):=may(\varphi_1) \vee may(\varphi_2)$	$must(\varphi_1 \vee \varphi_2):=must(\varphi_1) \vee must(\varphi_2)$
$may(\neg\varphi):=\neg must(\varphi)$	$must(\neg\varphi):=\neg may(\varphi)$

$$may(\exists v : \varphi):=\exists v : may(exist(v)) \wedge may(\varphi)$$
$$must(\exists v : \varphi):=\exists v : must(exist(v)) \wedge must(\varphi)$$
$$may(\forall v : \varphi):=\forall v : may(\neg exist(v)) \vee may(\varphi)$$
$$must(\forall v : \varphi):=\forall v : must(\neg exist(v)) \vee must(\varphi)$$

Fig. 5. May and Must rewriting rules for graph predicates

predicates in order to round $1/2$ values up or down for maximizing the result for $may(\varphi)$ predicates, or to minimize the result for $may(\varphi)$ predicates.

Secondly, as the lower part of Fig. 5 describes, *may* and *must* predicates are constructed from complex expression φ by recursively rewriting all subexpressions. It is important to note that the rewriting rule of the negated expression $\neg\varphi$ changes the modality of the inner expression from *may* to *must* and vica versa. Figure 6 illustrates the rewriting steps of an example graph previously introduced in Fig. 3 into a may predicate.

original pattern: $\mathtt{noOutgoing}(e) := \mathtt{Entry}(e) \wedge \neg\exists t, trg : \mathtt{from}(t,e) \wedge \mathtt{to}(t,trg)$

$$may(\mathtt{noOutgoing}(e)) := may(\mathtt{Entry}(e)) \wedge may(\neg\exists t, trg : \mathtt{from}(t,e) \wedge \mathtt{to}(t,trg)) =$$
$$= may(\mathtt{Entry}(e)) \wedge \neg\exists t, trg : must(exist(t)) \wedge must(exist(trg)) \wedge$$
$$must(\mathtt{from}(t,e)) \wedge must(\mathtt{to}(t,trg)) =$$
$$= (\mathtt{Entry}(e) \geq 1/2) \wedge \neg\exists t, trg : (exist(t) = 1) \wedge (exist(trg) = 1) \wedge$$
$$(\mathtt{from}(t,e) = 1) \wedge (\mathtt{to}(t,trg) = 1)$$

Fig. 6. Example graph pattern rewriting

Finally, $may(\varphi)$ and $must(\varphi)$ predicates are traditional 2-valued predicates, whose can be combined to encode 3 possible truth values:

- If $[\![must(\varphi)]\!]_Z^P = 1$ and $[\![may(\varphi)]\!]_Z^P = 1$ then $[\![\varphi]\!]_Z^P = 1$
- If $[\![must(\varphi)]\!]_Z^P = 0$ and $[\![may(\varphi)]\!]_Z^P = 1$ then $[\![\varphi]\!]_Z^P = 1/2$
- If $[\![must(\varphi)]\!]_Z^P = 0$ and $[\![may(\varphi)]\!]_Z^P = 0$ then $[\![\varphi]\!]_Z^P = 0$

3.6 Transforming MAVO Uncertainty to 3-Valued Partial Models

MAVO uncertainty (which stands for May-Abstract-Variable-Open world) is a well-known and user-friendly partial modeling formalism [10,27,28] with several use-cases and tool support [4]. In the following we present a mapping of MAVO partial models to 3-valued partial models, enabling the evaluation of graph constraints on it.

MAVO specifies partial models with a concrete instance model B called base model, and introduces uncertainty annotations on the objects and references of B. The transformation starts with the mapping of the base model, then the annotations are transformed separately.

Base Model. First, a logic structure $P = \langle Obj_P, \mathcal{I}_P \rangle$ of Σ is created from the base model B, where $Obj_P := Obj_B$, and $\mathcal{I}_P := \mathcal{I}_B$.

Mapping of May. In MAVO, *may* annotation marks uncertainty about the *existence* of an object or reference. For each object o marked by *may*, uncertain existence can be expressed by $\mathcal{I}_P(exist)(o) := 1/2$. For each reference R, holds that if a link between o_1 and o_2 is marked by *may*, then $\mathcal{I}_P(R)(o_1, o_2) := 1/2$.

Mapping of Abstract. Abstract objects marked by *set* annotation marks uncertainty about the number of elements represented by an object. In 3-valued partiality, this can be represented by uncertain equivalence: for each object o marked by *set*, $\mathcal{I}_P(\sim)(o, o) := 1/2$.

Mapping of Variable. *var* annotation marks uncertainty about the distinctness of an object from another (which is not necessarily marked by *var*). In MAVO, objects with the same type are compatible for merging. Additionally, a *var* annotation implicitly specifies that the incoming and outgoing references of the compatible objects may be added to each other. For example, in the partial model in Fig. 1, each incoming reference to *Init* may be redirected to *Filling* upon a merge. So for each object o_1 marked by *var*, and for each object o_2 with the same class predicate values ($\mathcal{I}_P(C)(o_1) = \mathcal{I}_P(C)(o_2)$ for each C) holds that:

- $\mathcal{I}_P(\sim)(o_1, o_2) := 1/2$, meaning that o_1 and o_2 may be merged
- for each incoming reference R from another object *src* to o_1 holds that: if $\mathcal{I}_P(R)(src, o_2) = 0$ then $\mathcal{I}_P(R)(src, o_2) := 1/2$. The outgoing references are handled similarly.

Mapping of Open. *open* is a *global property* of a MAVO partial model which marks uncertainty about the completeness of the model. If a model is *open*, then it can be extended by new objects and references in a refinement. Otherwise, only the existing elements can be resolved. In 3-valued partial models, this can be represented in the following way:

- a new object *other* is added to Obj_P, which represents the new objects.
- $\mathcal{I}_P(\sim)(other, other) = 1/2$, so *other* represent a set of objects.
- $\mathcal{I}_P(exist)(other) = 1/2$, so new objects are not necessarily added.
- for each class C: $\mathcal{I}_P(C)(other) = 1/2$, so *other* represents all types.
- for each reference R and each object pair o_1, o_2: if $\mathcal{I}_P(R)(o_1, o_2) = 0$, then $\mathcal{I}_P(R)(o_1, o_2) := 1/2$. Therefore new references can be added.

Cleaning of the Partial Model. During the translation of uncertainty annotations, new 1/2 references are added to the partial model without considering the structural constraints imposed by the target metamodel. Therefore, in order to exclude malformed instances from the analysis, when a $1/2$ reference is added during the translation, (1) the ending types, (2) the multiplicity, (3) the containment hierarchy and (4) possible inverse relations are checked. If a possible reference would violate a structural constraint, then it is not added to P, so the precision of the approach can be increased by excluding invalid extensions only.

4   Scalability Evaluation

We carried out an initial scalability evaluation[1] of our approach using 3 models (with 157, 347 and 1765 objects, respectively) and 5 queries available from the open TrainBenchmark [33]. We generated randomly assigned MAVO annotations for 5% of the model elements (e.g. with 7, 17, 88 uncertainties respectively). We evaluated the performance of (1) each graph query individually for (2) both may- and must-patterns ($may/must$) using (3) two pattern matching strategies ($incremental/local\text{-}search$) with (4) open world or closed world assumption ($open/closed$) after an optional (5) fault injection step ($valid/invalid$) to introduce some constraint violations. We measured the execution time for evaluating the queries in seconds with a timeout of 2 min using a laptop computer (CPU: Intel Core-i5-m310 M, MEM: 16 GB, OS: Windows 10 Pro). Our experiments were executed 10 times and the median of execution time is reported in Table 1 (table entries with a dash denote a timeout). We

Table 1. Evaluation time of validation patterns on partial models (in sec)

Local Search Incremental		#Obj = 157 #Ref= 604				#Obj=347 #Ref=1340				#Obj=1765 #Ref=6904			
		Open		Closed		Open		Closed		Open		Closed	
		Valid	Invalid	Valid	Invalid	Valid	Invalid	Valid	Invalid	Valid	Invalid	Valid	Invalid
Connected-Segments	must	1.40	1.36	1.39	1.37	1.79	1.96	1.73	2.07	28.41	68.97	27.96	68.71
	may	1.47	-	57.62	-	1.93	-	-	-	-	-	-	-
RouteSensor	must	1.40	1.30	1.35	1.45	1.72	1.92	1.74	2.20	25.28	70.70	26.79	70.23
	may	1.45	1.48	1.46	1.64	1.62	7.53	1.82	14.60	15.88	-	19.20	-
Semaphore-Neighbor	must	1.67	1.54	1.68	1.68	4.18	3.77	4.19	3.18	-	-	-	-
	may	1.49	-	46.93	-	2.80	-	-	-	-	-	-	-
SwitchSet	must	1.79	1.69	1.81	1.68	8.50	4.66	8.87	4.41	-	-	-	-
	may	1.88	8.86	4.14	-	8.62	-	117.79	-	-	-	-	-
Switch-Monitored	must	1.21	1.26	1.22	1.34	1.41	1.70	1.55	1.70	14.63	32.50	16.72	35.71
	may	1.13	1.11	1.06	1.12	1.27	1.30	1.31	1.30	12.55	31.30	12.46	29.22

Our main observations can be summarized as follows:

- *Pattern matching over partial models is complex.* To position our experimental results, it is worth highlighting that most solutions of the Train Benchmark [33] evaluate *graph queries for regular models very fast* (scales up to millions of objects) for all these cases thus pattern matching over partial models must likely be in a different complexity class.

---

[1] A detailed description at https://github.com/FTSRG/publication-pages/wiki/Graph-Constraint-Evaluation-over-Partial-Models-by-Constraint-Rewriting.

- *Fast inconsistency detection for must-matches.* The detection of a must-match over partial models is fast for both case of closed world and with open world assumption, especially, when using local-search graph pattern matching. It is also in line with previous observations in [29] using SMT-solvers.
- *Scalable detection of may-matches with closed world assumption.* Our approach may identify potential inconsistencies (i.e. may-matches) over partial models with closed world semantics containing more than 1500 objects using incremental pattern matching. It is more than one order of magnitude increase compared to previous results reported in [10,12] using Alloy.
- *Full match set of may-matches and open world is impractical.* As a negative result, calculating the full match set of graph patterns for may-matches *and* open world assumption frequently resulted in a timeout for models over 160 objects due to the excessively large size of the match set. For practical analysis, we believe that *open* annotation in MAVO should be restricted to be defined in the context of specific model elements.
- *Selection of graph pattern matching strategy.* In case of timeouts, we observed that large match sets caused problems for an incremental evaluation strategy while the lack of matches caused problems for local-search strategy.

5   Related Work

Analysis of Uncertain/Partial Models. Uncertain models [10] provide a more user-friendly language compared to 3-valued partial models but without handling additional WF constraints. Such models document semantic variation points generically by annotations on a regular instance model. Most analysis of uncertain models focuses on the generation of possible concrete models or the refinement of partial models. Potential concrete models compliant with an uncertain model can be synthesized by the Alloy Analyzer and its back-end SAT solvers [27,28], or refined by graph transformation rules [26].

The most related approaches [11,12] analyse possible matching and execution of model transformation rules on partial models by using a SAT solver (MathSAT4) or by automated graph approximation (referred to as "lifting"). The main difference is that their approach inspects possible partitions of a finite concrete model while we instead aim at (potentially infinite number of) extensions of a partial model. As a further difference, we use existing graph query engine instead of a SAT solver, which has a very positive effect on scalability (17 objects and 14 may annotations reported in [12] vs. over 1700 objects with 88 MAVO annotations in our paper).

The detailed semantic handling of matching graph queries over models with open world assumption is discussed in [30], which focuses to *open* uncertainty only, while our current paper handles all MAVO annotations for partial models. Furthermore, scalability evaluation is only provided in the current paper.

Verification of Model Transformations. There are several formal methods that aim to evaluate graph patterns on abstract graph models (by either abstract interpretation [23,24], or predicate abstraction [25]) in order to detect possibly invalid concretizations. Those techniques typically employ techniques called pre-matching to create may-matches that are further analyzed. In [22] graph constraints are mapped to a type structure in order to differentiate objects that satisfy a specific predicate from objects that do not which could be used in our technique to further increase the precision of the matches.

In the previous cases an abstract graph similarly represents a range of possible models, and graph patterns are evaluated on abstract models to analyze their concretization. However, all of those technique expect a restricted structure in the abstract model, which is not available in partial models that are created by the developer.

Logic Solver Approaches. There are several approaches that map a (complete) initial instance model and WF constraints into a logic problem, which are solved by underlying CSP/SAT/SMT-solvers. In principle, the satisfaction of well-formedness constraints over a partial model (i.e. may- and must-matches) could be reformulated also using these techniques, although the same challenge has not been addressed so far. Complete frameworks with standalone specification languages include Formula [15] (which uses Z3 SMT- solver [19]), Alloy [14] (which relies on SAT solvers) and Clafer [1] or a combination of solvers [29].

There are several approaches to validate models enriched with OCL constraints [13] by relying upon different back-end logic-based approaches such as constraint logic programming [8,9], SAT-based model finders (like Alloy) [18,32], first-order logic [2] or higher-order logic [6]. As a common issue of such SAT/SMT-based approaches, the scalability is limited to small models.

6   Conclusion and Future Work

Conclusions. In this paper, we proposed a technique to evaluate graph queries capturing constraints over partial models. Since a partial model may be extended by the designer in future refinement steps, we defined may- and must-matches of a graph query correspondingly to denote potential and real violations of constraints. We also defined conservative approximations of may- and must-matches by rewriting of graph patterns in accordance with MAVO semantics.

Our initial scalability evaluation using the open Train Benchmark [33] shows that (1) finding real constraint violations over partial models is fast; (2) identifying potential inconsistencies with either open world or closed world assumption may scale for partial models with over 1500 model elements (which is one order of magnitude larger than reported in previous papers).

Future work. Although we motivated our work to check well-formedness constraints over uncertain models, our current results provide a key milestone for an ongoing project, which aims at the automated generation of scalable and consistent domain-specific graph models (aka a graph-based model finder). While metamodels of industrial modeling language often contain several hundreds of classes, existing logic solvers fail to produce an instances model containing over 150 objects, which is a major limitation for industrial use. Since the actual validation of complex graph constraints consumes significant amount of time in existing SAT/SMT-solvers, our current approach (which exploits efficient checking of graph constraints) can nicely complement traditional logic solvers.

Acknowledgement. This paper is partially supported by MTA-BME Lendület Research Group on Cyber-Physical Systems, and NSERC RGPIN-04573-16 project. Additionally, we would like to thank Gábor Bergmann and the anonymous reviewers for their insightful comments.

References

1. Bak, K., Diskin, Z., Antkiewicz, M., Czarnecki, K., Wasowski, A.: Clafer: unifying class and feature modeling. Software Syst. Model. **15**(3), 811–845 (2016)
2. Beckert, B., Keller, U., Schmitt, P.H.: Translating the object constraint language into first-order predicate logic. In: Proceeding of the VERIFY, Workshop at Federated Logic Conferences (FLoC), Copenhagen, Denmark (2002)
3. Bergmann, G., Ujhelyi, Z., Ráth, I., Varró, D.: A graph query language for EMF models. In: Cabot, J., Visser, E. (eds.) ICMT 2011. LNCS, vol. 6707, pp. 167–182. Springer, Heidelberg (2011). doi:10.1007/978-3-642-21732-6_12
4. Bertolino, A., Canfora, G., Elbaum, S.G. (eds.): 37th IEEE/ACM International Conference on Software Engineering, ICSE 2015, Florence, Italy, 16–24 May 2015, vol. 2. IEEE Computer Society (2015). http://ieeexplore.ieee.org/xpl/mostRecentIssue.jsp?punumber=7174815
5. Biermann, E., Ehrig, K., Ermel, C., Köhler, C., Taentzer, G.: The EMF model transformation framework. In: Schürr, A., Nagl, M., Zündorf, A. (eds.) AGTIVE 2007. LNCS, vol. 5088, pp. 566–567. Springer, Heidelberg (2008). doi:10.1007/978-3-540-89020-1_37
6. Brucker, A.D., Wolff, B.: The HOL-OCL tool (2007). http://www.brucker.ch/
7. Búr, M., Ujhelyi, Z., Horváth, Á., Varró, D.: Local search-based pattern matching features in EMF-IncQuery. In: 8th International Conference on Graph Transformation (2015)
8. Cabot, J., Clariso, R., Riera, D.: Verification of UML/OCL class diagrams using constraint programming. In: IEEE International Conference on Software Testing Verification and Validation Workshop, ICSTW 2008, pp. 73–80, April 2008
9. Cabot, J., Clarisó, R., Riera, D.: UMLtoCSP: a tool for the formal verification of UML/OCL models using constraint programming. In: Proceeding of the 22nd IEEE/ACM International Conference on Automated Software Engineering (ASE 2007), pp. 547–548 (2007)
10. Famelis, M., Salay, R., Chechik, M.: Partial models: towards modeling and reasoning with uncertainty. In: Proceedings of the 34th International Conference on Software Engineering, pp. 573–583. IEEE Press, Piscataway (2012)
11. Famelis, M., Salay, R., Chechik, M.: The semantics of partial model transformations. In: Proceedings of the 4th International Workshop on Modeling in Software Engineering, pp. 64–69. IEEE Press (2012)
12. Famelis, M., Salay, R., Sandro, A., Chechik, M.: Transformation of models containing uncertainty. In: Moreira, A., Schätz, B., Gray, J., Vallecillo, A., Clarke, P. (eds.) MODELS 2013. LNCS, vol. 8107, pp. 673–689. Springer, Heidelberg (2013). doi:10.1007/978-3-642-41533-3_41

13. Gogolla, M., Bohling, J., Richters, M.: Validating UML and OCL models in USE by automatic snapshot generation. Software Syst. Model. **4**, 386–398 (2005)
14. Jackson, D.: Alloy: a lightweight object modelling notation. ACM Trans. Softw. Eng. Methodol. **11**(2), 256–290 (2002)
15. Jackson, E.K., Levendovszky, T., Balasubramanian, D.: Reasoning about meta-modeling with formal specifications and automatic proofs. In: Whittle, J., Clark, T., Kühne, T. (eds.) MODELS 2011. LNCS, vol. 6981, pp. 653–667. Springer, Heidelberg (2011). doi:10.1007/978-3-642-24485-8_48
16. Kleene, S.C., De Bruijn, N., de Groot, J., Zaanen, A.C.: Introduction to Meta-mathematics, vol. 483. van Nostrand, New York (1952)
17. Kolovos, D.S., Paige, R.F., Polack, F.A.C.: On the evolution of ocl for capturing structural constraints in modelling languages. In: Rigorous Methods for Software Construction and Analysis, pp. 204–218 (2009)
18. Kuhlmann, M., Hamann, L., Gogolla, M.: Extensive validation of OCL models by integrating SAT solving into USE. In: Bishop, J., Vallecillo, A. (eds.) TOOLS 2011. LNCS, vol. 6705, pp. 290–306. Springer, Heidelberg (2011). doi:10.1007/978-3-642-21952-8_21
19. Moura, L., Bjørner, N.: Z3: an efficient SMT solver. In: Ramakrishnan, C.R., Rehof, J. (eds.) TACAS 2008. LNCS, vol. 4963, pp. 337–340. Springer, Heidelberg (2008). doi:10.1007/978-3-540-78800-3_24
20. Nickel, U., Niere, J., Zündorf, A.: The fujaba environment. In: Proceedings of the 22nd International Conference on Software Engineering, pp. 742–745. ACM (2000)
21. The Object Management Group: Object Constraint Language, v2.0, May 2006
22. Radke, H., Arendt, T., Becker, J.S., Habel, A., Taentzer, G.: Translating essential OCL invariants to nested graph constraints focusing on set operations. In: Parisi-Presicce, F., Westfechtel, B. (eds.) ICGT 2015. LNCS, vol. 9151, pp. 155–170. Springer, Cham (2015). doi:10.1007/978-3-319-21145-9_10
23. Rensink, A., Distefano, D.: Abstract graph transformation. Electron. Notes Theoret. Comput. Sci. **157**(1), 39–59 (2006)
24. Rensink, A., Zambon, E.: Pattern-based graph abstraction. In: Ehrig, H., Engels, G., Kreowski, H.-J., Rozenberg, G. (eds.) ICGT 2012. LNCS, vol. 7562, pp. 66–80. Springer, Heidelberg (2012). doi:10.1007/978-3-642-33654-6_5
25. Reps, T.W., Sagiv, M., Wilhelm, R.: Static program analysis via 3-valued logic. In: International Conference on Computer Aided Verification, pp. 15–30 (2004)
26. Salay, R., Chechik, M., Famelis, M., Gorzny, J.: A methodology for verifying refinements of partial models. J. Object Technol. **14**(3), 3:1 (2015)
27. Salay, R., Chechik, M., Gorzny, J.: Towards a methodology for verifying partial model refinements. In: 2012 IEEE Fifth International Conference on Software Testing, Verification and Validation, pp. 938–945. IEEE (2012)
28. Salay, R., Famelis, M., Chechik, M.: Language independent refinement using partial modeling. In: Lara, J., Zisman, A. (eds.) FASE 2012. LNCS, vol. 7212, pp. 224–239. Springer, Heidelberg (2012). doi:10.1007/978-3-642-28872-2_16
29. Semeráth, O., Barta, A., Horváth, A., Szatmári, Z., Varró, D.: Formal validation of domain-specific languages with derived features and well-formedness constraints. Software and Systems Modeling, pp. 1–36 (2015)
30. Semeráth, O., Varró, D.: Evaluating well-formedness constraints on incomplete models. Acta Cybernetica (2017, in print)
31. Semeráth, O., Vörös, A., Varró, D.: Iterative and incremental model generation by logic solvers. In: 19th International Conference on Fundamental Approaches to Software Engineering, pp. 87–103 (2016)

32. Shah, S.M.A., Anastasakis, K., Bordbar, B.: From UML to Alloy and back again. In: MoDeVVa 2009: Proceedings of the 6th International Workshop on Model-Driven Engineering, Verification and Validation, pp. 1–10. ACM (2009)
33. Szárnyas, G., Semeráth, O., Ráth, I., Varró, D.: The TTC 2015 train benchmark case for incremental model validation. In: 8th Transformation Tool Contest, (STAF 2015), pp. 129–141 (2015)
34. The Eclipse Project: Eclipse Modeling Framework. http://www.eclipse.org/emf
35. Ujhelyi, Z., Bergmann, G., Hegedüs, Á., Horváth, Á., Izsó, B., Ráth, I., Szatmári, Z., Varró, D.: Emf-incquery: an integrated development environment for live model queries. Sci. Comput. Program. **98**, 80–99 (2015)
36. Varró, D., Balogh, A.: The model transformation language of the VIATRA2 framework. Sci. Comput. Program. **68**(3), 214–234 (2007)
37. Whittle, J., Hutchinson, J., Rouncefield, M.: The state of practice in model-driven engineering. IEEE Software **31**(3), 79–85 (2014)
38. Yakindu Statechart Tools: Yakindu. http://statecharts.org/

BXE2E: A Bidirectional Transformation Approach for Medical Record Exchange

Jeremy Ho[1]([✉]) [ID], Jens Weber[1,2], and Morgan Price[1,2]

[1] Department of Computer Science,
University of Victoria, Victoria, BC, Canada
{hojs,jens}@uvic.ca, morgan@leadlab.ca
[2] Department of Family Practice,
University of British Columbia, Vancouver, BC, Canada

Abstract. Electronic Medical Records (EMRs) are complex data models and developing medical data import/export functions is a difficult, prone to error and hard to maintain process. Bidirectional transformation (bx) theories have been developed within the last decades as a mechanism for relating different data models and keeping them consistent with each other. We believe that medical record exchange is a promising industrial application case for applying bx theories and may resolve some of the interoperability challenges in this domain. We introduce BXE2E, a proof-of-concept framework which frames the medical record interoperability challenge as a bx problem, providing a real world application of bx theories. During our experiments, BXE2E reliably transforms medical records correctly and with reasonable performance. With BXE2E, we demonstrate a method of reducing the difficulty of creating and maintaining such a system as well as reducing the number of errors that may result. BXE2E's design allows it to be easily integrated to other data systems that could benefit from bx theories.

Keywords: Bidirectional transformation · Electronic Medical Record · E2E · CDA · Medical record exchange

1 Introduction

The rapid adoption of Electronic Medical Records (EMR) in Canada has created an ecosystem of patchwork EMR systems across different provinces. Similar to the U.S., the availability of a number of different EMR systems have led to a high degree of market fragmentation, and many of these systems lack any robust form of interoperability [2]. As a result, EMR usage is limited to local functionality. While EMRs offer benefits over paper-only systems such as the ability to make practice related reflective exercises easier [16], the inability to digitally communicate and transfer medical record information to other EMR systems is currently a large roadblock for patient care continuity across different points of service.

© Springer International Publishing AG 2017
E. Guerra and M. van den Brand (Eds.): ICMT 2017, LNCS 10374, pp. 155–170, 2017.
DOI: 10.1007/978-3-319-61473-1_11

To provide a concrete and common example, consider a patient referral from a family doctor to a specialist. The referral requires sharing patient information with the specified consultant. They are expected to review the patient's information, schedule one or more encounters with them, and provide a consultation report back to the requesting practitioner with their second opinion or specialized advice. Providing proper medical care requires a proper exchange of patient information between practitioners.

Ultimately, this workflow example illustrates the importance of EMRs having some form of medical record exchange mechanism. While practitioners can still perform their job even with the lack of interoperability, it does significantly hinder their efficiency and could allow for potential human errors to slip in. Any viable import/export solution needs to satisfy three main factors: it must be correct and consistent with data presentation and semantics, maintainable and easy to understand for new developers, and the solution must emphasize performance and scalability comparable with existing solutions. Any solution that is unable to sufficiently satisfy all three factors mentioned above cannot be considered viable for live production use in the healthcare domain.

2   Background

2.1   EMRs, OSCAR and E2E

Electronic Medical Record (EMR) systems are responsible for storing and managing patient records specifc to a single clinical practice. EMRs also support physicians with their delivery of care with things such as clinical decision support, alert reminders and billing systems. The Open Source Clinical Application and Resource (OSCAR) is a web-based EMR system originally designed mainly for academic primary care clinic use, it has since grown to become a multifunctional EMR and billing system for primary care physicians.

E2E is a British Columbian (BC) implementation of Health Level 7 (HL7)'s Clinical Document Architecture (CDA) standard. CDA is a document markup standard which focuses on the exchange of health data between healthcare providers and patients. The markup is implemented in the eXtensible Markup Language (XML) format which is designed to store and transport data as both a human-readable and machine-readable format. As a CDA standard, E2E benefits from the structural organization of the Reference Information Model (RIM) [11], which provides models to represent health record content.

OSCAR eventually included E2E export functionality because multiple universities were interested and the BC province issued a mandate for E2E standardization [15]. OSCAR has had three distinct generations of E2E export functionality. The first generation was designed using the Apache Velocity library, a Java based templating engine. While it satisfied the E2E standard requirements, this approach rapidly became difficult to maintain since all transformation logic resided on a single monolithic template.

The second generation of OSCAR's E2E exporter, named E2Everest, replaced Velocity and instead uses the Everest framework [8]. It used a deferred model-populator design, where the models transform the data elements, and the populators assemble the elements together. As this was done completely in Java code, maintainability significantly improved as compared to the Velocity template approach. The capability of adding unit tests to the exporter greatly improved its reliability.

While the Velocity and E2Everest components were able to satisfy the export part of the E2E standard, neither of them were capable of safely importing E2E documents. Velocity is not capable of import transformations, and E2Everest's import would end up as an independent transformation function with no explicit connections to its export equivalent. We address this in BXE2E, the third generation exporter which is the focus of this paper.

2.2   Bidirectional Transformations

We define a *transformation* as a finite set of operations which converts a set of data values from one data model to another model. A *bidirectional transformation* (bx) is a mechanism for maintaining consistency between two or more sources of information [3]. Let S and T represent the sets of all source and target models, and R be the relationship between S and T. The source and target are considered to be in a relation if the relation $R \subseteq S \times T$ holds.

Given a pair of models where $s \in S$ and $t \in T$, $(s,t) \in R$ iff the pair of models s and t are consistent. The forward transformation $\overrightarrow{R} : S \times T \longrightarrow T$ and backward transformation $\overleftarrow{R} : S \times T \longrightarrow S$ enforces relationship R. The end result of applying either transformation should yield consistent models, i.e., $\forall s \in S, \forall t \in T : (s, \overrightarrow{R}(s,t)), (\overleftarrow{R}(s,t),t) \in R$. In general, a properly implemented bx must at minimum obey the definitional properties of *correctness* and *hippocraticness* [3]. Transformations which follow those two properties can be considered *well-behaved*. Correctness in bx is defined such that each pair of transformations shall enforce the relationship between the source and target [18].

Hippocraticness in bx is the property in which transformations avoid modifying any elements within the source and target which are already correct and covered within the specified relationship R [18]. Another way of putting this is that even if target models t_1 and t_2 are both related to s via R, it is not acceptable for $\overrightarrow{R}$ to return t_2 if the input pair was (s,t_1). Formally, transformation R is *hippocratic* if $\forall s \in S, \forall t \in T$, we have $R(s,t) \implies \overrightarrow{R}(s,t) = t$ and $R(s,t) \implies \overleftarrow{R}(s,t) = s$.

Triple Graph Grammars. The Graph Transformation community has a bx technique called Triple Graph Grammars (TGG). Drawing its influence from category theory, TGGs are a technique for defining correspondences between two differing models [12]. Originally introduced in 1994 by Andy Schürr [17], TGGs formally define a relation between two different models and provides a means of transforming a model from one type to the other. This is done by creating a correspondence model which defines how specific elements are related between the two models [12].

A TGG model consists of three sub-graphs consisting of the source model, the target model, and the correspondence model between the source and target. The correspondence graph describes the mappings and constraints that must be applied to the source and target in order to transform between the two models. A TGG rule is a form of graph rewriting which does pattern matching and graph transformations. We define a graph G as $G = (V, E)$ where V is a finite set of vertices and E is a finite set of edges. Let S be the source graph, C be the correspondence graph and T be the target graph. A TGG rule is a pair of morphisms between a source and target graph coordinated by the correspondence graph. As such, let a TGG rule be $r = (S \leftarrow C \rightarrow T)$ where $C \rightarrow S$ is injective. $C \rightarrow S$ must be injective in order to allow for rule pattern matching.

Let R be a set of TGG rules. Each TGG rule defines three graph transformation rules: one forward rule, one backwards rule, and one synchronization rule. Ultimately, each rule in R will assure that a given source S and target T is able to consistently transform between each other. Each correspondence C tracks the differences between S and T on an element-to-element basis. The total sum of all the rules in R defines a language which describes the transformation which can occur between the source and target. As seen in Fig. 1, a rule is denoted with the two colors: black and green. Black objects and links represent the rule's context, while green objects and links represent the mapping extensions of the context. Further details on TGG semantics can be found in Kindler's paper [12].

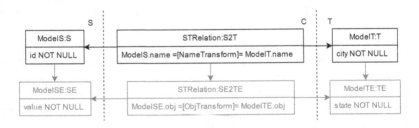

Fig. 1. An example of a Triple Graph Grammar Rule

A key property of TGG's rule matching and execution is *confluence*, or the property where the order rules are applied does not affect the final graph state. As long as all pattern matched rules are executed, the final result will be the same, regardless of order. The local Church-Rosser theorem states that two rules can be executed in any order and will *converge* to the same end result [4]. If all possible pairings of rules follows this theorem, the TGG is considered confluent.

Lenses. The Programming Languages community has developed separate approaches to handling bx. One prominent technique involves representing the get and put functions in the form of a *lens*. Simply put, a lens is a bidirectional program consisting of a forward *get* and a reverse *put* computation [6]. Formally, let L be the set of lenses which enforces relationship R between source model S and target model T. A lens $l \in L$ will define the three functions *get*, *put* and *create*. Get is defined as $l.get \in S \rightarrow T$, put is defined as $l.put \in T \times S \rightarrow S$, and create is defined as $l.create \in T \rightarrow S$.

Propagating any changes that appear in the models without losing information requires that our lenses to be well-behaved, or abiding to the properties of correctness and hippocraticness. This is achieved for lenses via the following *round-tripping* laws for all $s \in S$ and $t \in T$:

$$l.put \ (l.get \ s) \ s = s \tag{GetPut}$$

$$l.get \ (l.put \ t \ s) = t \tag{PutGet}$$

$$l.get \ (l.create \ t) = t \tag{CreateGet}$$

Round-tripping laws stipulate that information can pass through both transformation directions in such a way that information is preserved. GetPut requires the put function to restore any data discarded by the get function. PutGet and CreateGet force all propagated data to be reflected back onto the original models. These two laws are important because they ensure that any updates to t propagate to s correctly. These round-tripping laws tackle the classical view-update problem by reliably propagating any changes back to the source [6].

While round-tripping laws enforce well-behavedness, they are not sufficient for a well designed transformation. Leveraging the functional properties of lenses, we can use functional composition, or the chaining of functions. Lens composition facilitates modularized code creation by allowing transformations to be broken down to simpler units while maintaining overall transformation functionality [6].

In order to compose a lens, its get and put components each need to be properly composed together. Let lenses $l, k \in L$ and both lenses enforce relationship R between source model S and target model T. Suppose we want a new lens by composing the first lens l with the second lens k, where $s \in S$ and $t \in T$. We can do this with the following compose function [6]:

$$compose(l, k) = \begin{cases} get(s) & = k.get(l.get(s)) \\ put(s, t) & = l.put(k.put(s, \ l.get(s)), \ t) \\ create(t) & = l.create(k.create(t)) \end{cases} \tag{Compose}$$

By implementing our transformations with lenses, we have the liberty of designing simple lenses which do one specific, well-defined transformation. For example, a problems entry contains fields such as on id, code, effectiveTime, value and ICD9. As shown in Fig. 2, many small, simple lenses for each field can be composed together to create more complex transformation behavior.

Instead of a monolithic lens function which handles all these steps, we can instead apply each attribute's transformation step to a discrete lens. Chaining all these correct, simple lenses together allows us to recreate the same complex

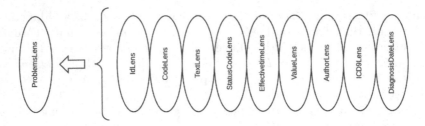

Fig. 2. Nine distinct sub-lenses are composed together to create the ProblemsLens bx definition.

transformation behavior as the monolithic lens. This addition of modularity also makes it easier to modify the overall transformation behavior by adding and subtracting lenses from the overall composition, improving maintainability [7].

3   BXE2E Design

3.1   Architecture Overview

The OSCAR data model uses a relatively simple Plain Old Java Object (POJO) representation. However, the E2E document model uses the MARC-HI Everest Framework library due to the complexity of HL7v3 data structures. Everest provides a consistent framework to represent HL7v3 data structures such as E2E with native Java patterns, objects and paradigms. The Everest framework allows for a methodical, reliable construction and serialization of the E2E document in a POJO format.

BXE2E is a bidirectional transformation framework which relates the OSCAR data model and the E2E document model of a patient record together using the Everest library as the CDA engine. BXE2E is effectively a POJO model transformer since the OSCAR model and E2E model are both represented as POJOs. Of course, a full import and export function does not rely only on POJO transformations. There are sub-transformations that convert between the POJO models to their respective OSCAR database tables and E2E XML models.

Although BXE2E is just one part in the overall import and export process chain, the sub-transformations around BXE2E simplify and group relevant data elements together, making it easier to map between the two different patient record models. These sub-transformations effectively provide an alternate way of viewing their data structures, whereas BXE2E transforms by defining and enforcing a mapping between the two models.

Taking inspiration from multiple facets of current bx theory, BXE2E utilizes a combination of Triple Graph Grammar Rules and Lens theory in order to enforce well-behavedness. Triple Graph Grammars have two main desirable properties, namely their declarative nature and their explicit representation of a correspondence between the source and target objects. Lens theory is desirable because a lens by definition is a pair of forwards and backwards transformations. As well,

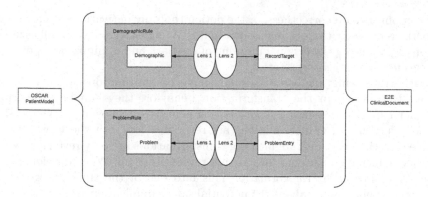

Fig. 3. An overview of how TGG Rules and Lenses are organized in BXE2E

lens theory has an emphasis on functional programming concepts, allowing for modular lens composition.

We chose a hybrid approach for BXE2E because TGGs focuses on enforcing graph and structural transformations, whereas lenses focuses on attribute level data transformations. While there are existing non-hybrid approaches for complex transformations [10], they do not provide a way to pragmatically separate different data contexts and transform at both the structural and attribute levels.

BXE2E combines aspects of both bx theories and applies them to our design of the transformation functions as shown in Fig. 3. Since a patient record is made up of multiple subcategories of information, we can define a TGG rule for each subcategory. This allows us to construct an explicit correspondence model and lets us take advantage of the non-deterministic execution property of TGGs. We then enforce attribute correspondences with lenses, making each rule have a tightly packaged forwards and backwards transformation. With modular lens composition, we can easily swap to different lenses if required.

3.2 Considerations

In order for BXE2E to be successful, it needs to be correct, maintainable and performant. As with any health-related application, we must avoid any potential patient safety issue by ensuring that the data transformation is correct. BXE2E's code organization must be easy enough to follow that any developer can pick it up and understand how to use and extend the framework. Lastly, BXE2E must also be designed with scalability and performance in mind.

Correctness and Safety. Since EMR systems are used as data repositories for patient health, we must ensure that the system is storing and representing data accurately. Although there are many facets regarding how providers interact with the EMR and the potential safety hazards that may arise from said interaction, that aspect of safety is outside the scope of this paper. Instead, our focus emphasizes on correctness, or the notion that any derivative data structure properly represents the original source data. We must strongly emphasize the notion of preserving the original meaning of the data and minimize any potential avenues for data misinterpretation.

Each transformation has a certain degree of information capacity preservation. Depending on the transformation behavior, they can be categorized as either capacity preserving, capacity augmenting, or capacity reducing [14]. Capacity preserving transformations are reversible for both the forwards and inverse direction, capacity augmenting transformations are only reversible, while capacity reducing transformations are not reversible at all. When developers can understand how each transformation falls into one of the three categories, it makes them more aware about the potential safety implications that could arise.

Ultimately, any developer working on health record transformations will require a significant degree of domain knowledge about how the data is handled and represented in order to minimize the amount of correctness that could be lost. While the act of preserving correctness is important in this domain, our paper focuses more on the software design of the transformation with the assumption that any relevant health domain knowledge is utilized to its fullest to minimize potential loss of correctness.

Maintainability. As with any active software project, it needs to be maintained over time. The readability of code plays a major factor as to whether a software project can easily be understood and contributed to by new developers. One way of quantifying this is with Cyclomatic Complexity which counts the number of linearly independent paths the code may take [13]. Essentially, it encourages designing software such that each module or section does not have too many potential execution paths.

Applying both Lens theory and TGG rules can minimize the cyclomatic complexity of the codebase. Lenses inherently have low complexity and very predictable behavior because they come from the functional programming domain. They also have the added advantage of having co-located forwards and backwards transformation functions. Lens composition can combine simple lenses together to build up more complex transformation behavior without compromising readability. TGG rules aid in minimizing complexity by limiting each rule's context to one independent and well defined topic. By grouping only related data together, each rule has a well defined purpose and works independently of other rules.

Performance. In order for the BXE2E framework to be successful, it needs to accommodate use cases which require a high degree of scalability. Once again leveraging the modular properties of lenses and non-deterministic execution property of TGG rules, we can tightly bind the units of transformation work into independent parts. This high degree of independence allows the framework to work efficiently and allow for concurrent operation.

This framework also natively uses Java as the programming language in part because the OSCAR EMR we are modelling after is written in that language. Although other languages were considered, ultimately there is no equivalent HL7 toolset similar to the Everest framework that could fit well in OSCAR's ecosystem. Our BXE2E framework leverages lambda function features introduced in the JavaSE 1.8 API to make lens implementation easier.

One of the big departures from current implementations of lens theory is that this framework uses objects as the transformation medium instead of strings [7]. Although it is possible to leverage existing string bx frameworks by serializing and coercing objects to strings and recasting them afterwards, this would add unnecessary overhead to a performance-sensitive environment. However, the techniques applied to string-based bx transformations can be extended upon to yield similar well-behavedness properties.

4 Implementation Details

Our BXE2E proof-of-concept implementation is implemented within the OSCAR EMR ecosystem. While BXE2E is mainly designed not to be reliant on other OSCAR modules, the OSCAR environment is complex and contains many other modules. Other OSCAR modules could significantly impact the performance measurements of BXE2E should they run concurrently with BXE2E. In order to minimize the potential of unexpected behavior caused by other modules, we built up BXE2E in a sandboxed OSCAR environment as shown in Fig. 4. As the sandbox emulates and OSCAR environment, we can "transplant" BXE2E from the sandbox back into an actual OSCAR environment and expect it to work with minimal modifications.

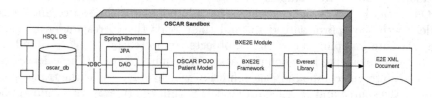

Fig. 4. An overview of the BXE2E Module and its sandbox environment

BXE2E relies heavily on OSCAR's Data Access Object (DAO) layer, which manages and represents the database tables as Plain Old Java Objects (POJOs). BXE2E transforms to and from E2E from the base POJO objects provided by OSCAR's DAO layer. We also leverage the Everest Framework because of its ability to enforce HL7v3 standards in a relatively intuitive POJO format for developers. The framework also emphasizes performance and standards flexibility with HL7v3, making it a suitable choice for creating and parsing E2E records.

BXE2E takes advantage of two main features of JavaSE 8: Lambda Function and Streams. The Lambda Functions are used to define the get and put functions of our lenses, and is a key component of making our lens compositions work. Java streams are good at converting loop-based operations into a parallel workflow. We use streams for a quick pool-based parallelization of our framework. Designing BXE2E to work with streams also has the added benefit of ensuring that we avoid any side-effects in each chunk of parallelizable work.

The overall design of BXE2E is split into three distinct parts: map-reduce, TGG rules and lenses. Referring back to Fig. 3, the map-reduce part coordinates what data needs to be transformed by a set of defined rules. The TGG rules part packages the incoming data and generates the local correspondence graphs and nodes for the data. Finally, the lenses part implements the correspondence graph portion of the aforementioned TGG rule. All three parts are written in separate Java packages, but work together in unison in order to divide and conquer the medical data and transform each data element consistently.

4.1   TGG Rule Implementation

While general-purpose TGG execution engines use a rule matching engine in order to decide what rules can be executed, our medical records are structured and predictable. We elected to use deterministic a map-reduce design in lieu of non-deterministic rule matching in order to take advantage of easier parallelization and reduce the amount of computation needed to determine which rules need to be run. Our TGG rules in turn are specifically designed to handle only one top-level topic or entry per rule, such as a medications or allergy entry. Effectively our TGG rules are all implemented as islands, or rules without context, while the map-reduce behaves as our bridge rules. Dividing the medical record up this way bounds the complexity of our bx into easier to process chunks.

On instantiation of the rule class, the rule populates the source and target models with the appropriate data, and then loads the correspondence graph. The attribute mappings between the objects connected by the correspondence graph are implemented by defining a set of required lenses. These lenses are composed into one compound lens definition which will serve as the transformer between the source and target data models within the rule. After a rule applies the lens transformation, both the internal source and target models will be consistent with each other. This correspondence approach improves maintainability by allowing lens definitions in the correspondence to be refactored as necessary.

4.2   Lens Implementation

Our lenses take advantage of three key principles of functional programming in order to enforce bx: Higher Order Functions, Pure Functions and Immutable Data Structures. HOFs are able to accept functions as inputs as well as yield functions as results. Pure functions are stateless, meaning they do not apply any side effects. Finally, immutable data structures are thread-safe and are critical for creating high performance parallel solutions. BXE2E emphasizes modularity and transformation reliability by using stateless and composable lenses. We use the Java Function API because it encourages functional programming approaches. However, it does not explicitly prohibit the creation and usage of impure functions because ultimately Java is still an imperative language.

In order to apply immutable data structures, we leverage the ImmutablePair construct from the Apache Commons library. This was chosen because it offers a clean and simple way of pairing source and target model objects together for the lens. ImmutablePair also has the added benefit of providing a common object type to pass around BXE2E, ultimately increasing its readability. The lenses are designed so that both the get and put function are on the same source file, making it easier for a developer to review and modify the lens transformations correctly.

5   Evaluation and Analysis

Our evaluation of the BXE2E framework is split into three parts, inspecting its correctness, maintainability and performance. The framework must be correct in order to maintain consistency between record model changes, be demonstrably more maintainable than other designs, and finally show decent performance under real medical workloads. We can only consider BXE2E to be effective if it satisfies those three criteria, and we do a comparison to the two older E2E frameworks as a reference.

5.1   Correctness

Medical record exchange involves the safety-critical act of transferring patient record data. Software is considered safety-critical if its failure could lead to the harm of human life. Because of this, we need to reduce the risk of software faults by deliberately designing software that focuses on increasing its own reliability. For a patient record transformation to be correct, it must be fault tolerant, satisfy requirements and capable of handling malformed data gracefully.

Bx theory allows us to perform round-trip testing, which ensures that information which passes through both the forwards and reverse transformations are properly handled and correct. This is because bidirectional transformations leverage the properties of correctness and hippocraticness. A transformation is coherent and well-behaved if those properties are satisfiable [18]. Essentially if we can demonstrate that the transformation can effectively enforce the relationship between the source and target, we know it is correct [18]. We also know that if the transformation follows a "check-then-enforce" behavior, or does not modify anything already within the relationship, then the transformation is hippocratic.

Since we also use TGGs in our framework, we can also factor in correctness through the property of confluence. As long as the order the TGG rules are executed does not affect the final result, we know that the resultant transformation is correct. Having confluent island rules means that the rules themselves will be unable to introduce potential errors that can arise from the order of rule execution. As each of our rules handle completely different medical record section topics, different rules have no opportunity to trample over each others output.

5.2 Maintainability

One aspect of software maintenance is its readability. Software readability is a subjective human judgement regarding the ease of understanding code. Software that is not written for humans is hard to understand, handle and ultimately maintain. Code maintenance typically takes over 70% of a software project's lifecycle cost [1]. Therefore it is important to minimize the burden of maintenance by making the code easy to understand and act upon.

The first generation exporter used a monolithic Apache Velocity template for its transformation logic. While it satisfied export requirements, it was a maintenance nightmare because both the E2E XML and logic code were mixed together in the same file. Finding and fixing any bugs in the template would require a substantial amount of effort.

The second generation exporter fixes this problem by having all of its business logic done in Java. It was designed with smaller and easier to test units of work, significantly improving its maintainability. However, this iteration was unable to import E2E documents with any guarantees of correctness. Both the import and export would effectively be independent functions, lacking any construct to influence each other's behavior. This is one of the main motivators for creating the third generation BXE2E framework for OSCAR.

5.3 Performance

We benchmarked all three generations of OSCAR E2E exporters against each other with the same tasks in order to perform a comparison between the three frameworks. All three exporters were tested inside their own respective OSCAR sandbox to minimize any outside interference. The standardized dataset included a hypothetical patient record named John Cleese. All sections of data (i.e. demographics, problems, etc.) that may be connected to the E2E patient record transformation workflow are populated fully in order to exercise all potential data paths. The tests were performed on a PC with Microsoft Windows 10 Home, Core i7-4770k CPU @ 3.50 GHz and 16 GB of RAM with the Java^{TM} 8 SE Runtime Environment on build 1.8.0_101-b13.

Our benchmark is split into two parts. The first part involves exporting John Cleese 10,000 times on each of the three frameworks and then comparing their performance results. While there is no major significance with the number 10,000, the number of repeat exports must be large enough to let the benchmark period last a couple of minutes. This allows us to increase our sampling time window and allow for any potential variances in transformation to be averaged out. The second part involves exporting and importing the John Cleese patient record 10,000 times in a full round-trip on the BXE2E framework only.

Table 1. Benchmark results of the single-threaded 10,000 patient export

Verification step	Velocity		E2Everest		BXE2E	
	No	Yes	No	Yes	No	Yes
Execution time	79 s	267 s	68 s	253 s	57 s	237 s
Avg memory use	458 MB	527 MB	298 MB	237 MB	379 MB	221 MB
Max memory use	1.28 GB	1.33 GB	1.01 GB	686 MB	1.25 GB	807 MB
Avg GC time	4.223 ms	3.886 ms	5.601 ms	2.864 ms	9.399 ms	2.949 ms
Max GC time	6.987 ms	8.305 ms	10.609 ms	6.167 ms	17.686 ms	5.421 ms
Avg CPU use	22.5 %	21.0 %	34.8 %	34.4 %	34.9 %	32.8 %
Max CPU use	66.1 %	65.5 %	71.7 %	73.4 %	69.5 %	71.9 %

Table 2. Benchmark results of the multi-threaded 10,000 patient export

Verification step	Velocity		E2Everest		BXE2E	
	No	Yes	No	Yes	No	Yes
Execution time	28 s	90 s	25 s	82 s	24 s	73 s
Avg memory use	710 MB	698 MB	622 MB	688 MB	671 MB	736 MB
Max memory use	1.35 GB	1.33 GB	1.34 GB	1.35 GB	1.34 GB	1.39 GB
Avg GC time	7.448 ms	10.143 ms	11.275 ms	9.780 ms	23.889 ms	13.260 ms
Max GC time	16.747 ms	18.521 ms	14.951 ms	17.482 ms	38.081 ms	20.591 ms
Avg CPU use	99.1 %	99.7 %	98.7 %	99.7 %	96.6 %	99.6 %
Max CPU use	100.0 %	100.0 %	100.0 %	100.0 %	99.6 %	100.0 %

Drawing from the survey of Java profilers done by Flaig et al., we determined that VisualVM and Java Mission Control were the best candidates [5]. These two tools were picked because they come with the Oracle JDK packages, had free usage licenses, provided useful runtime statistics in an easy to use interface, and had a minimal footprint on the executing program. Most of the relevant aspects of profiling were able to be gathered between both tools.

Results. OSCAR E2E transformers have a verification step which adds a constant amount of work to each processed record. This step scans the output and ensures that the output is conformant to E2E and CDA specifications. We performed our benchmarks both without and with verification to determine its impact on the results. In our single-threaded export-only benchmark, we find that BXE2E is the fastest at execution out of the three frameworks as seen in Table 1. However, the E2Everest framework is the most memory efficient with average memory use, and Velocity to use the least amount of average CPU.

The multi-threaded export-only benchmark as seen in Table 2 also paints a similar pattern, with BXE2E being the fastest and E2Everest being the most memory efficient. However, Velocity no longer has any noticeable difference in average CPU usage as compared to the other frameworks. While our BXE2E framework is not the most memory efficient algorithm, its memory footprint is not larger than the more memory efficient E2Everest design. What we gain in BXE2E over the other frameworks is a faster execution time as well as guarantees for well-behavedness through our hybrid TGG and lens approach.

For the round-trip portion of our benchmark, we only test without the verification step as it only adds a constant amount of work to the system. We find that in general, a round trip takes roughly twice as long as just exporting as we can intuitively expect. While memory usage does go up in a round-trip, this is expected as we are doing twice as much transformation work (Table 3). This also demonstrates that the execution time between both transformation directions is relatively equal, suggesting that BXE2E is indeed viable for production use.

Table 3. Comparison of BXE2E's 10,000 single-threaded patient export vs round trip without verification

Multithreaded	Export only		Round trip	
	No	Yes	No	Yes
Execution time	57 s	24 s	108 s	37 s
Avg memory use	379 MB	671 MB	516 MB	706 MB
Max memory use	1.25 GB	1.34 GB	1.34 GB	1.38 GB
Avg GC time	9.399 ms	23.889 ms	9.321 ms	12.152 ms
Max GC time	17.686 ms	38.810 ms	14.483 ms	19.507 ms
Avg CPU use	34.9 %	96.6 %	24.0 %	98.6 %
Max CPU use	69.5 %	99.6 %	59.1 %	100.0 %

Overall, we find that BXE2E has a faster execution time but at the cost of more time spent on garbage collection. Unlike the other two frameworks, BXE2E generates many small classes such as the lenses and rules. These classes are then manipulated and composed together to yield the transformation we want. Because of this step, there will be more objects that need to be cleaned up by the JVM, leading to longer average garbage collection windows. Our results indicate that BXE2E is performant under production loads and that our bx approach to record transformation is viable and worthwhile to pursue.

6   Conclusions

BXE2E as a proof-of-concept framework demonstrates that it is possible to apply bidirectional transformation techniques into an industrial use case. By leveraging the strengths of multiple bx approaches and using a common programming language such as Java, we show that bx theory is applicable to real-world issues. It's highly modular lens design wrapped in TGGs provide multiple degrees of flexibility for maintenance and offers a scalable approach to the transformation process. Compared to alternative OSCAR E2E export designs, we find that BXE2E is a suitable evolution for the medical record exchange problem.

Future work on this design includes investigating ways of reducing the large volume of stand-alone lens class objects in the codebase in order to minimize the garbage collection overhead. As well, advanced caching strategies for data flow could be explored in order to identify parts of the codebase with high memory usage. Since medical record structure are relatively repetitive, it may be possible to cache some of these redundant structures in order to reduce execution time as well. Our BXE2E source code is posted on Github [9].

References

1. Boehm, B., Basili, V.R.: Software defect reduction top 10 list. Computer **34**(1), 135–137 (2001)
2. Chang, F., Gupta, N.: Progress in electronic medical record adoption in Canada. Can. Fam. Physician **61**(12), 1076–1084 (2015)
3. Czarnecki, K., Foster, J.N., Hu, Z., Lämmel, R., Schürr, A., Terwilliger, J.F.: Bidirectional transformations: a cross-discipline perspective. In: Paige, R.F. (ed.) ICMT 2009. LNCS, vol. 5563, pp. 260–283. Springer, Heidelberg (2009). doi:10.1007/ 978-3-642-02408-5_19
4. Ehrig, H.: Introduction to the algebraic theory of graph grammars (a survey). In: International Workshop on Graph Grammars and Their Application to Computer Science, pp. 1–69. Springer (1978)
5. Flaig, A., Hertl, D., Krger, F.: Evaluation von Java-Profiler-Werkzeugen. 05 Fakultt Informatik, Elektrotechnik und Informationstechnik (2013)
6. Foster, J.N., Greenwald, M.B., Moore, J.T., Pierce, B.C., Schmitt, A.: Combinators for bi-directional tree transformations: a linguistic approach to the view update problem. ACM SIGPLAN Not. **40**(1), 233–246 (2005)
7. Foster, J.N., Pilkiewicz, A., Pierce, B.C.: Quotient lenses. In: Proceedings of the 13th ACM SIGPLAN International Conference on Functional Programming, ICFP 2008, pp. 383–396. ACM (2008)
8. Fyfe, J.: Mohawkmedic/jeverest. https://github.com/MohawkMEDIC/jeverest
9. Ho, J.: jujaga/bxe2e. https://github.com/jujaga/bxe2e
10. Hofmann, M., Pierce, B., Wagner, D.: Symmetric lenses. In: ACM SIGPLAN Notices. vol. 46, pp. 371–384. ACM (2011)
11. International, H.L.S: HL7 Reference Information Model. http://www.hl7.org/ implement/standards/rim.cfm
12. Kindler, E., Wagner, R.: Triple Graph Grammars: Concepts, Extensions, Implementations, and Application Scenarios. University of Paderborn, June 2007
13. McCabe, T.: A complexity measure. In: IEEE Trans. Softw. Eng. **SE-2**(4), 308–320 (1976). IEEE
14. Miller, R.J., Ioannidis, Y.E., Ramakrishnan, R.: The use of information capacity in schema integration and translation. In: Proceedings of the 19th International Conference on Very Large Data Bases, VLDB 1993, pp. 120–133. Morgan Kaufmann Publishers Inc., San Francisco (1993)
15. Price, M.: SCOOP Overview | SCOOP - UBC Primary Care Research Network. http://scoop.leadlab.ca/scoop-overview

16. Price, M., Lau, F., Lai, J.: Measuring EMR Adoption: A Framework and Case Study ElectronicHealthcare, vol. 10, No. 1. Longwoods Publication (2011)
17. Schürr, A.: Specification of graph translators with triple graph grammars. In: Mayr, E.W., Schmidt, G., Tinhofer, G. (eds.) WG 1994. LNCS, vol. 903, pp. 151–163. Springer, Heidelberg (1995). doi:10.1007/3-540-59071-4_45
18. Stevens, P.: Bidirectional model transformations in QVT: semantic issues and open questions. Softw. Syst. Model. 9(1), 7–20 (2010)

Rule-Based Repair of EMF Models:
An Automated Interactive Approach

Nebras Nassar[1](✉), Hendrik Radke[2], and Thorsten Arendt[3]

[1] Philipps-Universität Marburg, Marburg, Germany
nassarn@informatik.uni-marburg.de
[2] Universität Oldenburg, Oldenburg, Germany
Hendrik.Radke@informatik.uni-oldenburg.de
[3] GFFT Innovationsförderung GmbH, Bad Vilbel, Germany
thorsten.arendt@gfft-ev.de

Abstract. Managing and resolving inconsistencies in models is crucial in model-driven engineering (MDE). In this paper we consider models that are based on the Eclipse Modeling Framework (EMF). We propose a rule-based approach to support the modeler in automatically trimming and completing EMF models and thereby resolving their cardinality violations. Although being under repair, the model may be viewed and changed interactively during this repair process. The approach and the developed tool support are based on EMF and the model transformation language Henshin.

Keywords: Model driven engineering · Eclipse Modeling Framework (EMF) · Model transformation · Model repair

1 Introduction

Model-driven engineering has become increasingly popular in various engineering disciplines. Although model editors are mostly adapted to their underlying domain-specific modeling language, they usually allow to edit inconsistent models. While upper bounds of multiplicities are mostly obeyed, the violation of lower bounds and further constraints requiring the existence of model patterns is usually tolerated during editing. This means that model editors often use a relaxed meta-model with less constraints than the original language meta-model [7].

The result of an editing process may be an invalid model that has to be repaired. There are a number of model repair approaches in the literature which, however, are either purely interactive such as [4,5,11,12] or fully automated such as [1,6,8,17]. Our approach intends to integrate automatic model repair into the editing process allowing user interaction during repair. It does not leave the resolution strategy completely to the modeler as in pure rule-based approaches. Instead, it is semi-automatic and guides the modeler to repair the whole model.

In our approach, we consider modeling languages being defined by meta-models based on the Eclipse Modeling Framework (EMF) [18]. We present an

© Springer International Publishing AG 2017
E. Guerra and M. van den Brand (Eds.): ICMT 2017, LNCS 10374, pp. 171–181, 2017.
DOI: 10.1007/978-3-319-61473-1_12

algorithm to model repair that consists of two tasks: (1) The meta-model of a given language is translated to a rule-based model transformation system containing repair actions. (2) A potentially invalid model is fully repaired using the generated transformation system which configures the model repair tool according to the given language. An ordered list of used rule applications is reported as a second output. In summary, the contributions of this paper are: (1) an automatic derivation of repair rules (actions) from a given meta-model that is rooted and fully instantiable, (2) a rule-based algorithm for model repair, and (3) an Eclipse-based tool to automate the rule derivation and the model repair. Note, the correctness proof of the algorithm can be found at [10].

The paper is structured as follows: In Sect. 2, we introduce our running example. In Sect. 3, we present our repair algorithm, apply it at an example and sketch how a meta-model is translated to a rule-based transformation system. The developed Eclipse-based tools are presented in Sect. 4. An overview on related work is given in Sect. 5 while Sect. 6 concludes the paper.

2 Running Example

The running example is a simple *Webpage* modeling language for specifying a specific kind of web pages.

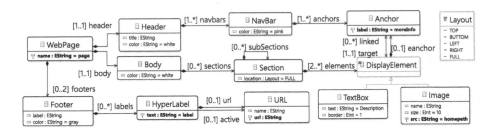

Fig. 1. *Webpage* meta-model

Our *Webpage* modeling language is defined by the meta-model shown in Fig. 1. Shortly, each web page has a *name* which requires a value *(being page by default)*. A web page contains a *Header*, up to two *Footers*, and a *Body*. A header includes at least one navigator bar *NavBar* which contains at least one *Anchor*. A body includes an arbitrary number of *Sections*. A section may contain subsections. A section is designed to contain at least two arbitrary *DisplayElements* of type *Image* or *TextBox*. Each display element may contain an *Anchor*. An anchor has a *label* which requires a value *(being moreInfo by default)* and must be connected to one display element. A web page must not contain more than two *Footers*. A footer may include an arbitrary number of *HyperLabels*. A hyper label may contain one *URL*. A url node has a *url* which requires a value. A hyper label may be connected to one url node.

Figure 2 presents the abstract syntax representation of an invalid *Webpage* model repaired to a valid one. The solid-line elements represent the invalid web page model. It consists of a blue header containing a pink navigator bar and three footers: footer *Appointment* contains a hyper label with text *calendar* including a url node with name *calurl* and a *url* attribute with empty value; the label *calendar* is activated. Footer *Address* contains a hyper label with text *floor 2*, and footer *Location* contains a hyper label with text *label3* including a *url* node with name *url3* and a *url* attribute with empty value. The label *label3* is activated.

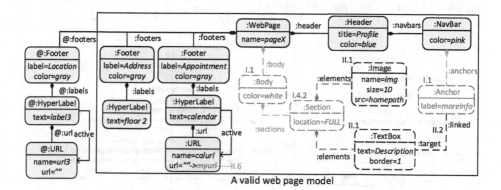

A valid web page model

Fig. 2. The abstract syntax of the invalid *Webpage* being repaired

To repair this invalid *Webpage* model, it is first trimmed and then completed: Since there are too many footers, one *Footer*-node and its children have to be deleted. The selection of the footer can be done automatically in a non-deterministic way or determined by the user. We select the footer annotated with @. Then, the trimmed web page still contains all solid-line elements shown in Fig. 2 without those annotated with @. To complete this *Webpage* model, at least the following missing elements (represented as dashed elements in Fig. 2) have to be created: A *Body*-node and an *Anchor*-node are needed to fulfill the lower bounds of containment types *body* and *anchors*, respectively. An edge of type *target-linked* is needed to fulfill the lower bound of non-containment type *target*. Therefore, a *Section*-node containing two nodes of type *DisplayElement* (e.g., an image and a text box) are demanded to fulfill the lower bounds of containment type *elements* and non-containment type *target*. The *url*-attribute value of the *URL*-node *calurl* has to be set (to, e.g., *myurl*).

3   Rule-Based Model Repair

Our approach to model repair consists of two activities: (1) *Configuration:* The meta-model of a given language is translated to a rule-based model transformation system (repair rules). (2) *Model repair:* A potentially invalid model is repaired yielding a valid model. The repair algorithm uses the generated transformation system and is presented first.

3.1 A Rule-Based Algorithm for Model Repair

As pre-requisite, our approach requires an instantiable meta-model without OCL constraints. Given an invalid model, i.e., a model that does not fulfill all its multiplicities, our algorithm is able to produce a valid one. The repair process is automatic but may be interrupted and interactively guided by the modeler.

The activity diagram in Fig. 3 illustrates the overall control flow of our algorithm which consists of two main parts: The left part performs *model trimming* eliminating supernumerous model elements. The right part performs *model completion* adding required model elements.

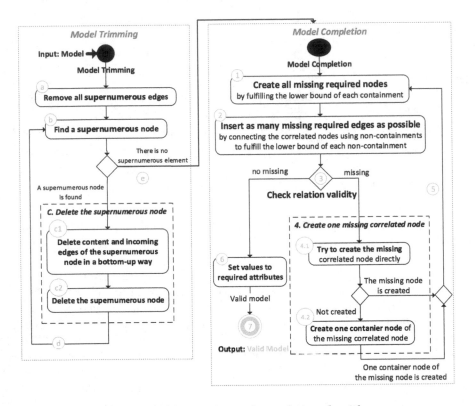

Fig. 3. Model trimming and completion algorithm

Model trimming: Step (a) in Fig. 3 removes *all supernumerous edges*, i.e. edges that exceed the upper-bound invariants of each non-containment edge type. Step (b) checks if there is a *supernumerous node*, i.e., a node which exceeds the upper-bound invariants of a containment edge type. If there is none, the model is ready to be completed (Step (e)). Otherwise, this node and its content have to be deleted; this is done in Step (c). It deletes all the incoming and outgoing edges of this node and its content nodes, and then deletes the content nodes in a bottom-up way (Step (c1)); thereafter, it deletes the node itself (Step (c2)). This bottom-up deletion process starts at all the leaves and continues with their containers. Step (d) calls again Step (b) to check if there is another supernumerous node.

Model completion: Once there is no further supernumerous element in the input model, the model can be completed: Step (1) creates *all missing required nodes*, i.e., nodes that are needed to fulfill the lower-bound of each containment edge type. Thereafter, we have a skeleton model which contains at least all the required nodes. At this stage, the model may contain nodes which are not correlated by required edges. Two node types being linked by a non-containment type are called correlated. Step (2) tries to insert *all missing required edges* by connecting the existing correlated nodes in the model. These edges are needed to fulfill the lower-bound of each non-containment edge type. This step may stop without having inserted all required edges due to potentially missing correlated nodes, i.e., it may happen that there is no further free node to correlate with.

Step (3) checks the validity of all required non-containment edge types. If all the required edges are already inserted, then we have a valid model w.r.t. all multiplicities of edge types. This also means that all the required nodes have been created. Otherwise, there is still at least one required edge missing. In this situation, Step (4) tries to add one missing node to fulfill the lower bound of a non-containment edge type. Although the number of missing nodes may be more than one, only one missing node is added in Step (4). If a missing node cannot be created directly, a (transitive) container node of a missing one is created. The added node may function as, e.g., target node for missing required edges. Hence, it may help to solve other inconsistencies in the model. The design decision of adding just one node in Step (4) helps to find a small completion.

Note that the type of a missing node may have several subtypes. In this case, there may be several possibilities to create a missing node choosing one of these subtypes. A further variation point are node types with several containers. This non-determinism may be solved by user interaction or automatically by randomly picking one. Thereafter, the next iteration of model completion starts with Step (5). Adding a node to the model may require adding further required nodes and edges. Starting a new iteration ensures that all those model elements are generated and that all missing nodes and edges will be created in the end. Once the instance model is valid w.r.t. edge type multiplicities, the values of all the empty required attributes are set (Step (6)). In Step (7) the algorithm stops.

3.2 An Example Repair Process

We illustrate our algorithm by applying it to the invalid *Webpage* model in Fig. 2. The invalid model is first trimmed and then completed. This process is described below and illustrated in Fig. 2. The annotations at the model elements refer to the corresponding iteration and step numbers.

Model trimming: Since the model does not have supernumerous edges, we go directly to Step (b). Here, a supernumerous *Footer*-node is found. Assuming that the *Footer*-node *location* is selected for deletion. In Step (c1), the edge *active* is removed between the nodes *label3* and *url3*. Then, node *url3* itself is deleted. Thereafter, node *label3* can be deleted. Finally, Step (c2) deletes the selected *Footer*-node *Location*. Step (d) calls again Step (b) but there is no further supernumerous node. Hence, the process of model trimming is finished and the output model is ready to be completed (Step (e)).

Model completion is done in two iterations. *Iteration I:* In Step (1), an *Anchor*-node and a *Body*-node are created to fulfill the lower-bound invariants of containment types *anchors* and *body*. In Step (2), a *target*-edge from the created *Anchor*-node is required but cannot be inserted. (3) The required non-containment edge type *target* has not been fulfilled yet. I.e., the node of type *Anchor* has to be connected to a node of type *DisplayElement* but there is none. Step (4.1) tries to create the missing correlated node directly: The creation of a *DisplayElement*-node fails since there is no available *Section*-node (used as container node). Consequently, Step (4.2) is required which creates a *Section*-node inside of the existing *Body*-node. In Step (5), the completion is continued. I.e, a second iteration is required. *Iteration II:* In Step (1), two *DisplayElement*-nodes are created inside of the *Section*-node to fulfill the lower-bound invariant of the containment type *elements*. As an example, a node of type *TextBox* and a node of type *Image* are created. In Step (2), a non-containment edge of type *target* is inserted between the existing *Anchor*-node and one of the existing nodes of type *DisplayElement*, e.g., the *TextBox*-node. Step (3) finds out that all the required non-containment edge types are available now. In Step (6) all remaining values for the all required attributes are set. Here, the *url*-attribute value of the *URL*-node *calurl* is set to *myurl*. A valid instance model is produced (Step (7)).

3.3   Deriving a Model Transformation System from a Meta-model

A pre-requisite of our repair algorithm is the existence of a model transformation system. It can be automatically generated from a given meta-model. In this section, we concentrate on the derivation of transformation rules and present a selection of rule kinds used for model repair. All rule schemes with examples can be found at [10]. They are generated from different kinds of meta-model patterns. The rule schemes are carefully designed to consider the EMF model constraints defined in [3]. They are generic and effective in the sense that the derived rule sets can be used to manage (fulfill) *any* lower or upper bound.

Set of required-node-creation rules: For *each* containment type *with* lower bound >0, a rule is derived which creates a node with its containment edge if the *lower-bound invariant* of the corresponding containment type *is not yet reached*. The container is determined by the input parameter p. The user gets the possibility to select the right container, otherwise it is selected randomly by the algorithm. Figure 4 illustrates the rule scheme used to derive this kind of rules. Note that for each non-abstract class B' in the family of class B such a rule is derived. Figure 5 presents an example rule; it creates a required *Body*-node being contained in a *WebPage*-node if there is not already a *Body*-node contained. This set configures Step (1) of the algorithm.

Set of required-edge-insertion rules: For *each* non-containment type *with* lower bound >0, a rule is derived which inserts a non-containment edge between two existing nodes if the *lower-bound invariant* of the corresponding non-containment type *is not yet reached*. This set configures Step (2).

Set of additional-node-creation rules: For *each* containment type of the given meta-model, a rule is generated which creates one node if *the upper-bound* of its containment type *is not exceeded*. These rules are used to add nodes without violating upper-bound invariants. This set configures Step (4) of the algorithm.

Set of exceeding-edge-removing rules: For *each* non-containment type with a limited upper bound of the given meta-model, a rule is generated which removes one edge if the *upper-bound* of its non-containment type *is exceeded*. This set configures Step (a) of the algorithm.

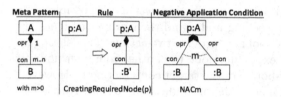

Fig. 4. Rule schema for creating a required *B*-node

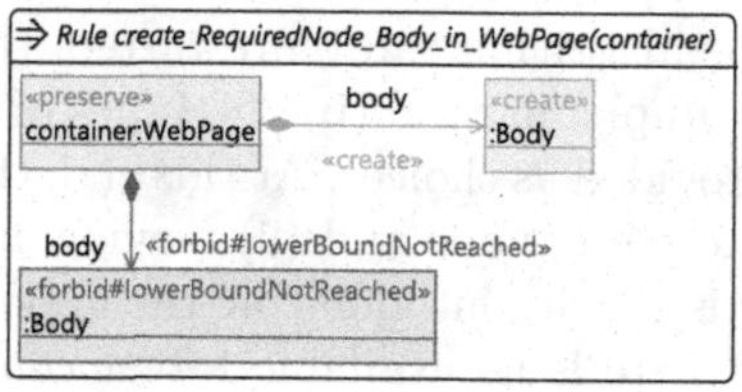

Fig. 5. An example rule for creating a required *Body*-node

4   Tool Support

We have developed two Eclipse plug-ins based on EMF: The first Eclipse plug-in automates the derivation of a model transformation system from a given meta-model. The input of this tool is an Ecore meta-model that is rooted and fully instantiable, and the output is an Eclipse plug-in containing the corresponding model transformation system. The generated model transformation system is formulated in Henshin. If the meta-model contains OCL constraints, they are not taken into account yet. The second Eclipse plug-in implements the repair algorithm presented in Sect. 3. This plug-in has two main inputs: The model transformation system being derived from the given meta-model and an instance model of it containing one node of root type. The main output is the repaired model fulfilling all the EMF model constraints. Thus, the EMF editor can open the resulting model. Note, the tool reports the user if a new node of root type is needed to complete a given model. More information is at [10]. The algorithm can be *automatically* executed in two modes: (1) *randomly* or (2) *interactively*.

Rule-based implementation of automatic random or interactive mode: The algorithm is configured with the rule sets in a way that at any point of the algorithm where choices have to be made, they can be random, or interactive. This applies to choices of rules (repair actions), matches (model locations or targets) and attribute values. The suggested choices of each step aim at repairing the whole model. Each algorithm step uses proper rule sets, e.g., Step (1) uses the set of *required-node-creation* rules. Step (1) is ended once there is no applicable rule of the set on the model. I.e., all the required nodes with all their required child nodes are created. Since the rule sets are designed to consider the EMF model constraints, identifying the applicable rules and their matches aim at finding the proper repair actions and matches w.r.t. the algorithm step and the given model state. To set attribute values of primitive types, the user can let this be done automatically by the tool or has to provide a set of values. Note, the user can not only select each suggested choice but also can randomly perform the current algorithm step or the whole algorithm at any time.

Since model trimming may lead to information loss, the tool is developed to manage that in two ways: (a) The repair process is able to be interrupted (stopped) anytime so that the user can manage the needed data. Thereafter, the algorithm can be restarted. (b) Suggesting moving actions (if possible). For example, in Step (b) the types of exceeding nodes and their proper matches are provided as choices. At this end, the tool may provide two actions: (1) deleting an exceeding node and (2) moving an exceeding node to another container node (if exists) without violating the upper-bound of the target container node. However, if there is no available target container node, an additional container node can be automatically added (if possible) to hold the exceeding node.

An interesting test case that motivates us to carry out a scalability study in the future is that we have applied the tool to randomly resolve more than 150 inconsistencies of 3 different kinds in a model with 10,000 elements. The tool just took about 58 ms to complete such a large model. The used meta-model composes 8 constrained element types and the test model is designed so that its structure is increased fairly w.r.t. the model size: The test model is composed of copies of an initial model part containing elements of all given meta-model types. The initial model is first designed to be valid and then is randomly changed to have 8 inconsistencies of three different types, namely missing nodes, missing edges, and missing nodes with their edges. The test has been executed 3 times and the average is calculated, thereafter. More information can be found at [10].

5   Related Work

In the following, we consider related work w.r.t. model repair and rule generation. We first relate our approach to existing model repair techniques that can be mainly categorized into syntactic and rule-based approaches on the one hand, and search-based approaches on the other hand.

Syntactic and rule-based approaches. In [11,12], the authors provide a syntactic approach for generating interactive repairs from full first-order logic formulas that constrain UML documents. The user can choose from automatically generated repair actions when an inconsistency occurs. Similarly, Egyed et al. [4,5] describe a rule-based technique for automatically generating a set of concrete changes for fixing inconsistencies at different locations in UML models and providing information about the impact of each change on all consistency rules. The designer is not required to introduce new model elements, i.e., the approach ignores the creation of new model elements as choices for fixing inconsistencies. In [14], Rabbi et al. propose a formal approach (with prototype tooling) to support software designers in completing partial models. Their approach is based on rule-based model rewriting which supports both, addition and deletion of model elements. In all these approaches, inconsistencies can be considered by the user one after the other; possible negative side effects are not taken into consideration. It is up to the user to find a way to get a valid model (if any). Moreover, they are not shown to be fully consistent.

Search-based approach. A search-based repair engine starts with an inconsistent model state and tries to find a sequence of change actions which leads to a valid model. Another approach is model finding, using a constraint solver to calculate a valid model. Many approaches such as [1,6,8,17] provide support for automatic inconsistency resolution from a logical perspective. All these approaches provide automatic model completion; however, may easily run into scalability problems (as stated in [9]). Since the input model is always translated to a logical model, the performance depends on the model size. Badger [13] is a search-based tool which uses a regression planning algorithm to find a valid model. It can take a variety of parameters to let the search process be guided by the user to a certain extent. The authors argue that their generation of resolution plans is reasonably fast showing that the execution time is linear to the model size and quadratic to the number of inconsistencies. They do not show the time needed to apply a repair plan on a model. This approach may support some configuration before model repair but do not allow user interaction during model repair. Although being rule-based, the refinement approach in [16] basically translates a set of rules with complex application conditions to a logical model and thereby completes models. This completion is performed automatically by rule applications; user interaction is not considered in this process.

Our approach is designed for integrating the best of both worlds: It is a rule-based approach; therefore, it is easy to allow user interaction in the repair process, in contrast to search-based approaches. But it does not leave the resolution strategy completely to the modeler as in pure rule-based approaches. Instead, it guides the modeler in an automatic interactive way to repair the whole model. Our approach yields valid EMF models which can be opened by the EMF editor. How all the EMF constraints are specified and how valid EMF models are constructed are not clearly shown by most existing approaches. On the downside, our approach cannot yet handle OCL constraints being covered by most of the approaches mentioned above. It is promising to translate OCL constraints to graph patterns [2,15] functioning as application conditions of rules and thereby extending the automated interactive model repair approach.

Rule generation. In [7], model transformation rules are generated from a given meta-model as well. The main difference to our work is that consistency-preserving rules are generated there while we generate repair rules allowing temporarily inconsistent models w.r.t. the multiplicities. Hence, rules are generated for different purposes: There, consistency-preserving rules are generated to recognize consistent edit steps, while we generate repair rules here to configure our model repair algorithm yielding consistent EMF models as results.

6   Conclusion

In this paper, we present a rule-based approach to guide the modeler in repairing models in an automated interactive way and thereby resolving all their inconsistencies. Different sets of model transformation rules (repair actions) are derived from a meta-model considering it pattern-wise. A rule-based algorithm of model trimming and completion is presented yielding consistent EMF models. Two Eclipse plug-ins have been developed to automatically translate meta-models to model transformation systems and to repair corresponding instance models. First test cases show that our algorithm is fast and motivate us to carry out a scalability study. We plan to extend this approach to support OCL constraints as well. Translating OCL constraints to graph patterns [2,15] and further to application conditions of rules is promising to achieve an automated interactive model repair approach for meta-models with OCL constraints.

References

1. Apt, K.R., Wallace, M.: Constraint Logic Programming Using Eclipse. Cambridge University Press, Leiden (2006)
2. Bergmann, G.: Translating OCL to graph patterns. In: Dingel, J., Schulte, W., Ramos, I., Abrahão, S., Insfran, E. (eds.) MODELS 2014. LNCS, vol. 8767, pp. 670–686. Springer, Cham (2014). doi:10.1007/978-3-319-11653-2_41
3. Biermann, E., Ermel, C., Taentzer, G.: Formal foundation of consistent EMF model transformations by algebraic graph transformation. SoSyM **11**, 227–250 (2012)
4. Egyed, A.: Fixing inconsistencies in UML design models. In: ICSE (2007)
5. Egyed, A., Letier, E., Finkelstein, A.: Generating and evaluating choices for fixing inconsistencies in UML design models. In: IEEE/ACM, pp. 99–108 (2008)
6. Hegedüs, Á., Horváth, Á., Ráth, I., Branco, M.C., Varró, D.: Quick fix generation for DSMLs. In: VL/HCC, pp. 17–24. IEEE (2011)
7. Kehrer, T., Taentzer, G., Rindt, M., Kelter, U.: Automatically deriving the specification of model editing operations from meta-models. In: Van Gorp, P., Engels, G. (eds.) ICMT 2016. LNCS, vol. 9765, pp. 173–188. Springer, Cham (2016). doi:10.1007/978-3-319-42064-6_12
8. Macedo, N., Guimarães, T., Cunha, A.: Model repair and transformation with echo. In: ASE, pp. 694–697. IEEE (2013)
9. Macedo, N., Tiago, J., Cunha, A.: A feature-based classification of model repair approaches. CoRR abs/1504.03947 (2015)
10. EMF Model Repair. http://uni-marburg.de/Kkwsr

11. Nentwich, C., Capra, L., Emmerich, W., Finkelstein, A.: xlinkit: a consistency checking and smart link generation service. ACM **2**(2), 151–185 (2002)
12. Nentwich, C., Emmerich, W., Finkelstein, A.: Consistency management with repair actions. In: Software Engineering, pp. 455–464. IEEE (2003)
13. Puissant, J.P., Straeten, R.V.D., Mens, T.: Resolving model inconsistencies using automated regression planning. SoSyM **14**, 461–481 (2015)
14. Rabbi, F., Lamo, Y., Yu, I.C., Kristensen, L.M., Michael, L.: A diagrammatic approach to model completion. In: (AMT)@ MODELS (2015)
15. Radke, H., Arendt, T., Becker, J.S., Habel, A., Taentzer, G.: Translating essential OCL invariants to nested graph constraints focusing on set operations. In: Parisi-Presicce, F., Westfechtel, B. (eds.) ICGT 2015. LNCS, vol. 9151, pp. 155–170. Springer, Cham (2015). doi:10.1007/978-3-319-21145-9_10
16. Salay, R., Chechik, M., Famelis, M., Gorzny, J.: A methodology for verifying refinements of partial models. J. Object Technol. **14**, 3:1–3:31 (2015)
17. Sen, S., Baudry, B., Precup, D.: Partial model completion in model driven engineering using constraint logic programming. In: Proceedings of the INAP 2007 (2007)
18. Steinberg, D., Budinsky, F., Paternostro, M., Merks, E.: EMF: Eclipse Modeling Framework 2.0, 2nd edn. Addison-Wesley Professional, Amsterdam (2009)

Author Index

Printed in the United States
By Bookmasters